LETTERS FROM HELLES

Colonel Sir Henry Darlington, 1925.
(Walter Stoneman, National Portrait Gallery, London)

THE UNCENSORED CORRESPONDENCE OF
A BATTALION COMMANDER AT GALLIPOLI

LETTERS FROM HELLES

By

COLONEL SIR HENRY DARLINGTON

K.C.B., C.M.G., T.D., D.L.

WITH A FOREWORD BY HIS GRANDSON
HUGH DARLINGTON

AND A PREFACE BY
GENERAL SIR IAN HAMILTON
G.C.B., G.C.M.G., D.S.O.

EDITED BY
MICHAEL CRANE & BERNARD DE BROGLIO

LITTLE GULLY PUBLISHING
2025

'Turk shell. Krithia Road. Clapham Junction.'

Copyright © 2025, the descendants of Col. Sir Henry Darlington, Michael Crane, Bernard de Broglio.

All rights reserved. No part of this book may be reproduced in any form by electronic or mechanical means, including information storage and retrieval systems, without permission in writing from the publisher, except by a reviewer who may quote brief passages in a review.

First published in February 1936 by Longmans, Green & Co. This second, annotated and illustrated edition was published in October 2025.

ISBN 978-1-7636268-8-1 (hardback)
ISBN 978-1-7640773-2-3 (paperback)
ISBN 978-1-7640773-3-0 (ebook)

Little Gully Publishing
littlegully.com

A catalogue record for this book is available from the National Library of Australia

CONTENTS

FOREWORD—HUGH DARLINGTON 1
EDITORS' NOTE 3
PREFACE—GENERAL SIR IAN HAMILTON 5
INTRODUCTION—COLONEL SIR HENRY DARLINGTON . . 9

    I. PREPARATION 11
    II. GALLIPOLI 19
    III. THIRD BATTLE OF KRITHIA 39
    IV. IMBROS—TRENCH WARFARE 45
    V. 127TH INFANTRY BRIGADE 63
    VI. BATTLE OF 6/7TH AUGUST AT HELLES 87
    VII. MORE TRENCH LIFE 93
    VIII. THE WAY HOME 137

APPENDICES

    A. BIOGRAPHY OF HENRY CLAYTON DARLINGTON . . 143
    B. TIMELINE 163
    C. EMBARKATION STATE 178
    D. ORDERS AND MESSAGES, THIRD KRITHIA 180
    E. ORDERS AND MESSAGES, 6/7 AUGUST 183
    F. NOMINAL ROLL, OFFICERS, 6 MAY — 1 OCT 1915 . 187
    G. CASUALTIES 190
    H. BIOGRAPHIES, 1/5TH MANCHESTERS 191
    I. BIOGRAPHIES, OTHER UNITS 219
    J. 42 DIVISION ORDER OF BATTLE AND FIELD STATE . 248

RECOMMENDED READING 253
ABBREVIATIONS AND ACRONYMS 256

MAPS

    1. 5TH MANCHESTERS COMPANY DISTRIBUTION . . 259
    2. GALLIPOLI 260
    3. HELLES, SOUTHERN AREA 261
    4. OBSERVATION HILL 262
    5. KRITHIA SPUR 263
    6. MORNING OF 4 JUNE 264
    7. NIGHT OF 4 JUNE 265
    8. MORNING OF 6 AUGUST 266
    9. MORNING OF 7 AUGUST 267
  10. AFTERNOON OF 7 AUGUST 268
  11. 42ND DIVISION SECTION FROM 19 AUGUST . . . 269
  12. OPPOSING LINES, HELLES, 30 SEPTEMBER 1915 . . 270

TRENCH MAPS *(1st edition endpapers)*

    TRENCH DIAGRAM OF CENTRE SECTOR, JULY 1915 . 62
    TRENCH DIAGRAM OF LEFT & CENTRE SECTORS . 109

INDEX 180

FOREWORD

By HUGH DARLINGTON

Grandson of the late Henry Clayton Darlington

Letters from Helles is a compilation of letters written by my grandfather, affectionately known as Hal, to his first wife Mabel (née Hirst). They were penned while he was engaged in the harrowing events in Gallipoli in 1915. Sadly, Mabel died in 1916 following the birth of their fourth child, with Hal away fighting in Egypt. In June 1919 he married Mabel's sister Daisy, and they went on to have a further five children —number seven being my father.

I was in Wigan in August 2024 with my son Jack, at the unveiling of a Memorial at the site of the Wigan Drill Hall, home to the 5th Battalion Manchester Regiment. Michael Crane introduced himself and expressed an interest in putting together a book, similar in format to *Gallipoli Diary 1915*, by Alec Riley, that he and Bernard de Broglio had produced. I had been researching my grandfather's military career over the last twenty-five years and had hoped to be able to publish an illustrated volume ten years ago to coincide with the Gallipoli centenary. Both work and family commitments intervened so Mike's proposals were readily accepted and I am indebted to Mike and Bern who have facilitated the republishing of this new and expanded volume of *Letters from Helles*.

I first read *Letters from Helles* as a teenager when staying in Chelsea with Hal and Mabel's eldest child, Aunt Esther. And it was whilst staying with another of their daughters, Aunt Margaret and her husband Stephen Phillips, that I discovered their passion for genealogy and at the age of 50 began my own investigation of the Darlington family history.

LETTERS FROM HELLES

I was incredibly fortunate to be bequeathed a large archive of family documents including scrap books, newspaper cuttings, original negatives and photos (loose and in albums) and letters. Many of these relate to my grandfather's military exploits during the second South African War, the First World War, and the period leading up to and including the Second World War. Among the above are assorted orders, maps, telegrams, post cards and other memorabilia relating to the war years which he, and later my grandmother Daisy, had kept. I was also fortunate to have in my possession my grandfather's Army Record, which chronicles his various appointments, periods of leave and sickness, etc. I am especially grateful to my cousin Richard Phillips, another of Hal's grandsons, for the boxes of documents passed on from his late parent's archive.

My grandfather was a keen photographer right from his school days. He took his camera with him when in 1896 he sailed to Tasmania, via Cape Town, capturing many fascinating images. He also carried a camera throughout his military service in South Africa, and later during the First World War in Egypt, Gallipoli, and France. His remaining negatives have survived in better condition than many of the photos originally developed from them. Many of the photographs have scribbled notes on the reverse or on the album pages where they have been pasted. Within this archive I discovered an album containing his original photographs taken in the Gallipoli campaign, sadly the negatives have not survived.

Over the years I have endeavoured to locate copies of *Letters from Helles* to give to my children, and to the many other descendants of Henry Clayton Darlington and the Hirst family. This new publication makes it possible to pass on my grandfather's story to current and future generations, and makes this important piece of history available to a wider audience.

HUGH DARLINGTON.

EDITORS' NOTE

Colonel Sir Henry Darlington's letters give us unique insight into the daily life, actions, and thoughts of a commanding officer (CO) at Gallipoli. Colonel Darlington arrived at Helles at the head of the 1/5th Manchesters on 6 May 1915, 10 days after the first landings. He and his battalion quickly gained a reputation for reliability and resilience in the face of great challenge, exemplified by the 1/5th Manchesters' steadfast performance in the June and August battles.

Except for three weeks in charge of the 127th Brigade, Colonel Darlington remained continuously at the head of his battalion until his medical evacuation on 30 September. By that time, he was the last of the twelve COs in the division who had landed in early May, and the only remaining officer of the 34 who had disembarked with the 1/5th Manchesters.

During his time at Helles, Darlington led his men through three battles and through the many challenges unique to Gallipoli, earning a reputation throughout the division as an exemplary leader.

Letters From Helles was first published in February 1936 against the backdrop of what Sir Ian Hamilton described as an 'unnerving and distracting impending calamity'—the approaching Second World War. That calamity would ensure the book's scarcity. On 29th December 1940, during one of the most devastating raids of the Blitz, a firestorm engulfed the area around St Paul's Cathedral, destroying the publisher's warehouse at 39 Paternoster Row. The following July, Longmans, Green & Co. wrote to Sir Henry Darlington confirming that the entire remaining stock of *Letters from Helles*—424 copies—had been 'destroyed by enemy action.'

A fortuitous meeting in 2024 with Colonel Darlington's grandson, Hugh Darlington, at a commemoration ceremony in Wigan, gave rise to this new, expanded edition of *Letters from Helles*.

LETTERS FROM HELLES

The editors have supplemented the original work with 12 maps and seven additional appendices, among them a full, illustrated biography of the author. The most valuable addition, however, is undoubtedly the many previously unpublished photographs taken by Colonel Darlington himself. All the photographs in this book are from his camera, except for some portraits that accompany the biographies.

The main text has been faithfully reproduced here, with all footnotes being Darlington's own. Where clarification is needed, we have used [square brackets] to correct minor discrepancies that arose from the fog of war or typographical errors. These include clarifying a common confusion at the time between Gully Beach and Y Beach, correctly identifying the torpedoed battleship as HMS *Majestic*, and amending a trench designation and several officers' names in an appendix. Three appendices from the original work have been retained and are now re-lettered D, F and G; all footnotes in the new appendices are the editors' own, save for two by the author in appendix D.

Darlington often used his initials 'HCD' when captioning 'self' in photographs; the editors have retained that usage for image captions, Darlington's biography and other appendices.

We are indebted to Hugh Darlington for the opportunity to re-present this classic account. We could not have completed this edition without his assistance, and the generous access he gave to his grandfather's photographs and original documents from his personal archive. Our gratitude also extends to his cousin, Richard Phillips, who kindly allowed us to supplement this collection with photographs from his own archive.

         MICHAEL CRANE,
         BERNARD DE BROGLIO.

PREFACE

By GENERAL SIR IAN HAMILTON
G.C.B., G.C.M.G., D.S.O.

Commanding Mediterranean Expeditionary Force, 1915

THUS spake unto me not very long ago my own private Oracle: "write Finis to the story of thine own Life without pausing to write Prefaces to the Lives of others, lest haply thou stumblest unawares over a tombstone!"

Since then I have clasped my own life as closely as if it were a football and have been striving to get across with it, eluding the tackle of Publishers, Freelance journalists, Autograph hunters and other Time-poachers who are lined out between me and the goal posts.

How comes it then that this New Year finds me at my old game of passing the ball and making pause in my own undertaking? Well, quite simply, it is the unnerving and distracting sense of impending calamity which makes me, like everyone else, unable to settle down quietly to my own ordinary business. The effect of these heavy clouds darkening at once the horizons of so many parts of the world is to make me feel we may not be able to keep out of it. And if we are not going to be able to keep out of it, how necessary (amongst many other necessities) that students should lose not a moment in learning how to write home to their mothers, as well as bridegrooms from the battlefield to their brides.

There could not be a better model for this purpose than the *Letters from Helles* by Sir Henry Darlington. I have been privileged to read a good many letters circulated to friends during the Great War and some of them were very bad, talking about the Angel of Death in the most familiar, eerie and uncomfortable way. These—when they got back to the home front—were as much out of place there as was the man who wrote them out of place at the war front! All will, however,

LETTERS FROM HELLES

I think, agree that this naive and original story by Colonel Darlington of the adventures of himself and his Officers and Rank and File at the Dardanelles must have heartened up the friends who read them at the time and I think, too, that even now when we know that they only gave one half of the story they will do us all good to peruse. For although I am a very old campaigner and have been in many wars where the British soldier has always played his part as to the manner born—I must say that the happy way in which these Manchester men encountered their ghastly mix-up of mud, flies, stinks, bombs, corpses, was an eye-opener. Had those men all been killed (and they very near were) still they would have refused to be defeated, and they would not in fact have been defeated. Of such were, not necessarily the Kingdom of Heaven, but anyway, certainly Colonel Darlington's own Battalion, the 5th Manchesters, miners from Wigan. The 6th Manchesters were another brand of the same breed, just as a Corona cigar may be out of a box marked Claro or Colorado. These boys were Claro. I happened to be standing by as they disembarked on the Peninsula and I scanned every one of them— mostly young school teachers, many of them fit to be officers right there. A beautiful battalion! Had they and the rest of this Division been with us on the date of the first landing, i.e., five days earlier, what a wonderful story would have been given to old Mother Europa to paste into her book of reminiscences. But I must not spoil my preface by making it a vehicle for publishing my own thoughts; I want to devote it entirely to helping Sir Henry Darlington to portray those men he commanded so bravely and so well, as they answered back the death's head grin of the trenches with a cheery smile, whilst for three weeks the Dardanelles Committee were eating good dinners and sleeping the sleep of the just.

Here are a few samples taken from the book:

"... when a cookhouse (an open-air one) was blown sky high and the surrounding landscape littered with rice, all the Master-Cook said was, 'It favvers a b——— wedding.'"

"Our men on the left had some shooting, but nothing much. They slew one Turk, I imagine a scout, who put his head up out of the scrub and had a good look round. Our men were very amused the way he poked his head up and peered round. He was christened 'Audacious Alfred,' and one man said, 'He was looking for his iron ration,' which caused much laughter."

PREFACE

Now for a few samples of the tone in which officers on service should write home to their relatives.

"The sniper has just hit the top of my dugout a fearful smack. Ernest Fletcher, who is reading, said, 'Bow-wow.'"

"You must not picture us in deadly danger and doing the death and glory act *a la* Graphic. We live absolutely underground, do our turn in the fire trenches, which is absolutely the safest place in the Peninsula and spend the rest of our days digging and doing road making and other fatigue work day and night."

"I am still very fit and untouched. You will be glad to hear that in case of an attack the Authorities do not allow the C.O.s to lead their men, they say that is the job of platoon commanders and that C.O.s should be in the rear of their commands, where they can watch and influence events and keep in touch with their commands and with Brigade. So don't imagine me charging at the head of the Battalion. One has to sit on a telephone in comparative safety. It will not be your idea of my functions, but it seems sound if you think of it. They say that things go wrong when a C.O. gets knocked out."

"It is very much worse to think of at home than it is really. It becomes one's normal life and you don't care twopence for the minor discomforts there are. If you could just change places with me for a week and see things from inside my brain, you would go home after your week was up and never worry any more. At home one thinks of it as 'so dreadful.'"

So now good-bye and a happy new year to the survivors of the Dardanelles in Manchester. You are already being regarded as "old soldiers" by the youngsters. "Old soldiers," they say, "never die; they only fade away." But you will hardly fade away until the sun slowly fades out of the sky and the earth sinks into the universal blackness. For already you form a part of that Great Tradition of the Dardanelles which began with Hector and Achilles. In another few thousands of years the two stories will have blended into one, and whether when "the iron roaring went up to the vault of heaven through the unharvested sky," as Homer tells us, it was the spear of Achilles or whether it was a 100 lb. shell from Asiatic Annie won't make much odds to the Almighty.

IAN HAMILTON.

January, 1936.

Lieutenant-Colonel Henry Clayton Darlington (HCD).
Probably taken in Egypt in early 1915.

INTRODUCTION

By COLONEL SIR HENRY DARLINGTON
K.C.B., C.M.G., T.D., D.L.

Before the outbreak of war in August, 1914, the 5th Battalion The Manchester Regiment was recruited in Wigan with outlying companies at Atherton, Leigh and Patricroft. The battalion formed part of the East Lancashire Territorial Division, subsequently the 42nd Division.

The Division in Egypt was made up of the following units:

Cavalry:—"A" Squadron, Duke of Lancaster's Own Yeomanry.

Artillery:—The 1st (Blackburn) and the 3rd (Oldham Standish) East Lancashire Brigades.

R.E:—1st and 2nd Field Companies and Signal Company.

Infantry:—(125th) Infantry Brigade: 5th, 6th, 7th, and 8th Battalions The Lancashire Fusiliers.

(126th) Infantry Brigade: 4th and 5th Battalions The East Lancashire Regiment and the 9th and 10th Battalions The Manchester Regiment.

(127th) Infantry Brigade: 5th, 6th, 7th, and 8th Battalions The Manchester Regiment.

A.S.C., R.A.M.C., Army Service Corps, and three Field Ambulances.

The Division was mobilized on August 4th, 1914, and on the 10th Lord Kitchener asked the Territorial Force to volunteer for service overseas. This invitation was quickly accepted and on September 5th Lord Kitchener ordered the Division to Egypt.

On the 9th about 40 trains conveyed close on 16,000 officers and men with horses, guns and equipment to Southampton and on September 10th the Division sailed for Egypt, the first Territorial Division to volunteer for foreign service and the first to leave these shores.

The men of the 5th Manchesters were mostly colliers and allied trades. They were blessed with an unquenchable sense of humour, an ability to stick it, great self-reliance and an apparently natural *esprit de corps*: the last two virtues being due, I imagine, to the fact that they worked down pit and were very loyal to their trades unions. I never knew them rattled and their outlook on affairs is well instanced by the following incident: Not being in France on Nov. 11th, 1918, I afterwards asked my Pioneer Sergeant, who was in the front line at the Armistice, whether there was great excitement amongst the men at 11 a.m. on that day. His reply was, "I have seen more excitement at a beer issue."

Of the officers I could never say enough.

MELLING,
17th Nov., 1935.

I.—PREPARATION

Anchor Line,
Twin Screw Steamer,
"Caledonia"

Bay of Biscay.

We left Southampton via Spithead, as the Needles entrance is mined, at 5 p.m., on September 10th, 1914, with orders to rendezvous off Eddystone at 10 a.m. on the 11th. We loafed around all the 11th and finally left for Gib at 7 p.m. on the 11th.

The convoy is fifteen troopships in three lines ahead and the escort is the cruiser *Minerva* and the battleship *Ocean*. It will take us six days to Gib as we are tied down to about nine knots or less owing to a slow ship.

A strange ship attended at the rendezvous, and after cruising about among us for some hours the cruiser sent a boat aboard and found she was a Dutchman and she was arrested and the cruiser took her into Falmouth.

We had a calm down Channel and in the Bay thick mist and a heavy roll.

We run at night with all lights out that are not actually wanted and no deck lights.

We are getting some Marconi news through, although it is tapped news and not intended for us.

Most of the officers have been more or less sick, I think all of them.

The battleships get very angry if we get out of station. It is very curious being part of a convoy and seeing so many ships together.

We arrive Gib to-morrow, Thursday 17th, and the 8th Middlesex go ashore there.

I was inoculated the night before last (enteric). It is not pleasant, but I expect to be quite right by to-morrow.

It is very hot and we have beautiful sunny days.

We had to stop our Marconi yesterday as the battleship signalled "Enemy reported in vicinity, and no more wireless or lamp signalling."

However, our escort looks well after us, and the cruiser does scouting work at intervals.

I suppose we shall have the ship to ourselves after Gib.

I am writing this in my shirt sleeves and shall go into drill to-morrow, the sun is getting a bite.

Our men are all being inoculated I am glad to say.

The food is excellent and the boat very comfortable in every way. I have a cabin to myself. Everybody is enjoying it very much now except those suffering from inoculation. I feel as fit as a fiddle.

We don't know yet where we go in Egypt.

Mediterranean.

We stayed at Gib all Thursday and were ordered to ship naval stores for Malta, so we have to call there.

I did not go ashore as the men were not allowed to, but most of the officers did by my permission. There was a rumour at Gib that we had been sunk by a mine off Spain. I hope you did not get it in England.

The weather has been extremely hot and the horses have been dying like flies, so yesterday our horse boat, a fast one, was sent on to get to Egypt as quick as she could and take her risks.

The battleship *Ocean* left us at Gib so our only escort is the cruiser *Minerva*.

We have plenty of room now the Middlesex are gone and I am O.C. Troops and have to go round the ship followed by the Captain every morning.

We have formed our double Companies and Archie Brook[1] comes under Milward Rogers.[2] Milward says he will make a very good officer, he thinks.

Captain Bankes, our old Quartermaster of the 1st Manchesters in South Africa, came on board at Gib to see me. He was very surprised to find me in command.

---

1 Lieut. A. C. Brook, my brother-in-law. Killed June, 1915.
2 Capt. H. M. Rogers. Killed May, 1915.

I.—PREPARATION

Everybody is very well, one or two of them feel the heat.

It is a very damp heat and this ship was built for the N. Atlantic, the result is very hot cabins, saloons, etc., and we have to have all blinds down over lights at night, which makes it worse.

We got orders to leave the convoy yesterday about 4 p.m. and go to Malta at full speed (17 knots), so we are now by ourselves.

Sanders[1] and I sat up last night trying to decipher code wireless which kept coming in from the cruiser *Minerva*. We at last came to the conclusion they had changed the code word and had not let us know, so went to bed. This turned out to be correct, as we managed by an awful fluke to guess the code word and so were able this evening to decipher the messages.

September 23rd. After Malta en route for Alexandria.

This has been an extraordinary voyage and I think our men are beginning to realize that we have an Empire.[2]

We spent all Monday in Malta and whilst in there six French Dreadnoughts came in to coal right up into the inner harbour where we were.

Our men swapped lies and cigarettes and whilst one of the Dreadnoughts was being towed past us to have some guns put in her, one of the French sailors shouted, "Are we downhearted?" There was a roar of "No" from our whole Battalion.

When we left to go out and find our convoy we had a tremendous send off which impressed our men very much. The Band of the Dreadnought *Danton*, which you may remember at the Coronation Review, played our National Anthem for us and the whole of the crews lined the sides and cheered. All our own ships did the same, including the crew of a Russian boat, not to mention a great part of the populace of Malta.

One of our wits invited a French sailor to dine with him in Paris, but the French sailor said, "No, no, ve vill dine in Berlin togezzer."

The next thing we met was a huge convoy escorted by a big cruiser,

---

1 Capt. J. M. Sanders, Leinster Regiment, my adjutant.
2 Whilst in Malta Harbour, one of the men was overheard saying to a friend, "Well mate, I suppose this is this here b——— Empire we have heard about."

which we imagine to be the Indian troops.[1] Our cruiser and theirs stopped to have a chat and to make arrangements to change convoys.

Whilst this was going on we had the curious sight of 40 troopships and two cruisers all lying together in a heap.

I don't suppose that has ever been seen before or will be again.

It made us think what a haul it would be for the *Goeben* and *Breslau*.

The "Command of the Sea" seems to be more than a phrase now.

We have been very well treated on this boat and everybody has gone out of their way to be kind to us. I have written a letter to the Captain and Officers of the ship thanking them and we drank their healths to-night.

We are all very fit and have only four men in hospital out of 1,013 and these are not serious cases.

We have organised our double Companies and things are going quite well.

A man was buried this morning from one of the other ships, but I heard no details. We have lost a great number of horses I hear.

Alexandria.

We are at Mustapha Pasha Barracks, Alexandria, with the 6th and 8th Battns.[2]

It is the coolest station in the Mediterranean and very healthy.

I do not mind the heat and feel very well. I have a nice cool room in Barracks and we have an excellent Mess.

The sun is very hot and the glare tremendous. I have one Company in a fort[3] in the Town. We also supply the Town Guard, which has to be smart, and we deal with all passports.

There is ripping sea-bathing, and I had a lovely swim before breakfast.

We have a guard boat out for bathing and don't allow anyone to get far out.

You can dive off the rocks into five feet of water.

---

1 The Lahore Division, bound for Marseilles.
2 The Manchester Regiment.
3 Fort Kom-el-Dik.

I.—PREPARATION

The fatigues we have to find are enormous. We arrived here Friday evening and yesterday had every man in the Battn. on eight hours fatigue at the Docks six miles away. It is very hard on both officers and men.

Sanders' mare died on the voyage out, but both my horses[1] have come. I have engaged a native syce.

CAIRO.

21/1/1915.

We have now arrived at Cairo! Our last train got in at 8 p.m. last night and we got orders on arrival for a big divisional field day to-day. Incidentally I was informed I could not have a haversack ration for the men, so I had to go down late last night and have a slight argument with one[2] of the divisional staff. Eventually I got my ration and we parted the best of friends.

We settled down in camp pretty late and had our breakfasts in the dark at 5.30 a.m. We paraded at 6.30 a.m. and got in at 4.30 p.m. after doing an attack, digging ourselves in and finishing up with another attack. This as well as a good march out and back. Not a man fell out, so I think we have come through a pretty severe test.

We are all under canvas in bell tents. I am living in one and am very comfortable, although it is nothing but sand on the edge of the desert and it is very cold at nights. I am writing in our small ante-tent now in my thick khaki, a thick sweater, my thick waistcoat and a greatcoat. You would probably think it as warm as a summer evening at home.

24/1/1915.

I have been very busy all morning getting things right in Camp, routine, etc. Things are inclined to slack off after a move. It is just as well I did as I hear Gen. Douglas[3] is coming round in about an hour. Yesterday we had a pow-wow on the field day. We escaped pretty

---

1 My horse "Bob" survived the War.
2 Col. R.J. Slaughter, C.M.G., D.S.O. One of the best.
3 Major-General Sir William Douglas, K.C.M.G., C.B., D.S.O., commanding the 42nd Division.

lightly and Gen. Douglas said one of the four features of the day was the spirited attack of the Manchester Brigade.

Yesterday I went with Gen. Lee and H.L. Knight,[1] Brigade Major, to write my name in the calling books of the Sultan, McMahon and Maxwell.[2] Cairo is a beastly filthy town, and I shan't go down there more than I can help.

ABBASSIA.

11/2/1915.

I am sitting outside my tent (4 p.m.) writing and watching a very dusty football match. I am very fit indeed; they say you don't get Egyptian tummy at Cairo like you do at Alexandria. It is very hot here in the summer, but not at all unbearable, I don't suppose any hotter than South Africa.

To-morrow we are having a very interesting day, the five seniors from each Battalion leave here at 6.45 a.m. for the Canal, Kantara and Ismailia to see the fortifications and where the scrapping has been.[3]

Gen. Douglas has arranged it as a tour of instruction for us and I am very much looking forward to it. I went to a Concert on Tuesday and Gen. Douglas made a speech, in which he told us all about our division in the scrap. Our Engineers have been practically responsible for the whole of the defences of the Canal, and our guns did good work. Seven hundred dead Turks were found opposite one of our Batteries.

The Battery Commander[4] found he could not observe properly from the trenches, so went 800 yards forward under a heavy fire and carried on from there until the Turks chased him back. Whilst he was being chased back, the senior Captain[5] climbed a tree, and directed from there until he was shelled out of it, so he moved to a flank and

---

1 Brig-General Noel Lee, was I believe the first Territorial Brig-General.
  Major H.L. Knight, Royal Irish Fusiliers.
2 Sir Henry McMahon, High Commissioner of Egypt.
  Lt.-General Sir John Maxwell, Commanding in Egypt.
3 The first Turk attack on the Suez Canal on February 3rd, 1915.
4 Major B.P. Dobson, Bolton Artillery.
5 Capt. P.K. Clapham.

I.—PREPARATION

carried on from another tree. They all seem to have done very well, although I should imagine it is fairly soft fighting, judging from our casualties.

I personally don't think we shall see France for a long time, if ever; they must have a garrison here and I don't think the Turks have finished with the Canal by any means.

We have found one of our ex-officers, Walter Brown[1] by name, serving as a private with the Queenslanders. He has only just found out we are here.

The football match is awful and I shall have to move; I can now and then see a figure emerging from an enormous and stifling cloud of dust.[2]

13/2/15. Saturday, 9.30 a.m.

I am writing in the sun outside my tent waiting for orderly room. Saturday is our slack day, kit inspection and close order drill.

We had a most interesting day yesterday on the Canal; a party of 20 from our Brigade went. We caught the 7 a.m. train from Cairo, had breakfast on board and got off at Kantara; incidentally we passed over the battlefields of Kassassin and Tel el Kebir,[3] where Arabi's trenches are still to be seen. We were taken round the Kantara defences and shewn where the fighting took place and had it all explained.

The defences on the Canal are wonderful. We then went by train to Ismailia and had tea on board. At Ismailia we had another account of the scrapping there and saw the pontoons in which the Turks tried to cross the Canal; they were made in Germany of aluminium, and were painted "G.4. CONSTANTINOP*EL*" like that; observe the spelling, it betrays their origin I think! They were very full of shot holes and there are still a lot of Turks at the bottom of the Canal. A diver went down once, but refused to go again. I fancy their ammunition keeps them down.

---

1 Captain W.S. Brown, afterwards killed.
2 Neither heat nor dust nor any other adversity ever stopped football.
3 The scenes of Arabi Pasha's defeats by the British under Sir Garnet Wolseley in 1882.

We then went down by ferry-boat to Toussoum, where the Turks actually got down to the Canal bank and launched their boats, and where the toughest fighting took place. All the Turkish scratch trenches are along the bank and in every one was a pair of boots; there were hundreds lying about. I fancy they took their boots off when they got orders to embark in the pontoons and rafts they brought. We found lots of ammunition (empties) and some full clips. Sanders found some full clips in a boot, so started looking for more. He caught hold of one boot and tried to pick it up, but found it was on a dead Turk. The Indians have only partially buried them in some cases and their limbs stick out of the sand. There were piles and piles of kerosene tins; they brought their water in them on camels, then when they arrived they were used to make rafts of. Very clever idea.

We went to see the grave of "Major von Hagen," who is supposed to have played the white flag trick on the Punjabis.[1] He was found with a white flag just where the incident happened. The marvel of it all is how they ever crossed Sinai with pontoons, guns, baggage and water. It is an amazing feat. Their casualties were about 2,000, ours were 4 officers, 17 men killed, and about 70 wounded. It must have been very gentlemanly fighting from our point of view. If they come again, after this reconnaissance, and I feel sure they will, it will not be quite so genteel. We came back on a dining train and arrived here about midnight. In fact it is the only way to see war, and I feel I could have sold my ticket to any American for about £1,000!

---

1 This was merely a rumour and almost certainly untrue.

II.—GALLIPOLI

Abbassia.

30/4/15.

We are under orders to fit out at once. We are told Sir I. H.[1] cabled home asking to have us.

Everybody is fearfully pleased and although I don't thirst for blood, I shall be very glad for the Battalion to get a show. They have worked very hard and been very keen, soldierly and well disciplined, and I think they are quite capable of giving a first-class account of themselves.

I send you a cable from C.L.B., H.Q.,[2] on the occasion of our meeting when 500 were present.

Sunday.

We are off to-night. The Battalion is fearfully bucked as you can imagine. I am very fit and certain the men and officers will do very well. I am quite glad to go and give them their chance. As you know the thought of scrapping does not spoil my sleep or appetite.

3/5/15.

Just a line from the Transport *Derflinger*,[3] captured from the Germans. We are on board and probably go soon but do not quite know yet.

I am glad you got Mrs. Lindsay's[4] cable. The men are very bucked and in excellent spirits. I feel quite sure they will do well.

---

1 General Sir Ian Hamilton.
2 A meeting of ex-Church Lads Brigade Members was held and cables were exchanged with H.Q. in London.
3 This ship was afterwards renamed the *"Hunslet."*
4 The Hon. Mrs. Ronald C. Lindsay, Cairo.

LETTERS FROM HELLES

British Med. Force. 5/5/15.

I am writing before we land in the hopes it will get to you some time if I leave it on the ship.

We get there to-morrow early and don't know what we shall do or what is going on. I am very well and the two days at sea in lovely cool weather has bucked us all up tremendously after the heat at Cairo.

The bags that were issued to carry our emergency rations in were white, so we boiled them all in tea to-day and the result is quite good—they are distinctly khaki.

Gerald Allen,[1] I fancy, has jaundice, and will probably have to go back to Egypt to get over it.

I am sharing a Cabin with Knight.

The islands we are going through remind me exactly of the West Coast of Scotland.

Several people we know came to see us at Alexandria including Mr. Valentine[2] and Mr. K. Birley,[3] who is running a teashop on the quay for the men.

I hear we are going to a splendid climate, like Alexandria only cooler, and it is certainly ripping here. We shall get our orders to-morrow morning, and I suppose shall land to-morrow.

I went to early service on board. The Dean of Sydney took it. We have a Chaplain attached to us as well, a very young one, but I like him. Everybody is keen on a show.

DARDANELLES.

In the Trenches, 10/5/15.

Just as I started this letter the Turks started to shell our aeroplane, which was very high right over us. We could hear the pieces of shell falling and actually see them in the sunlight. They fell quite close.

I am very well and not taking any risks.

We are at present in the second line trenches, a good way behind the firing line.

---

1 Afterwards Lt.-Col. G. E. Allen, commanding the 5th Manchester Regiment.
2 The Vicar of Ramleh, Alexandria.
3 Of Alexandria.

II.—GALLIPOLI

As is usual in support we get a lot of "overs," and are also shelled some time during the day. We are quite safe, however, in our trench and I fancy the Turk is short of ammunition.

We have had one officer (Jim Walker's brother)[1] very slightly wounded, he has not left duty, and about 12 men are wounded, all slightly.

More shells at our aeroplane and more pieces.

I wish the beastly thing would go away.

We had a good voyage on a filthy ship and I sent a cable back by Allen who had jaundice.

We landed in tugs and I went in the first one with A Coy.

We had three shells in the water fairly near us from a gun[2] called "Asiatic Annie," so you know where she is.

We have bivouacked since and have no kits, no blankets, no camp kettles and no nothing, but we are very well fed.

There was a devil of an attack by us the day before yesterday; we were in reserve and I was ordered up to support part of the attack in the afternoon. We went up[3] and got into some support trenches just at dusk and were shelled and fired at mildly coming up. Our casualties were only three though.

We are still in these trenches, but don't know for how long.

We watched, earlier in the fight, the most extraordinary bombardment by our guns and saw the French charge the trenches and chase the Turks out. They caught it from our guns as they left.

The usual evening bombardment and rifle firing is starting.

Last night I got a message about 1 a.m. to stand by for an expected counter attack, which never came off.

Both sides, I fancy, were nervy and expecting an attack, the result was firing of all sorts all night. I slept pretty well between times.

The snipers here are very clever.

It is getting dusk now and I must stop, also letters have to go down to the base at once.

---

1 Lieut. T.C. Walker, killed June, 1915.
2 A big gun on the mainland, which used to shell us from the rear.
3 As we went up a rather exposed nullah one of the inhabitants put his head out of a hole in the ground and said, "They call this hell fire valley, sir." It cheered the men more than anything.

'HCD, Sanders, E. Fletcher.'
In dug-out, left to right: HCD (bare-headed), Captain J.M.B. Sanders and Major E. Fletcher. Sitting left of picture, Captain A.C. Leech.
Photograph probably taken at 'Bridge Bivouac,' 7/8 May 1915.

II.—GALLIPOLI

It is very cold at nights, but a lovely climate, absolutely perfect. Only one shower of a few drops since we came and the flowers and birds are lovely. I feel very fit and quite like old times. It is very funny how all the different people take shells. I find I am the only one, from my South African experience, who can tell where they are coming, and the range is just right, you have time to tumble into your trench.

Trenches. 14/5/15.

I am *very* fit. Sleep as I used to in S.A.[1] and eat enormous quantities of food.

The weather is perfect again. We had one day's rain and our trenches were a quagmire. We are still in the firing line reserve trenches and have to be careful showing up. Their snipers are very good, and they now and then shell the trenches. They hit my dugout three times with shrapnel the night before last and my last dugout twice.

Young Walker was hit slightly in the head. Cyril Ainscough[2] got a spent bullet in his foot and Cunningham[3] was hit slightly in the face. They are all nothing and only Cunningham went to hospital. He was up here to see us to-day.

We have still no kits and I want a bath badly. I have a ground sheet and one blanket and no change, but it is much nicer having no luggage to bother about. The men take it very well, but of course have not faced much yet.

We had rather a bad time coming up, but it was more frightening than dangerous.

We have had one man killed and 20 wounded. The Turk aeroplane guns are beastly. The pieces fall and you can hear them coming for ages, also sometimes you can see them falling in the sunlight, very slowly like a penny through water.

The Turks have a big gun up. They killed Frank James'[4] horse with it yesterday. I am perfectly filthy with mud and want of a bath and change, but I am shaving. Archie Brook looks like a Turk himself with his beard.

---

1 The South African War.
2 Lieut. C. Ainscough, killed August, 1915.
3 Capt. Cunningham, R.A.M.C.
4 Lieut. F. James, killed Sept., 1915.

I have stripped my badges, wear putties and a web kit and carry a short rifle.[1]

Here comes Archie.[2] He wants leave to go out and bury 20 dead Turks just in front of his Trench. He is now with the Machine Guns. The aero is right over me now, I hope they won't shell it. It is a very good life this and makes you feel so fit.

5.15 p.m. I have been up and down the trenches all day driving people to deepen and improve. One gets sniped all the way. The country is a mass of furze and the snipers lie out in it for weeks with tinned food and snipe all day.

They are apparently behind the lines and in between and are almost impossible to spot, the scrub is so thick.

I tried for an hour to-day to spot one that annoys us all day, but I can't.

The food is good of a sort, and plenty of it, and we live on tinned stew, which we heat up, and we sometimes can buy bread and eggs. We have plenty of jam and bacon and tobacco, and make out with bully beef and biscuits.

I had a mail to-day up to Apl. 20th.

We had a quiet night last night for once, as a rule there is a devil of a racket some time or other during the night, rifle fire and big guns and the ships and as everything comes over our heads the noise is appalling.

It is a lovely bit of country, agricultural and moorland dotted with trees, and in configuration something like Slaidburn[3] only very few trees. The daisies and poppies are lovely, the landscape is rather spoilt by dead Turks on close inspection.

A.C.B.[4] has 15 to bury to-night as soon as it is dusk. You can't do it by day, only sometimes it is more dangerous at night, as the Turks have a habit of opening a devil of a fire when they think we are relieving trenches or bringing up supplies. Our guns are now starting the usual

---

1 A very necessary precaution in Gallipoli.
2 Lieut. A. C. Brook.
3 A village on the borders of Lancashire and Yorkshire, where my father-in-law had a grouse moor.
4 A. C. Brook.

II.—GALLIPOLI

evening bombardment, and we have our high tea at 6 p.m., and then turn in. Our tea to-night is fried bacon, bread and jam, figs and tea, also a drop of ration rum.

I *am* hungry too. My dugout is rather damp, but it does not seem to affect me and it is safe enough from shrapnel. I sometimes wake rather rheumaticky, but that may be the hard ground. I shall be glad when we are relieved from the trenches to get my valise again. I have nothing here.

You ought to hear the big guns fire, it is an education. I won't mention any names.[1] The guns are fairly at it now, they make the whole place rock.

I will finish to-morrow.

15/5/15.

I am very well. A quiet day except for sniping and interminable shelling.

18/5/15. 6.15 a.m.

I am writing this between standing to arms and breakfast, we stand to every day at 3 a.m.

I am very fit and safe and sound.

We are now in the fire trenches about 450 yards from the Turks' fire trenches.

We moved up here the night before last after dusk and got up without a casualty, which was lucky as the Turk generally shells the donga we come up after dusk to catch the reliefs and ration parties.

All our food and water has to be carried up during the night and brother Turk often opens heavy fire to catch parties doing so.

I have an artillery officer here and can use guns when I want to.[2]

The Turks opened a very heavy fire as the troops we relieved were going out, so we fired five shells at the offending trenches and stopped it.

I was afraid the outgoing troops would suffer. We did not reply with rifle fire.

---

1 H.M.S. *Queen Elizabeth.*
2 I found my mistake very soon, owing to the shortage of ammunition.

'Looking back from my H.Q., Redoubt Line (just where Brig. Gen. Lee was killed). Dead Australian.'

Probably taken between 16–21 May 1915, or possibly between 3–7 July 1915.

Brigadier-General Noel Lee, commanding 127th (Manchester) Brigade, was mortally wounded by shrapnel around 12 noon on 4 June 1915. He died in hospital on Malta on 22 June 1915.

II.—GALLIPOLI

It is safer here than it is in support or reserve. The bullets cannot come into your trenches at the short range like they do further back, also the Turks' guns very seldom shell us like they do the support and reserve trenches. I fancy they are too close to do much harm to the fire trenches.

By day we have observers and snipers who watch for enemy snipers.

The men are very keen on the job and we have quite got the superiority, altho' their snipers are very good shots. The worst of this place is the stench. The whole place is stiff with dead Turks and Australians. We have buried a few and do what we can altho' it is dangerous work. We shall manage to get the near ones under soon.

The sniper has just hit the top of my dugout[1] a fearful smack. Ernest Fletcher[2] who is reading said "Bow wow."

The Turks started firing this morning about 3 a.m. and some of our men replied.

One or two had the jumps so I went and threatened to fall them in as soon as it was light and send them out in front to bury all the Turks they had killed. It amused them. The men are wonderfully steady and let the Turks simply blaze away without replying. It is an N.C.O. now and then who gets the jumps and opens fire.

We don't reply unless there is a good reason, as it only starts the whole Turk line firing, and our ration and water parties catch it badly.

The climate is ripping and I fancy the rain is finished with, and they feed us very well.

We can now and then get eggs and this morning for breakfast we are having cooked ham and eggs, bread, jam and tea. For lunch we shall have hot tinned stew and figs and probably the same for tea with some cheese. We cook in the fire trenches,[3] and I drink quarts of hot tea.

Yesterday we got hold of a tin of milk and some tinned butter of sorts.

---

1 Dugouts did not exist in Gallipoli. We lived in holes in the ground governed as to the depth by water and as to roofs by the fact that we had no roofing materials of any sort.
2 Major E. Fletcher, my Second in Command.
3 Our trenches were outlined each morning by a haze of smoke. The Turks had an issue of charcoal.

We have no kit, but I have got a horse blanket and a ground sheet and my air pillow, and I never wake till I am woken or unless heavy firing starts.

I prowl around a bit at nights, altho' there is no need, as the Company organisation is pretty good now and the men are fast getting settled.

Any extras in the food line you can think of will be very welcome. Any variety in the meat line (we have very good bacon and ham issued), such as tongue or sardines, potted meat or a cake or plum pudding, chocolates or sweets.

We are all dressed like tommies, and I carry web kit, pack and all, and a rifle. It is safer with these snipers, but the kind of warfare we are engaged in is not dangerous if you keep your head down, which I do.

We have a couple[1] of periscopes, but it would be a good thing if you were to send me one.

I am extremely fit and eat and sleep like anything, and now we are in more or less dry trenches I have no rheumatism at all when I wake up. Don't worry, I don't, and the men are very steady and reliable and *splendid* diggers,[2] which means a lot.

Sat., 22/5/15.

We were relieved from the firing line last night and came down near the base at the cost of only one casualty.

We are now for some days in a so-called rest camp, which is a collection of dugouts in a field. It is not much of a rest camp as it is shelled all day at unexpected moments, and you have to stick close in your dugout.

I tried to get out this morning after breakfast with Freddy Brown[3] and half-way across we heard two shells coming; we went flat just in time, but it wounded three men close to us. Luckily the Turk shrapnel is fairly innocuous and has very little effect.

Poor Milward Rogers was laid out by the previous shell. He was outside his dugout and got hit in the thigh; it is not at all bad as far as we know.

---

[1] "A couple" is literally true.
[2] The men were mostly Wigan and district colliers, and the whole Battalion literally sank into the ground wherever we halted.
[3] Capt. F. S. Brown. Killed May, 1915.

'HCD in Dugout at Rest Camp—22 May 1915.'
Probably taken at 'Shell Bivouac.'

'The Dugouts at Rest Camp. Cronshaw, Fletcher, self.'
Left to right: Major A.E. Cronshaw, Major E. Fletcher and HCD.
Probably taken at 'Shell Bivouac' between 22–25 May 1915.

'Bivouac Gallipoli.'
Probably taken at 'Shell Bivouac' between 21–25 May 1915.

'Ainscough, Woods, Hewlett, K. Burrows, F. Brown, A. Johnson.'
Back, left to right: Lieut. C. Ainscough, Capt. W.T. Woods, Capt. A. Hewlett.
Front, left to right: 2nd Lieut. M.K. Burrows, Capt. F.S. Brown, Lieut. A.E. Johnson.
Three of these officers were wounded, and two killed, at Gallipoli.
Captain Brown was killed on 26 May 1915, a few days after this photo was taken.

'A.C.B. shaving.'
2nd Lieutenant A.C. Brook. The canvas bucket over his left shoulder is marked
as the property of Lieutenant G.S. James (KIA 4 June 1915).

It is a bonny expedition. The rest camps are miles more dangerous than the fire trenches. We lost three killed and one wounded during our six days in the fire trenches and already this morning we have had four wounded before 10 a.m. However, I have played the game before and am not taking unnecessary risks.

I slept in my valise last night with my boots off for the first time since we landed on May 6th, and shall have my first bath and change later on.

Our men are very steady and not at all liable to the jumps and I feel great confidence now in both officers and men. There was not a night in front when the Turks did not start blazing away on the French or someone, and our men never fired unless ordered. They also quite got the Turk snipers down.

They all dig, too, on their own and nearly every man in the Battalion now carries a pick or spade which he has snitched or picked up, left by other units who are too lazy to carry them, as well as their other kit. Our trenches have been splendid wherever we have been, and the Divisional and Brigade Staffs and the R.E. are very pleased with them. Our trench casualty list is far below anyone else's.

I had a ripping night's sleep from 2 a.m. to 8 a.m., and altho' the Turks shelled us at 5 a.m. it did not even wake me. I sleep well anyhow now in the fire trenches, altho' I generally turn out once or twice if firing starts.

It rained last night and I got somewhat wet, but the sun this morning has dried everything.

There is a devil of a musketry scrap going on ahead, and both sides have their guns going, but it usually means very little.

We have not had a shell here for an hour. I feel very fit and fat and eat tons and sleep well and consequently I don't have any nerves and the shelling and shooting does not bother me.

The French [1] are fairly going it just at this moment. Brother Turk is a bit of a humorist, he signals washouts with a spade when our snipers miss him. We drew him all right yesterday, we rigged up a dummy and put it up, he had some shots at it and then got suspicious and stopped,

---

1 Corps Expéditionnaire d'Orient.
    1st Division: Zouaves, Foreign Legion, Colonial Regiments, and
    2nd Division: 175th and 176th Regiments

II.—GALLIPOLI

so I told a man to lower the dummy, poke up a rifle on the parapet, and then shove the dummy up as if it was one of our snipers; that fairly fetched the Turk and when he had quite finished we shoved the dummy right up and waggled it at him.

The Turks put their bucket up to draw our snipers, and if one fires the Turk signals a miss.

We put a bully beef tin up to represent the end of a periscope and he hit it first shot. Two of our men played the ass and crawled out behind the trench to get a bit of kit. They had both been cautioned before about being fools and they were both killed first shot.

They are now shelling our field again, but their shrapnel is rotten. Freddy Gordon[1] and several men have been hit and only bruised and Fred Brown was knocked down by the burst of one quite unhurt.

We score over France very much here in the climate, it is perfectly lovely and the acres of poppies and daisies and the birds are simply beautiful.

The only thing that spoils the view up in the front is the big number of dead Turks and Australians. We bury what we can at night, but it is dangerous work especially if a flare goes up. The smell is appalling. However, it is restful here and the responsibility of the front line is not there. Bar the shells I shall get a walk later on as one needs exercise in this kind of warfare.

I have my camera[2] here and am taking a few photos, but goodness knows when or where I will get them developed. There is no town here and no inhabitants[3] so far as I can see. All the farms are in ruins. I did hear a cock crow the other day, but it was behind the Turk trenches. I think they have dogs in their trenches, as we heard them bark the other morning. It might have been a fox or something of that sort.

My Aunt, what a rest Camp. They are at it again.

24/5/15.

We are still in our rest bivouac and shelled at odd times.

---

1 Lieut. F.C. Gordon.
2 Cameras were allowed at Gallipoli.
3 An officer joining us asked the Military Landing Officer where the nearest pub was.

'*Trench Decoys. Fire Trench 5th Mans. With dummies.*'
Probably taken in the Redoubt Line between 16–21 May 1915.

'*Lieut. F.C. Gordon.*'
Probably taken in late May or early June 1915.

II.—GALLIPOLI

I found Postlethwaite[1] the night before last presiding over our dressing station in the next field, so I went and had a talk with him. He had dressed Milward's wound and said it was only slight in the thigh.

You must not picture us in deadly danger and doing the death and glory act *à la* the Graphic. We live absolutely underground, do our turn in the fire trenches, which is absolutely the safest place in the Peninsular and spend the rest of our days digging and doing road making and other fatigue work day and night.

I hear now Milward's wound was more serious than they thought, but he is much better to-day and it is not quite to be catalogued as "dangerous."

Yesterday I went down to W Beach to see the ships, &c., and also had a paddle, and in the afternoon I went to Y Beach [Gully Beach] and watched two of our Companies bathing.

This morning I walked down on to the cliffs to have a look at the aeroplanes. I soon cleared off as brother Turk started to shell the aerodrome. The first shell fell right in the middle but did no damage.

It rained hard this morning early for several hours, but we don't mind as the sun soon comes out and dries everything very quickly.

It is ripping country and weather, and we thoroughly enjoy walking down to the shore and getting some exercise and at that long range you have plenty of time to get to cover, when you hear a shell coming your way, which is really not often.

29/5/15.

I have had no time to write lately. We were moved forward again to the fire trench and have since been making new forward trenches.

It is extraordinary how you can go out into the open and dig close to the Turk trenches. Poor Freddie Brown was killed dead during our first advance and we have had our Quartermaster, Taylor, G. Johnson,[2] P. C. Fletcher and Parker[3] (joined at Alexandria) wounded.

We have been relieved of the forward work for a day or two and are having more or less of a rest, altho' we are still close up. We suffered rather yesterday in our forward trenches. The night we came here

---

1 Capt. J. M. Postlethwaite, R.A.M.C.
2 Lieut. W. G. Johnson, killed in France.
3 Lieut. P. C. Parker (Alexandria).

there had been heavy thunder storms and the trenches were full of water. The communication trench coming up took me well over the knees. I can't say I went to bed soaked as I never went to bed at all, the relief took the whole night. I am very well indeed and the wet did me no harm.

I still keep shaved and have no hair. I keep it cropped with clippers, but I don't get many baths.

It is getting very hot in the trenches by day, but the weather is ripping. Anchusa grows wild all over the place here.

The G.O.C. the force has expressed his satisfaction with the work done by our Brigade. Our officers and men are better than I hoped, and they don't care a damn for anything. The men are very calm and cool, and think things out for themselves.

Our digging is already known throughout the Peninsular, and it is quite a stock joke now.

I was on the cliffs the other day with my glasses and watched the torpedoing of one of our battleships, H.M.S. *Ocean* [H.M.S. *Majestic*]. It was close in and nearly all were saved. It was very interesting as you can imagine, but very sickening and made one very angry.[1]

Poor old Coy. Sgt.-Major Spencer was killed yesterday. He was with me in S.A. and was Arthur Simpson's[2] Col. Sergt. of the Leigh Company.

Copy of Order.

O.C. 5th, 6th, 7th, and 8th Battns.

Following message received begins:

> I congratulate you and your gallant Brigade on their achievement under difficult circumstances, and I am confident that it is only a prelude to further good work.

Major-Genl. Douglas ends.

From G.O.C., 127th Brigade.

---

[1] The Turkish batteries on shore shelled the *Ocean* [*Majestic*] until the rescue boats started picking the crew out of the water; after that not another shell was fired.

[2] Afterwards Lt.-Col. A. W. W. Simpson, O.B.E., commanding 5th Manchester Regiment.

II.—GALLIPOLI

Fire Trenches, 2/6/15.

I am still very fit and untouched. You will be glad to hear that in case of an attack the Authorities do not allow C.O.'s to lead their men, they say that is the job of platoon commanders and that C.O.'s should be in the rear of their commands, where they can watch and influence events and keep in touch with their commands and with Brigade. So don't imagine me charging at the head of the Battalion. One has to sit on a telephone in comparative safety. It will not be your idea of my functions but it seems sound if you think of it. They say that things go wrong when a C.O. gets knocked out.

We are all fairly tired (I am not particularly, as I get a fair amount of sleep), but the Battalion is.

They have been digging without rest ever since May 6th, and our Brigade seems to be doing front line permanently. The others are behind and do not take their turn in relieving us. It is undoubtedly a compliment.

We are now "127 Brigade." Our battalion's casualties are mounting up, altho' we are still less than other people.

I am not supposed to tell you numbers, but the total is about twice my age,[1] rather more. We had 15 killed and 10 wounded three days ago in one trench from enfilade fire. All in one day.

I don't want any clothes or anything except as written in my letter from Cairo to you and I like Abdulla cigarettes.

I got a box containing chocolate, tobacco, cigs, etc., from you and very much appreciated it.

We were warned that old man Turk was going to have a shy at us last night, but he never came, altho' we could hear him chanting his prayers and shouting Allah, &c., &c., in his trenches about 9 p.m. He makes the most weird noises at times.

3/6/15.

We were warned of a Turk attack again last night, but it never came off. I am very fit and will post this and write you another.

---

[1] Thirty-eight years.

'Gallipoli.'
Graves of Captain Arthur Clive Leech, 2nd Lieutenant Arthur 'Archie' Charles Brook, and 2nd Lieutenant Thomas Cartmell Walker. All three men are buried in the Redoubt Cemetery, Helles, Turkey.

III.—THIRD BATTLE OF KRITHIA

June 5th, '15.

You will by now have seen in the papers that we had a big scrap yesterday, of which I can tell you the details later. Our casualties were heavy, and worst of all poor old Archie Brook, Sidney James and C. Leech[1] were killed.

It does not do under these circumstances to think too much about things, but I cannot help thinking of Sidney and Aunt Ruth and Mrs. Leech.

I cannot mention casualties, but they were

Officers, the last numeral[2] in the year we were married in.

Men, about four-fifths of my Wigan Office telephone number.[3]

Poor old B Co. got rather mauled, but it was not their fault, they hung on long after the French retired on our right; so did A Co.

I am very fit but of course tired to-day, the strain of a modern fight is big. I got through without a scratch. My puggaree was cut slightly, and I had two bullets through my periscope. I spent most of my day in a trench at the end of a telephone.

Both officers and men did perfectly splendidly, and I feel proud of them, and those that were killed were killed as men should be.

Brig.-Gen. Noel Lee was slightly wounded and Lord Rochdale[4] is in command.

He congratulated me on the Battalion and said they had astonished him and that he considered them magnificent.

---

1 Lieut. G. S. James, brother of Lieut. F. James, killed Sept., 1915.
   Capt. A. C. Leech.
2 Nine.
3 Telephone No. 215.
4 Colonel Lord Rochdale came out with the Division in command of the 1/6th Bn. Lancashire Fusiliers.

'Fire Trench. Vineyard E. of Krithia Nullah. 5th Manchesters.'
Probably taken on 5 or 6 June when the 5th Manchesters held the firing-line that ran along the southern boundary of the Vineyard.

'Fire Trench. 5th Manchesters.'

III.—THIRD BATTLE OF KRITHIA

I enclose the Corps Commander's chit and Gen. Douglas' on the same chit.

We are the 127th Brigade now. We have not been relieved from the front line yet altho' we have now had 15 days hard.

The other two Brigades were not in the front line and I fancy we were kept here to take the job on.

Our artillery bombardment was appalling, and I saw one of our Black Marias send a Turk at least 100 feet in the air. The Turks had the cheek to counter-attack our Battalion twice last night in small numbers.

We wiped the lot out as far as I can tell, only one reached the trench and he was promptly bayoneted.

Our men loved getting in with the bayonet. One man coming back with a bullet in his leg and one in his arm patted me on the back as he passed and said, "I don't care a damn, Colonel, I got three on the bayonet."

7/6/15.

We are still in the fire trench. Why, I don't know.

The rest of the Brigade have been relieved, but we are still here.

Our men are played out for want of sleep, but are splendidly game. We have been counter-attacked three times and stopped it each time and our flanks have been bombing Turks and being bombed back by Turks in the same line of trenches[1] all the time. Sidney James was killed that way.

Archie Brook was killed absolutely outright whilst getting one of the guns or ammunition up.

Young Walker[2] was killed, too, and Clive Leech, Archie and Walker were all buried next to each other by our Brigade Chaplain.[3] I could not go as we were scrapping and have been for the last few days without ceasing. We have nine officers left for duty, including four battalion staff.

---

1 One was so used to being mixed up with the Turks that when a (naturally) excited officer of the Royal Naval Division rushed into Bn. H.Q. and shouted, "Do you know the Turks are in your front line?" Major Ernest Fletcher merely said, "Well, have a drink."

2 Lieut. T.C. Walker, a brother of Capt. J.S.A. Walker.

3 The Rev. E.T. Kerby.

The Battalion has been splendid, but the Authorities are trying them up and I can't get them relieved. I think they rely on us a good deal.

I am *very well*.

42nd (East Lancs.) Division.

The following message from Lt.-Gen. A. G. Hunter Weston, C.B., D.S.O., received at 6.33 p.m. on 4th June is published for information:—

"Please express to the 42nd Division and particularly to the 127th Brigade, my appreciation of the magnificent work done by them to-day. The 127th Brigade attacked punctually on time, and exactly in the manner ordered, dashing forward with gallantry and holding on to the objective with tenacity. It was a very fine performance."

Please convey this to all the troops of the Division where possible and tell them that I deeply appreciate their gallant conduct and devotion to their duty. The renown they have gained for the Division will not only reach the ears of all Lancashire, but throughout the British Empire.

I feel sure that the same tenacity will be maintained to-night and throughout the Campaign.

W. DOUGLAS,
Major-General,
Commanding 42 (E. Lancs.) Division.

9/6/15.

I am very well and we are having a much needed rest. We were relieved from the fire trenches yesterday after 15 days of it, one big fight and nearly incessant minor fighting, we were ordered to 3rd line trenches, but I fancy Lord Rochdale, now commanding our Brigade (*vice* N. Lee,[1] wounded in the face), intervened, so we have been brought back to corps reserve for a rest. It is delightful to get rid of the responsibility of first line after 15 days, but they shell us like blazes here.

---

1 Brig.-General Noel Lee died of wounds.

III.—THIRD BATTLE OF KRITHIA

However, I stick in my dugout mostly. I got smack in the middle of a shrapnel[1] burst yesterday and for the second time came out untouched.

The Division has been badly cut up and for very little so far as we can see. The last few days were very trying as we had the Turks in our trenches on both flanks, and it was bomb, bomb, bomb, morning, noon and night. Of course we were short of bombs and not old man Turk! Our strength now is eight officers and the following number of men: multiply my Wigan office telephone by two and subtract 13. The other battalions are less by a long way. However, we manage to keep cheery and the men are splendid, they were quite steady to the end and only suffered from lack of sleep. They had none for three days and nights as we were counter-attacked three times[2] during the nights. They are now starting to shell us again! However, we are so used to it we hardly notice. They can actually shell the beach. People coming out here from France are utterly astonished at the fighting here.[3] We are all quite certain the true facts are being kept back from the British public.

We had a tophole dinner last night. Bacon, sardines, potted meat, tinned apricots, cocoa (the first we have seen), a drop of port and a cigar.

I turned in about 10.30 and slept till 9 a.m. I shall sleep again this afternoon as I have a lot of arrears to make up.

It is difficult to sleep by day as the sun is so hot and there is nothing to make a roof of.

Don't think I am downhearted. One could not be so with my battalion, what is left of them. They are so cheery and steady. They simply loved getting in with the bayonet on the 4th. Our men did not fire a single shot when we charged.

They jumped out of their trench, legged it splendidly across the 200 yards of open and bayoneted every Turk in the trench. Only two escaped that I could hear of. One of our men saw five Turks escaping

---

1 This shell apparently had no lead bullets in it, but was loaded with old brass clock wheels and other scrap.
2 It was not certain whether one of these attacks was Turks or some belated Fusiliers trying to regain our front line. Private G. Carr of the 5th said, "I'll damned soon see," climbed over the parapet, ran towards the enemy trenches, flung himself on his face, and shouted, "Fire, They're Turks." Private Carr got back untouched, but was afterwards killed.
3 Whether in rest or not the troops were in every battle, as there was no depth in our position: also the proportion of killed to wounded was high and few prisoners were taken.

LETTERS FROM HELLES

down a communication trench, so he jumped out in the open, ran down the trench, jumped in in front of the Turks and drove them back on to our men's bayonets. There were no wounded.

Two of our Companies then went on to the next position and collared that. However, the French on the right retired, then the Naval Division and then the 7th Manchesters leaving B Co. with their flank 800 yards in the air. They hung on splendidly[1] for about three hours and then gradually fell back as the Turks were then round them. This left A Co.'s flank in the air. They hung on from 1 p.m. to 7 p.m., when I ordered them back on my own. They were gradually being cut to pieces. Both companies lost nearly 40 per cent, and stuck it.

They came back cursing and swearing that there were no reinforcements to help them to stick it, and quite calm only *very* angry.[2]

I tried to get reinforcements of course, *but there were none*. There *never* are here.

That is our experience in every show.

Don't send me blankets or heavy stuff. I can't cart them about. I only have what I and my servant can carry about.

We have no transport and all our pack-horses and mules have been killed.

I got three more mules last night and they were killed this morning during the shelling. It is astonishing how happy and cheerful we keep. Good food and a rest now and then make one feel that one would not call "King George one's Uncle."[3]

I am lying on my bed now quite comfortable and happy, have had a good lunch and am smoking a cigar and just comfortably sleepy.

The dust and flies are beastly and these shells, but they don't disturb me much.

Mrs. Ronald Lindsay sends me a plum pudding every so often, which is very nice. Cakes are the things we like.

The 6th Manchesters have nearly been wiped out. It is sickening.

I shall sleep now. I am very well and quite happy, and very comfortable and my nerves have stood the strain without any give at all.

---

1 Sir Ian Hamilton in his "Gallipoli Diary" says, "By all the laws of war they ought to have tumbled back anyhow, but by the laws of the Manchesters they hung on and declared they could do so for ever."
2 I was unpopular for several days for having forced them to come back.
3 A Wigan expression of well-being.

IV.—IMBROS—TRENCH WARFARE

June 14, '15.

I am *very* well and we are having a ripping rest away from even odd shells.

The whole brigade the night before last was put on to trawlers, etc., and sent across to a neighbouring island (Imbros) to reorganize. It is a ripping island, exactly like Lewis or Harris. We have got tents. This morning I had a bathe in the sea before breakfast and then we had breakfast, bacon and eggs and jam, among the rocks, just like we do at Tarbert. The great relief is to be in a place where you can walk about without getting shot at or shelled. Annie from Asia can't even reach us and we don't care a damn for aeroplanes. One came over yesterday and dropped bombs on us. We were very lucky getting across: we came in the dark and Annie never fired a shot. She generally shells the beach at nights. You don't know the tremendous relief it is to feel really safe, especially after 15 days in the first line and one big scrap thrown in. There are not 30 officers left in the Brigade, and only about 40 per cent. of the men. How long we shall be here I don't know, but I am afraid it will only be for four days. It *may be* longer. I don't think anyone at home has an idea of the kind of fighting here unless they can gather from the enormous casualty lists.

Our trouble is that when we are sent in reserve it is more dangerous than the fire trenches, as every inch of the Peninsula is systematically searched and shelled.

We have just heard that old Milward Rogers has died from wounds, and I am afraid it is true.

The worst of being out of the fighting is that one, for the first time perhaps, realizes one's losses. One cannot afford, however, to think of them too much.

Old man Turk is such an excellent fighter that one has to keep one's tail up and one's officers' tails up to compete with him.

'A Coy, Imbros, after June 4th.'
'A' Company would have begun the battle around 180 strong.

'Camp of Manchester Brigade, Imbros, after June 4th.'

IV. — IMBROS — TRENCH WARFARE

My Battalion and the 6th Manchesters have been magnificent and utterly steady throughout it all. One thing is certain that the 5th and 6th Manchesters[1] could not have done much better and when loosed they went as straight as dies and what is more in all the stress carried out the orders.

"A" Co. under Talbot Woods[2] hung on all day splendidly with the Turks on their flank and rear and suffered very much.

I have sent in Frank James' name for bombing up a Turk trench with only one man, also Kenneth Burrows[3] for climbing out of a trench under heavy fire from the Turks and *from our own artillery* and holding up a red screen to show our guns they were firing on his Company. How he escaped I don't know.

16/6/15.

We are still on this island reorganizing, but are afraid we shall have to go back soon to the Peninsula.

It is raining like anything this morning, and I am thankful we are here under canvas and not squelching in the trenches. I did not have my before-breakfast bathe to-day, as it was so wet and blowing such a gale. Did I tell you that Parson Komlosy[4] is on the Peninsula, he rolled up in my dugout the other day. We are hoping they will leave us here until some drafts come out from home to fill us up. We are only a nucleus now, but if we go back again now we shall soon cease to be even that and the best course would seem to be to fill us up, when our old hands would train the new drafts. This island is ripping. I went a walk yesterday with Rochdale and it reminded me every step exactly of the west coast islands.[5] Rocks and scrub.

17/6/15.

I went a walk yesterday over the Naval flying station; they gave us tea there, honey and bread and *butter*. The first butter I have tasted since I left Cairo. A tin of butter is a good thing to send.

---

1 The 5th and 6th were working together and relieved each other in the trenches.
2 Afterwards Col. W. T. Woods, D.S.O., M.C.
3 Capt. M. K. Burrows, M.C.
4 The Rev. F. Komlosy, formerly a curate in Wigan, attached 29th Division.
5 W. Coast of Scotland.

'*Our dining room, Imbros.
E. Fletcher, Cunningham, self, Sanders, Hutchinson.*'
Major E. Fletcher, Capt. H.H.B. Cunningham, R.A.M.C., HCD, Capt.
J.M.B. Sanders and Major W.A. Hutchinson, OC, 'W' Company, 1st Royal
Munster Fusiliers. Hutchinson was attached to the 1/5th Manchesters
from 25 May 'to assist in training them in their duties.'

'*Woods, F. James. Imbros.*'
Capt. W.T. Woods and Lieut. F. James.

'Imbros.'

Views of the camp and harbour at K Beach (top and centre). Below, a bathing party, with Major Hutchinson, Capt. Cunningham, and HCD on the shore, and Hutchinson and Cunningham pictured swimming in the sea.

LETTERS FROM HELLES

18/6/15.

I am very well. Sir Ian Hamilton inspected the Brigade this morning and seemed very pleased with the appearance of the men. They certainly look a hardy lot now. They are attaching officers to us from K.'s armies. I wish we had our own from home instead.

We are still on this island, much to our surprise, and are afraid we may be biffed back to the Peninsula any day.

We are hoping with luck to be left here till our drafts arrive, but of course we may be wanted. I wonder what Manchester and Wigan will think of our losses, 86 officers killed and wounded out of 129 is a bit thick. I am sorry for the Walkers, one brother killed in France and one killed here. Jim Walker[1] has now been sent away sick with neuritis.

The cream you sent me was ripping. We had it last night for dinner with cherries, which you can buy here.

Sir I. H.[2] asked me when I got command. I told him, and he said, "I suppose you have had lots of chances of getting rid of it lately." I expect you will think it sorry wit.

Sunday, 20/6/15.

I have just come in from early service and am waiting for breakfast. The service was on the hillside.

We still have no orders to return to the Peninsula, but as we have now had a week's rest we may get them any time, unless we are to be here till our drafts come.

One of the German submarines was nearly bottled yesterday. She got foul of our nets in the Straits and had to come up, and those French lost their opportunity and never fired at her. One shell or a maxim would have sent her to the bottom.

The French guns cover our sector of the trenches and we are great friends with their observing officer who lives with us when we are up there, Lt. Marie. I have got a photo of him in our dugout, if it is ever developed.

---

1 Major J. S. A. Walker.
2 General Sir Ian Hamilton.

'Lt. Marie F.O.O. French Artillery, Sanders, Hutchinson.'
2nd Lieutenant Marie, Forward Observation Officer, 51st Battery
(*Canon de 120 mm L modèle 1878*), 1st Group, 30th Artillery Regiment (*30ème régiment d'artillerie de campagne*), Capt. J.M.B. Sanders, and Major W.A. Hutchinson.

'Hutchinson, Corpl Seddon, Sanders.'
Major W.A. Hutchinson, Corporal Seddon, Capt. J.M.B. Sanders.

Did you read the official account of the 4th of June in the ——— of the 7th? Goodness knows who compiles these things, but it is a rotten account and extremely inaccurate to say the least of it.

Breakfast is ready, so I will write more later. The guns on Gallipoli have been busy all morning and are still at it. Turk guns, you bet, not ours.

21/6/15.

We have just had orders to go back to the Peninsula.

It will interest you to know who are left with the Battalion: Self, E. Fletcher, Cunningham, Cronshaw, Sanders, Bryham, Woods, Slaughter and Frank James. The others are casualties except Simpson, who was sent back medically unfit to Alexandria, and Holden,[1] who was injured, Jim Walker, who is in hospital. Cunningham has been wounded once and recovered.

22/6/15.

We got orders to embark for the old spot[2] at 6.30 p.m. yesterday, and within 1 ½ hours we (the 5th) were on board two trawlers which brought us back to the old spot and the old noise. We saw nothing of our friends the submarines and Annie from Asia (she apparently has had triplets[3] in the last week) was taking a rest, so we had an uneventful crossing. Our new Brigadier has taken over, by name Herbert Lawrence,[4] an old cavalry officer. He seems very nice, but we are sorry to lose Rochdale.

We have had a Taube over this morning and during breakfast watched an aeroplane chase it with no result. No doubt the Taube was over to spot for Annie, who was firing all the time about 300 yards short of our dugouts.

---

1 Lt.-Col. H. C. Darlington, Major E. Fletcher, Capt. Cunningham, R.A.M.C., Major A. E. Cronshaw, Capt. J. M. Sanders (Adjutant), Capt. A. L. Bryham, Capt. W. T. Woods, Lieut. A. Slaughter, Lieut. F. James, Capt. A. W. W. Simpson, Lieut. J. N. Holden—all these officers survived the War except F. James.
2 Helles, Gallipoli.
3 The reputed father was "Quick Dick," a quick firing neighbour of Annie's.
4 General Sir H. A. Lawrence, afterwards Chief of Staff to Earl Haig.

IV.—IMBROS—TRENCH WARFARE

I suppose we shall go into the trenches to-night or very soon. The week at "Blackpool" has done us all a lot of good and I thoroughly enjoyed it, altho' it was all too short.

Arthur Slaughter[1] has gone back now, but I hope a day or two will see him back. It makes us shorter than ever. I wish some of the wounded officers would come back. Old man Turk is distinctly aggressive just now and has, I fancy, been chasing ——— in our absence. I think our fellows will teach him a lesson with any luck.

Albert Smith, Labour Member for Clitheroe, has just been attached to our 8th Bn. from K.'s army. I hope these K.'s lot are good. They *look* pretty mixed. When we are asked, as we have just been, for a fatigue party to go to the beach, we actually have to send them in small driblets, or else they get shelled like blazes. Just fancy being shelled at your base! We think it a bit thick to chuck our Brigade back into the trenches so short of officers that are old hands, why we cannot get some from our home Battalions I can't think.

I am enclosing a letter I have just got from Major Hutchinson of the Munsters, Regulars. He was all through the landing here and was attached to us. The first thing I did when we arrived was to apply for someone to be attached to give us the tips about trench warfare, so they attached a regular to each Battn. You will see what he thinks about the Battalion.

Gen. Douglas has just been round to see us. He is a changed man, so very friendly and affable and no grouses. He is very bucked with our brigade, and I heard him tell some of our men that they had done splendidly and that no troops in the world could have done better.

Brig.-Gen. Lawrence, our new Brigadier, told the C.Q.'s he was very proud to come and command our Brigade as it had made a reputation for itself on the Peninsula. Altogether we are in great favour at the moment. I hope it will last, especially after we get our drafts! We are so few now that two-thirds of the Brigade will be new stuff, who had not the training we had in Egypt and an enormous percentage of new officers. However! The poor 8th had all their seniors killed and are at present commanded by a new Sub from K.'s army and no adjutant. The 7th are commanded by their adjutant.

---

1 Lieut. A. Slaughter.

We go up into the trenches to-morrow. I have only three old officers for four Coys.

I am writing in my dugout and it is very hot and the flies defy description.

I am thinking of going and having a bathe shortly (it is now 4 p.m.), but shall have to see, as it is almost time for Annie and her whelps to tune up, and walking about is very unhealthy when she starts throwing Jack Johnsons about.

Komlosy came to lunch to-day, but had no news. Ernest Fletcher and I are dining to-night with Gen. Douglas.

28/6/15. 2.15 p.m.

I am quite fit again and on full work and full food. I was on my way up to the trenches two nights ago when I heard the Brigade was coming down. We went into rest dugouts and yesterday went up again and took over a section of fire and support trenches we had not been in before.

We could not understand why, but we know now. There has been another push on to-day on the left, quite successful so far. We were put on the right of the attacking troops to be responsible for a very difficult piece of ground and a muddle where our trenches and the Turks are absolutely mixed up. The Authorities expect, if a counter attack is made, that it will be made against the trenches we are in. It is a great compliment to the Brigade to be chosen. The counter attack has not come off so far, but to-night is the dangerous time, if old man Turk can face it after the artillery punching he has had to-day. My head rings now with the noise of our guns, we have had no show yet except a very thorough shelling. No damage done that I know of, altho' very unpleasant at times when they start rafales on you, according to their unpleasant habits. Our dugout has a good many shrapnel balls lying about it, but they did no harm. The flies are awful and so is the smell in places, as there are a lot of dead up here who have not been able to be got at yet.

IV.—IMBROS—TRENCH WARFARE

I do hope you won't worry, I am very well and get lots of good food and sleep like a log. I don't worry myself at all and find my nerves are all right and that I don't get the jumps at all. In fact I am quite content and enjoy it all in a way, altho' I shall be very glad when it is over and don't pretend, I prefer it to Parbold.[1]

It is very much worse to think of at home than it is really. It becomes one's normal life and you don't care twopence for the minor discomforts there are. If you could just change places with me for a week and see things from inside my brain, you would go home after your week was up and never worry any more. At home one thinks of it as "so dreadful."

Is it blazes? It is unpleasant at times, but it is your normal life and a good shelling now worries us just about as much as getting caught in a rainstorm at home without an umbrella. I am not piling it on. As I wrote the last sentence the Turks put four shells on to our line within 50 yards of here. Result no damage and nobody even looked up. There goes another! I am *not* pulling your leg, I am writing the literal truth for your comfort if you will only believe it. There's another shell. Sanders has called it an unprintable name!

I shall post this to-day. Everything is quiet now (4 p.m.) except intermittent rifle fire and shelling.

You ought to see me with my new way of wearing the hair, I keep it clipped off with clippers.

It is much healthier and very comfortable. Probably I shall take to it when I get home.

I am glad Jules[2] is getting to the front, it will just suit him and he will thoroughly enjoy it, except at times.

The parcels you sent have not turned up yet, but no doubt they will in time. I am looking forward specially to the cigars and cakes, cafe au lait, sweets and shortbread. Bullseyes are A1. Both cigars and cakes are tremendously welcome.

We get chits here every day telling us the Turkish morale is gone, we haven't noticed it in the trenches.

---

1 A pre-War camping place for the Wigan Companies of the 5th Manchester Regt.
2 My brother-in-law, afterwards Col. C. J. Hirst, M.C., commanding the Yorkshire Dragoons.

LETTERS FROM HELLES

29/6/15.

I finished a letter yesterday telling you about yesterday's scrap, but it started again later and went on all day. A Company of our new T.'s were driven out of a trench (they had a frightful gruelling and can't be blamed), and then others tried to retake it. I saw two attacks nearly wiped out and one Turk counterattack completely wiped out, and the trench so far as I know still belongs to old man Turk. They shelled us here badly all day till dark at a cost of five men wounded. I should think it cost about £300 a man at least! The 6th and part of the 5th were in our firing line and the expected counter attack by the Turks never came off. I spent all night up till 2 a.m. in the fire trench with Philip Holberton,[1] who was at Shrewsbury with me, the adjutant of the 6th. Nothing happened except shooting and bombing. Holberton and I were near one bombing station when a Turk bomb was thrown over. One of the 6th Coy. Sgt.-Majors [CSM 44, Frederick Hay, DCM, 1/6th Manchesters], who has already been wounded twice and got a D.C.M., picked up the bomb and tried to throw it back. He was too late and the beastly thing went off. It wounded the Sgt.-Major in 14 places and broke both his wrists, as far as we could tell.

No one else was touched luckily.

The Sgt.-Major was patched up and *walked* out of the trenches. He is a bank clerk at home. Stout fellow.

I have just had a wash all over in my bucket in our washing dugout, and a complete change and feel very clean. The set of underclothes I have on now are in absolute rags.

I think things are going pretty well here now, but fancy it will take some time and cost us a heap of casualties.

I shall shave now.

---

1 Capt. Phillp Holberton of the Manchester Regiment and adjutant of the 1/6th Manchester Regt. Killed in France, to the great sorrow of all. A first-class soldier, and a man of infinite jest, a good companion in peace or war.

IV.—IMBROS—TRENCH WARFARE

30/6/15.

We were ordered up last night to take over the firing line with the remains of the battalion and a nice place it is too. A regular mix-up with the Turks and three bombing stations where we bomb each other over a barricade. I was talking last night to one of our new subs[1] from K.'s army when a bullet came and killed him dead. Poor chap! There was a lot of firing and scrapping again last night, and I was up most of the night again. I sleep in snatches at any time when I can and it does not seem to affect me. Our battalion always seems to do more time in the fire trenches than any other for some reason or other, and the difficulty is the shortage of officers. The strain is very big on them and they have no one to relieve them, we want officers and reorganization badly.

7.15 p.m. We have had an exciting day. The Turks at one of our bombing stations have about three places they can bomb us from and we have only one. They were playing Old Harry this morning until one of our snipers managed to kill one of their bombers and hit another, since when their bombing has ceased and we have been stirring them up with a trench mortar. To-night we are going to do some scrapping and try and get even with them.

I went up to the place this afternoon with a R.E. officer to decide what we should do and was there about half an hour. I can tell you I was very glad to get away without having a bomb over.

Col. Tufnell,[2] chief of our divisional staff, was coming up the trenches this afternoon and got hit in the arm. A chit has just come in saying it is important to deepen our communication trenches!

The trenches we take over are usually rotten, like these, and our men work like n-----s and gradually make them safe. It is rather hard on our men, but they undoubtedly have got a lot of kudos from the Authorities for it. They certainly do work well. These trenches are perfectly beastly and in some places you can't dig at all as they are full of dead Turks. However, one looks on a dead Turk, poor chap, rather as one looks on a sardine or a dead cockroach at home.

---

1 Lieut. Iveson, 16th D.L.I.
2 Col. A. W. Tufnell, C.M.G., D.S.O., G.S.O.1., 42nd Division.

The heat yesterday was terrific, but it is cooler this evening, which is a blessing. The weather keeps very lovely all the same.

Here is dinner; soup, cold mutton, bread and jam, cheese and tea.

There has been another scrap to-day on the French side which went very well and I saw a fair number of Turks running back like rabbits with the French 75's plunking shrapnel right on them. They laid out most of them.

I have just had the soup, thick mutton broth with real onions in it. Absolutely tophole and very hot. Our battalion H.Q. Mess Cook got badly wounded in the back to-day, so one's servants are cooks for us, or rather my Stuart[1] is. Here is the cold leg of mutton (mutton is a rarity round here), with boiled potatoes and onions. Sanders is cursing and swearing.[2] Toasted cheese has just arrived.

3/7/15.

I am waiting for my breakfast after a round of the trenches. It poured last night and about 11 p.m. my roof made of ground sheets fell in full of water and drowned me out. I was pretty tired as I did not go to bed the night before. I sat down on a seat cut in the side of my dugout and slept solid till 4 this morning. It is extraordinary how you can sleep anywhere on these shows, we got word on the 1st that the Turks were landing more troops and as our piece of ground is very tricky and the nearest to the Turks anywhere on the Peninsula, I thought I would stay up all night in the fire trenches. About 1 a.m. our observers reported that the Turks were reinforcing their trenches in front of us. I could not see anything at first but after a bit I could see small parties of them not more than 150 yards away advancing across the open and dropping into the trenches.

---

1 Private Alexander Stuart of Wigan. Shot through the shoulder later on. Hearing the noise, I went to see who had got it. Stuart's companion informed me that Alec was a hard lad and that it sounded same as hitting a plank. I entirely agree. Alec came through the War in spite of being torpedoed.
2 I don't remember why.

IV.—IMBROS—TRENCH WARFARE

We got about 10 men and opened controlled fire on them when we got the chance, and about 2 a.m. I ordered the "stand to" and reported to Brigade. It is very funny they did not attack us, I made certain they intended to, but it never came off. Our men did very well bombing. When we got up there the Turks had absolutely got the upper hand, and when we left yesterday we were top dogs.

We managed to kill their most impudent bomber by a judiciously placed sniper and we adopted the policy of "2 bombs to 1." It succeeded very well. The 6th Manchesters[1] relieved half our battalion yesterday and half of us came back into support.

We always have to leave 2 Coys. up as the 6th are so short of men.

It is rough luck on our men, but they never complain, and we always seem to do more than our share.

The trenches were utterly unsafe when we got in, and we have left them good trenches, but it means hard work. Goodness knows what the previous inhabitants do. The R.E. told me previous units refused to work and did nothing but sleep. It is a damned shame.

We have got five more officers from K.'s army, who seem quite all right, but none of our wounded are back yet. I wish they would come.

Noon. The sun is blazing again and all my things are out drying. In fact it is very hot and I am sitting in my shirt sleeves, my usual costume, under the shade of a ground sheet. The only thing which saves us from the very trying heat is a cool breeze, which very rarely drops except at night.

The whole country is a perfect maze of trenches, the Turks and ours, and you can walk miles and miles underground, if you want to. I have had quite a long walk this morning underground. I met Gen. Lawrence, who congratulated me on the tremendous improvements we had made.

---

[1] The men of the 5th and 6th worked particularly well together in spite of social distinctions. The 6th called us "the flashy fifth" and they were known as "collars and cuffs."

'E. Fletcher, HCD—H.Q. Redoubt Line W. of Krithia Nullah.'

'E. Fletcher, Sanders.'
The two photographs were probably taken between 3–7 July 1915.

IV.—IMBROS—TRENCH WARFARE

I got a lot of your parcels yesterday and they are very welcome. The shortbread, cafe au lait, cakes and cigars are very much sought after and everything arrives in splendid condition. Thank you for taking such a lot of trouble packing and sewing up, it just makes all the difference.

The cigars are a great treat, and we smoke them after dinner with cafe au lait on the rare occasions when we have either of them.

I wish the "Ross" periscope[1] would turn up as it would be valuable and very often save one the necessity of using glasses over a trench, which I don't do often, I can promise you. It is 6.30 now in the evening; late rounds are going on, both our guns and the Turks. The Turks are shelling the beach, so I don't mind. The noise of a shell is rather soothing when it is going *high* over you.

4/7/15. 6 a.m.

It poured again last night! I have reopened this to dry it. What a game, but I feel very well.

---

[1] An inconspicuous periscope with a fairly high magnification. The only one I ever used in Gallipoli which was not smashed by snipers.

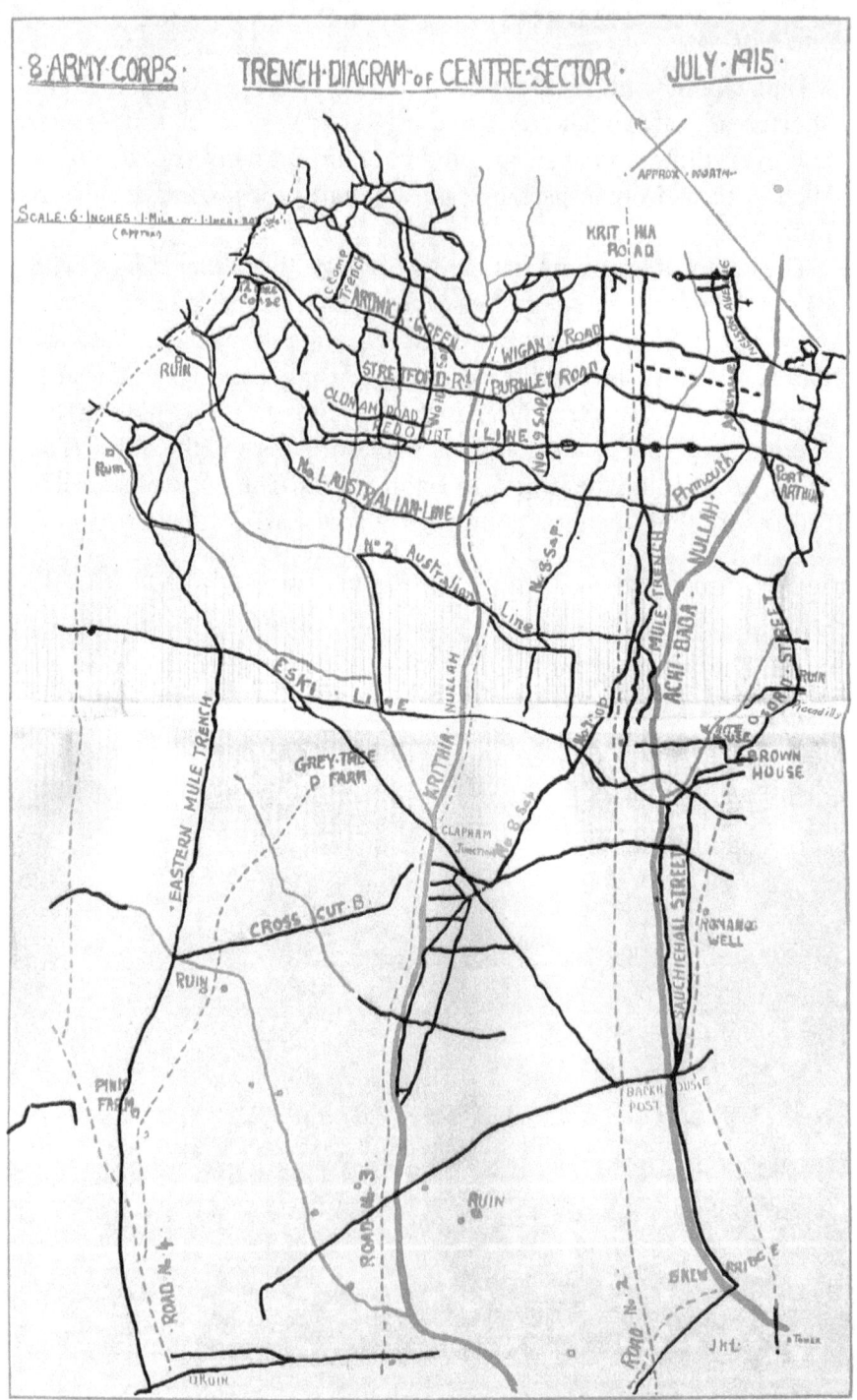

Trench diagram, centre sector, July 1915, included in first edition endpapers.

V.—127TH INFANTRY BRIGADE

7/7/15.

The day before yesterday the Turks made an attack at dawn which was supposed to be a great attack along our whole front.

The attacks on our left and right came on and were repulsed with apparently heavy losses. The attack against us in the centre never came home, and we now hear that the Turks for this attack could not be driven on.

Our men on the left had some shooting, but nothing much. They slew one Turk, I imagine a scout, who put his head up out of the scrub and had a good look round. Our men were very amused the way he poked his head up and peered round. He was christened "Audacious Alfred," and one man said, "He was looking for his iron ration," which caused much laughter.

It seems rather rough luck on "Alfred," our men had five minutes' hilarity at his expense and then plugged him through the head. They bagged a few more as well.

Yesterday I got a chit about 3 p.m. to hand over command temporarily to E. Fletcher and report to Brigade office. I could not imagine what was up and thought perhaps I was to be stellenbosched.[1] When I reported, Gen. Lawrence told me that he was going on a special mission and that I was to take command of the Brigade until his successor was appointed, so here I am living in a proper dugout with a roof, in command of the 127th Inf. Brigade until some regular can be found to take over. If he turns up to-day I can at any rate say I have commanded a brigade in war.

I know you will be proud to think that I have been entrusted with the Brigade and an important sector of the fire trenches. I live in a maze of dugouts, telephone wires, etc., about a mile behind the firing line,

---

1 A South African War term. The equivalent in this war was "getting a bolar hat."

and had a bath last night in a proper canvas bath and a whole night in bed without disturbance.

I met one of our men the other night climbing back out of the Turk trench over the sandbag partition where we play with bombs now and then. I asked him where he had been and he said he had been collecting firewood!

Our men absolutely take the prize, they do the most extraordinary things and look at everything from such a curious point of view, when one of our observers was shot through the head and killed the other night, a voice from the darkness said, "Has he got his rations on him, sergeant?"[1]

I have had my breakfast like a gent for once, at a table and nice and cool under a roof. The only drawback is a dense cloud of flies. I don't feel any qualms about leaving the battalion with Ernest Fletcher. He has done very well and is quite cool and collected, also the men are very good now and are only very keen for the Turks to attack them.

The French 75's are going through their usual performance of deluging some wretched Turk trench with shells, they really are magnificent gunners. All the same I don't think old man Turk minds. Guns on trenches don't seem to matter much unless it is a regular deluge of high explosives. We sit happily whilst the Turks put a few hundred shells round and about our trenches and as a rule there are very few casualties. Frank James had two practically in his dugout the day before yesterday. There were three officers in it and no one was hurt, although they were deafened.

It seems very quaint, even temporarily, to be in command of a brigade in war and how long it will last I don't know, anyhow it is pretty safe, and one gets a bath, comfortable meals, shade from the sun (which is worth more than you imagine) and with good luck a good sleep every night. There is not a great deal to do as things are running smoothly, and everything is quiet for the moment. It is funny having to deal with questions as Brigadier which yesterday I was arguing with Brigade!

---

1 A member of the staff who was with me at the time was rather shocked. He did not come from Wigan as I did. On another occasion when a cookhouse (an open-air one) was blown sky high and the surrounding landscape littered with rice, all the Master-Cook said was, "It favvers a b——— wedding."

'*South bomb barrier W. of Krithia Nullah.*'
The south bomb barricade formed a barrier at the southern end of Turkish trench H11a.

'Inside Turk Trench. Taken through Loop-hole. Dead Turk bomber.
South bomb barrier W. of Krithia Nullah.'

'South bomb barrier W. of Krithia Nullah.
Loophole through which photo of Turk trench was taken.'

V.—127TH INFANTRY BRIGADE

I tried to take a photo of a Turk we had slain yesterday, but I don't think it will come out.[1] At any rate it should show the inside of the Turk trench! The periscopes have not turned up yet. They will be very useful as the Turk snipers smash a lot. They are of course issued to us but get broken very quickly.[2] We are carrying respirators now, altho' so far no gas has been used against us. We always carry them on us in the trenches.[3]

6 p.m. I have just come back from Divisional H.Q. with my four Commanding officers from a pow-wow. Gen. Douglas was very polite.
My Commanding Officers consist of two Majors and two Captains.—

Major E. Fletcher, 5th Manch. Regt.
Major C. R. Pilkington, 6th Manch. Regt.
Capt. P. Creagh (Leicesters), 7th Manch. Regt.
Capt. Ross (Soudanese), 8th Manch. Regt.

11/7/15.

I enclose some odds and ends, especially Ian Hamilton's order of June 8th. You need not address my letters to "Brig.-Gen. Darlington," as I feel certain the Brigade will get a regular[4] pretty soon. But at any rate for the moment I am a General, and am addressed as such! The whole thing is pretty humorous and I don't know what is going to happen.

It happened like this: Division got a wire from G.H.Q. (Ian H.) for Brig.-Gen. Lawrence to report there and to hand over 127 Brigade to next senior until a successor was appointed. Gen. Lawrence handed over to me and went to G.H.Q. to report himself. Division never heard anything more until they saw the enclosed orders, which came as a great shock to them! There are two explanations: (1) that the promotion to Brig.-Gen. was a routine mistake, or (2) that General Lawrence recommended me to G.H.Q.

---

1 It came out very well indeed.
2 Our trenches were so close to the Turks that snipers were probably shooting at not more than 30 yards.
3 The Turk never used gas.
4 I was a civilian.

'HCD commdg 127th Inf. Bde.
Major C. Pilkington, commdg 6th Man. Major E. Fletcher, commdg 5th Man.
Capt. Creagh, commdg 7th Man. Capt. Ross, commdg 8th Man.'
HCD is second from left, standing between Majors Pilkington and Fletcher.

'Turk Shell. Krithia Road. Clapham Jn.'
Probably taken at 127th Brigade H.Q., between Clapham
Junction and Krithia Road, on 11 July 1915.

V.—127TH INFANTRY BRIGADE

I feel pretty certain that (1) is the correct solution, as I don't think G.H.Q. would give the promotion without consulting Division.

However, the matter remains that I am "General D." until the promotion is cancelled or until a regular is appointed to take over, when I go back to being a common Lt.-Col. It causes me a good deal of amusement anyway. I am very fit and have only a slight common rick in a neck muscle. The cause was not common.

I was up in the dugout[1] of the 6th Battn., H.Q., yesterday when the Turks started to shell it; they shelled us out all right and we cleared. When it was over we went back to have our tea and had not properly started when old man Turk opened again and burst one on the near parapet. I got some of the back blast right in the face, it was as hot as blazes and jerked my head back.

Hence my rick, which, however, is nearly all right to-day.

Old man Turk is very busy shelling us this morning, but this dugout is very good and has a splinter proof roof.

Unfortunately he thinks there is a battery close to and keeps trying to knock it out. He knocked out the tail of the Staff Captain's[2] shirt yesterday, but that is the only damage. It was hanging out airing. This job keeps me pretty busy and I get a lot of exercise now touring the trenches, but it is most awfully interesting, and I should of course like to keep it, altho' I am quite certain that it is sound to give Brigades to regulars only.

They never promoted Rochdale whilst he was in temporary command. Anyway I don't expect to keep it, but they can't do me out of having been a General and they can't do me out of anyhow a week's pay at the rate of about £1,000 a year!

I keep very fit.

Since finishing, they have been shelling us and I hope I have got some very good photos of their shells bursting just outside on the road.[3]

---

1 A hole in the ground open to the sky.
2 Capt. T. N. C. Nevill, 6th Manchester Regt.
3 These photographs came out very well.

12/7/15.

The Brigade were taken out of the fire trenches last night to rest trenches. As soon as the 5th arrived in theirs, a shell came right in and killed one man, took the leg off another and wounded a third.

I am afraid our rest will be very short. Now it is past history, it will interest you to know that the Brigade went into action on 4th June about 2,700 strong and came out about 1,400. Of course these figures are only approximate.

There is a terrific bombardment by our guns going on now and they are chucking simply tons of high explosives on to the Turk trenches opposite the French. There has already been a scrap this morning on the left, so we are all standing by for a noisy day. In other words, there is a show on, but we are not in it unless it develops unexpectedly. I am very glad to get the Brigade out, they have done 18 days in the front trenches on end and the 6th Battn. are so weak that two Coys, of the 5th had to be permanently in the fire trenches the whole 18 days. It comes rather stiff on them, but does not seem to make much impression on them. They are quite happy and have no imaginations and no nerves of any description.

As long as they get a bit of firewood to fry their bacon with and a limited amount of sleep they are quite satisfied, and they look upon the Turk as a comic of the deepest dye. Their one hope always being that the Turk will muster up enough courage to attack them.

The din of our guns is simply appalling. Luckily we are not very close to any, but we are so packed up on the Peninsula that you can't get away from anything.

You will be glad to hear that my ricked neck is practically right this morning.

If you see my name in the paper at any time as wounded don't get excited, you are probably returned as wounded if you get a scratch. The Brigade M.G. officer [1] who is sitting opposite me now was returned as wounded for a scratch on the head and has never been off duty for a second.

---

1 Capt. F. Hayes, M.C., 7th Manchester Regt.

'Lt. Hayes. M.G. in fire trench.'
2nd Lieutenant Frank Hayes, 1/7th Manchesters (on the left).

The majority of wounds are very slight, as the Turk bullet is very merciful and they don't tamper with it. In fact they seem very gentlemanly fighters, and I have a great respect for them.

I wish breakfast would turn up. The head and lung wounds that recover are simply extraordinary. You see dead men taken out on stretchers and a few weeks after hear that they are all right.

Noon. The French, I believe, have rushed some more trenches. The bombardment has stopped, but I should think we chucked 7 or 8,000 high explosives at the Turk trenches between 6 and 10 a.m.

Annie from Asia put a big one in one of our batteries about 500 yards from here about an hour ago. I don't know what happened to the guns, but I can see 3 or 4 dead gunners lying about and the stretchers were pretty busy afterwards. There is only desultory gun fire now, but heavy rifle fire and several men have been wounded.

There is a white flag out just in front of Krithia village, it means nothing, I fancy, as the Turks seem to use them as artillery marks or something of that sort. Anyhow I have reported it to Division.

13/7/15.

There was an attack yesterday, which I think went all right, but have no definite news yet.

I never saw such a sight in *my life* as the bombardment of the Turk trenches and of Achi Baba by our guns and the 75's, all throwing high explosives. It is utterly impossible to describe and beyond anything you can imagine.

The ground is so dry and sandy here that a big shell throws up earth, etc., probably several hundred feet high and 3 times I saw Turks flung up over 100 feet.

A Turk shell killed 2 and wounded 4 of the 5th. Bad Luck.

I got your letters up to June 23rd and parcels. The underclothes came and the Trench periscope.

APPOINTMENTS, COMMISIONS, REWARDS, ETC.
APPROVED BY
THE GENERAL COMMANDING MEDITERRANEAN
EXPEDITIONARY FORCE

(Subject to War Office approval where authority is not quoted).

List No. 6.

General Headquarters,
8th July, 1915.

Command and Staff.

(*n*) Lieut.-Col. H. C. Darlington, 1/5 Battn. The Manchester Regt., is appointed to temporarily command 127 Infantry Brigade *vice* Brig.-Gen. The Hon. H. A. Lawrence, appointed Deputy Inspector Gen. of Communications, and is granted the temporary rank of Brigadier-General while so employed, dated 6th July, 1915.

14/7/15.

I have had to-day more letters from you up to June 27th. You ask me if my hair is going grey!

V.—127TH INFANTRY BRIGADE

I don't think so, as I feel very fit and not a day older, but anyhow I can't tell you what colour it is, as I have it cropped close to my skull every week with clippers. In fact, I don't wear any hair now at all. It is more sanitary and if you do get a scalp wound much better for you.

There is no need for you to picture me tired and hungry. I get tons to eat and with your parcels live very well. One does get tired of course at times, but it does not seem to have much effect. I am not dismal either, we are very quickly teaching old man Turk that we are better than he is. He is a good fighter and full of pluck, but we have undoubtedly got his tail down now and can take his trenches when we please. Of course, it is costly work and slow, as he has line after line of them, and it is bound to be a tough and long job, but we have no fear of him now. In fact our men regard him as a comic with a nasty bite in his tail.

I have not been deposed yet! I am still drawing pay!

We have had a rotten time in these trenches, and have lost in the Brigade 7 killed and about 50 wounded during the last 3 days' fighting without coming out of our dugouts or firing a shot.[1]

Partly shells and partly bullets coming over from our right front and fired at the French. A bullet hit a piece of our roof rafters last night at tea, ricochetted off and went through the table top right in the middle of the tea things. It is very different living at a brigade H.Q. than up in the trenches. (I spoke too soon, they are shelling us now like blazes for some reason. Two have burst within 20 yards and now two more! what a life!)

Half an hour later, 5.50 p.m. I really did speak too soon. I stopped writing to have tea and if they put one shell within 50 yards they put 30.

It has stopped now except for an occasional one.

However, we are used to it and went on with our tea (there's another beast about 50 yards off). I have had a good rest here, plenty of work really, but regular meals and all my nights in bed.

I have made the most of that I can tell you.

How long it will last I can't tell. It is very hot now and you can't get the breeze into these dugouts, we live in our shirt sleeves and never wear a coat.

---

1 We were not "on" in this fight.

The new officers from England have felt it very much, and our new drafts have suffered and a lot gone sick. I think it is a good thing we came from Egypt as we really don't notice it.

I hear there are plenty more troops supposed to be coming to these parts and I think our Division will probably be taken out to reorganize in a few weeks.

16/7/15.

I am very well and still in command of the Brigade.

18/7/15.

I am still at the old spot in Brigade H.Q.[1] in the nullah, but have had a busy time since I wrote last owing to the quantity of orders that have come in, each time cancelled at the last minute.

Twice we have been ordered to take over a section of the defences and twice I have been put in command of that section and twice we have got well on with the relief and twice it has been cancelled in the middle; this amongst all kinds of other diversions which I am unable to mention. I am still in command of the Brigade and have not been demoted and do not even blush now when I am addressed as General, altho' it takes a lot of getting used to—in war time.

It really is a funny show. Two old dugouts [Lt.-Col. A. Canning and Lt.-Col. D.F. McCarthy-Morrogh] have been sent here from England to command two battalions. They are ex-regulars at least 55 years of age and covered with ribbons, and I can tell you they stare at me; one of them asked me yesterday what my regular battalion was! They both seem quite old gentlemen,[2] but I don't like them getting up and standing when they talk to me, and I give them about a fortnight in this place and then home.

It is an absolute record here the number of Brigadiers, Colonels and other senior ranks who have only been able to stick it from 3 days to about a fortnight, and who have then gone home with shattered nerves. Regulars just as much as Territorials. In our division (12 battalions) there is not one single C.O. now commanding who was at

---

1 Close to Clapham Junction.
2 They don't seem so old now and were both very stout fellows.

V.—127TH INFANTRY BRIGADE

Cairo with us. Three have been killed, 8 have gone home (3 wounded and 5 invalided), and I am the only one left and not with my battalion.

It is a very soothing sight to see these full strength battalions of K.'s army coming in. Some of them are as strong as and can actually relieve the whole of the trenches held by our Brigade! We have felt all these two months that there was no one at our backs and that we had to fight it out on our own, and it is very pleasant to feel that we have backing now. They will soon settle down and are excellent troops, but at present a bit jumpy and inclined, as last night, to make night perfectly hideous with sudden rifle fire. However, we sleep through it mostly, unless a C.O. gets the jumps and telephones back (as last night) to the guns close to my H.Q. to open fire. They'll get over that soon. I fancy it is being so very close to old man Turk that worries them at first. Annie and her pups have taken to throwing shells around promiscuously at night, but I fancy the American Ammunition Contractor has done old man Turk down a bit.

The night before last I counted 27 within possibly 300 yards of here and only 5 burst, and last night I got tired of counting and went to sleep. None seemed to be bursting.

The heat is rather bad just now and everybody is finding it trying, altho' I keep very well. It is awfully hot in the nullah, so this afternoon I went up to the 6th Battn. H.Q., which is under a tree and cannot be seen from Achi Baba. I had a nice cool sleep under the tree in the open and feel much refreshed.

One is inclined to get rather jaded at times, but I find if you don't worry and take any time you can spare wandering down to the shore, you soon shake it off. You see we have done over two months now, almost entirely in the fire trenches and always under shell and rifle fire, which you never get away from, with only one week's proper rest. One longs for a week away from it all. Thank goodness it has no effect on my nerves or on my spirits, which are A1, or on my appetite or sleeping powers. Only one feels jaded at times, naturally.

The evening hate is starting now and the Turks are shelling promiscuously at goodness knows what. It is really quite safe wandering about as long as you keep away from wagons and groups! At this range you can judge the shell and get down somewhere.

Anyhow everybody does it.

'*127th Inf. Bde H.Q.*'
127th Brigade HQ near 'Clapham Junction' around 20 July 1915.

V.—127TH INFANTRY BRIGADE

20/7/15.

I got a parcel from you to-day: they are simply ripping and the lemonade fisslets are just what one appreciates in this heat when one can't get a fizzy drink for love or money.

We have moved Brigade H.Q. out of that beastly nullah to a ripping breezy spot under some trees, where you hardly ever get a shell. I had a topping sleep under a tree this afternoon in the open and feel very fit. The change from the nullah has quite taken away my jaded feeling.

I had to go up into the fire trenches this morning to look at some work up there. It was as hot as blazes and smelly and dusty. K.'s army were in possession, very keen but rather ignorant as yet of trench work. We all wear shirt sleeves and it is very funny they generally take me for the adjutant of the 5th Man. (by my helmet). I don't undeceive them, but if by any chance they find out who I am it is very funny the way they apologize. The trenches here are extraordinary, I walked about 5 miles this morning and 4 miles of the trip was entirely underground. It is like a huge warren, but I know every turning in it now, and all the short cuts as well as I know the walks round Parbold.

K.'s army are lost in it absolutely at present and the fire trenches are so intricate, a lot of the officers don't know yet which are Turk and which are their own trenches.

The Asiatic guns are a nuisance, they seem to have got a lot of big new ones and they use them nearly always at night. Last night was very noisy, as they were chucking Jack Johnsons four at a time on to the Peninsula from about 11.30 to 2 a.m. I woke up at first, but went to sleep again very soon and left them at it. No one takes much notice, as long as it is near somebody else.[1]

21/7/15.

It is much cooler to-day and the air is really fresh, very pleasing after the heat we are having.

---

1 This paraphrases the Soldier's Prayer, "O Lord, give us victory but not in our sector."

Two men have turned up here with K.'s army, one a Major Mott whom I used to meet out with the beagles and another Brig.-Gen. Baldwin,[1] who was in the Manchesters and who used to act Brigade Major of our camps years ago.

He remembers me as a 2nd Lieut, and is highly tickled to find me the same rank as himself!

I have just had breakfast with him and Brig.-Gen. Lord Hampden, who now commands one of the Brigades in our Division, at Division. We had to go there for a pow-wow and had a better breakfast than pow-wow, porridge, eggs and bacon, raspberry jam and butter. I mix in most select circles nowadays.

I may go back to the battalion any time, altho' so far there are no signs of it so you had better make the most of it.

We have a ripping Mess here under the trees, and I am afraid we shall have to leave it very soon, probably today.

Old man Turk seems to have had a present from Germany yesterday. He is most lighthearted with his shells this morning. Probably he is very pleased at having some that burst and likes watching them, also it is rumoured that he has got a select party of Mudirs and journalists from Constantinople to see how things are going. We hoped the select party were picnicking on Achi Baba yesterday about teatime as some of our guns put about a dozen Jack Johnsons right on the top.

We are all thoroughly prepared for gas here, but it is not a good spot for its use as there is always too much wind, except occasionally at night. If the old man does use it, it will just about be the end of him, as our troops will show him no mercy afterwards and he has not the backbone of the Germans to stand up against active hate, and a bit of hate is just what our men want here. They are too inclined to look on the Turk as a very bad old comic. One old boy came over the parapet one night, probably to give himself up; he was received on the point of a bayonet by one of the 5th Colliers, who thought he might be leading an attack. The old man was not much hurt and our men were so sorry for him they gave him several rum rations and made him most indecently tight.

---

1 Killed at the Suvla landing.

V.—127TH INFANTRY BRIGADE

22/7/15.

We moved up into front trenches yesterday evening and I spent most of the night till 1 a.m. in walking round and finding where everybody had got to. It is unpleasant work walking about at night. You have to walk a good deal in the nullah and the open; you don't get shelled, but bullets come in intermittently the whole time. I suppose the odds are very much against one being hit, but there are quite a lot of casualties all the same.

We are expecting old man Turk to make a devil of a biff against us in the next few days, and shall give him a good hiding.

7.0. Have been very busy all day.

24/7/15.

We are now in a dugout in Krithia Nullah awaiting events! Mr. Turk has apparently got a lot of reinforcements and new guns and is fairly lavish with his ammunition. Our friend Hunter-Weston has been invalided home. Gen. Douglas has taken over the 8th Army Corps *pro tem.*

I am still in office.

Our second draft (small) has arrived, but I don't know any of the officers of the 5th.

I am very well indeed in spite of a very busy 3 or 4 days, getting tons of orders and arrangements cut and dried for eventualities. I walked round our trenches with Ian Hamilton the other day.

We hear that it is thought at home that the Turks may give in any day! I hope so, but we don't believe a word of it. There are no signs of it here anyway. The old man is as lively as ever, altho' he does not hanker after attacking us. If he can be screwed up, he is bound to have a big go at us in the next day or so.

He tried on a mild attack yesterday, but got badly mauled. It is a sight for the Gods to see the 75's really get at him in the open. They keep on him so wonderfully and make everything very comfortable.

It is really extraordinary warfare, when we attack we break in his communication trenches every 100 yards with high explosives, his trenches are blown to blazes and then the infantry are let loose. The guns are then cocked up to deal with the supports coming up and make a big cloud of dust behind, so that his artillery can't see what we are doing and then, as soon as the old man climbs out to run away, the 75's chase him out of sight. It always reminds one of well-trained sheep-dogs rounding up a flock of sheep. It is really quite pretty, but one feels very sorry for the individual altho' absolutely bloodthirsty against the mass, and one feels inclined to shout when one watches it.

A shell has this moment burst within 20 yards of this dugout and covered us all with dust and filth not to mention several more holes in our tarpaulin roof.

A pleasant life! It is just lunch time too and the food will be sandy now as well as fly-blown. There is one complete shell hole in the roof, but it was just before we moved in luckily. I see practically all our wounded officers have been sent home to England. I could do with a week or so myself. It does not seem nearly 3 months since we landed here. I think we all deserve a bit of leave, we have had none for nearly a year, and undoubtedly have borne the brunt of this show bar the actual landing, and that was only a week before we arrived.

I *thought* the publication of our casualties would open people's eyes a bit and they must be nearly double that now.

27/7/15.

I got another parcel from you to-day with a cake in and two pots of salmon, etc. We have had the potted stuff and part of the cake for lunch.

I don't know if it was Aunt Constance's cake, but at any rate it is simply top hole and I hope you will give her my love and thank her very much for me.

You don't know what an enormous difference your parcels make to me. The parkin was simply ripping and the potted meat and tongues and sardines are exactly what we love for lunch. It is so hot at mid-day we can hardly face bully beef!

The cafe au lait is absolutely priceless, also oxo. I find all the other officers' parcels are so utterly idiotic, full of beef lozenges and fancy things that are invented by shopkeepers to catch the public with.

Sweets and toffee are always prized and a small amount of chocolate. Everybody sends piles of that, and at present no one can eat it, there has been so much sent. Butter and tinned sausages are good.

'Self, Sanders. Mule Track, Krithia Nullah.'

'Eski Line.'
The 1/5th Manchesters occupied this section of the Eski Line (immediately west of Krithia Nullah) from 21–29 July 1915. Mule Track in foreground.

LETTERS FROM HELLES

There are 6 of us in the Brigade Mess and the other members' parcels are negligible, being filled with rubbish mostly. I have not got Jack's cigars yet. Cigars are like gold dust and it is really too hot for a Pipe.

W. R. Marshall,[1] a very good soldier, has got the 42nd Division.

6.0 p.m. It is getting bearable now as the sun is going down.
You may like to hear my day.

I did office work till 10 a.m. and then went to test a new bomb with the R.E. Had a meeting of C.O.s at 11 to talk over a possible attack scheme.[2] Wrote orders and chits nearly all afternoon and after I have finished this I am going round the trenches. At present the evening hate is on so I am better here. They have already put shrapnel on this dugout twice within the last half-hour.

Re cakes, the only suggestion I can make is, *don't* make them rich. Parkin, *seed cake*, sponge cake, lunch cake and shortbread are the best. They always arrive in good condition and you need not make them very wet if you put them in a tin.

I am very well and the life suits me, altho' the heat is trying, but I don't feel it like some of the others do. A fortnight's rest, out of range of Annie and her pups, Quick Dick and various other guns, is what we all could do with, altho' we can do without it and most certainly shan't get it!

I got the lined Burberry, thank you, and it will be invaluable when the rains start. At present it makes a most comfortable pillow.

I don't fancy my films are doing much good in this weather, so I am going to send them to you and chance them getting through.

We are getting some nice crosses for our officers' graves made of wood and are getting some photos taken of them.

We go up to the firing line again very soon and shall have to get the Turk sniper down again. He has quite got the better of K.'s army, but of course they are new at the job. It will take us 2 or 3 days.

I must go off now as the hate seems to have died down for the moment, at any rate just here.

---

1 Major-General W. R. Marshall, afterwards commanding in Mesopotamia.
2 Our attack of August 6th to cover the landing at Suvla Bay.

'Watching own guns bombarding Achi Baba. July 1915.
Welch, 127th Bde Ammo officer, Williamson, 127th Bde Signals, Nevill, Staff Capt.
127th Bde, Holberton, Adjt., 6th Man., Knight, Bde Major, 127th Bde.'

'Officers watching bombardment, 127th Headquarters.'
Taken at 127th Brigade HQ, close to 'Clapham Junction,' prior
to The Action of Achi Baba, on either 12 or 13 July 1915.

28/7/15. 6.45 p.m.

I have to-day packed and sent off my films to date.

There is a general post on here to-day and to-morrow and our H.Q. are back, for to-night only, in our nice cool dugouts under the trees.

Since we were here last the Turks have taken to shelling the place, which really does not make much difference.

They gave us a good shelling[1] this afternoon, but no damage, and they put one big one right in the middle of the horses in a little wood just behind us.

I have been all round to-day as usual.

Some of my photos may just be a landscape or may show Achi Baba in the distance more or less hidden by dust and bursting shells. I am afraid it was too far off for the photos to come out, but I took 2 or 3 on the off chance during the terrific bombardment prior to one of our attacks. In the same roll is one of several officers looking at the bombardment through glasses.

The evening hate has just started, so I have moved my seat, a box with a blanket on, up against the wall of the dugout nearest old man Turk. It is difficult to know what you like to hear in my letters, one day very much resembles another, especially when you are at Brigade and don't have to live in the fire trenches. One writes and chats about a 1,000 and 1 matters of varying importance and futility and goes round one's battalions and looks at work going on and attends pow-wows.

The only excitement is the ubiquitous shell and when you get into a zone on your walks that is being shelled, you dive into the nearest dugout and sit tight—or take no notice occasionally when in a hurry. After all the chances are very much against getting bagged by promiscuous shelling.

29/7/15. 9.15 a.m.

We move again to-day as the Brigade is taking over the fire trenches.

We have been sitting around here now for a week expecting a heavy Turk attack, but it has not come off yet and I don't think it will now.

---

1 A shell partially buried one of the 6th Manchester signallers, but his astonished face was sticking well out of the debris. His companion ran away. By the time I arrived at the spot the companion was back with a spade and a camera. The camera was used first.

'"Temp Brig Gen" H.C. Darlington. Major Knight. Bde H.Q., Clapham Junction.'

'Captain T.N.C. Nevill, Staff Capt. Major Knight.
127th Inf. Bde H.Q., Clapham Junction.'
Photographs taken between 7 July and 1 August 1915.

Our Intelligence (there's a sudden shell nearly on our dugout) warned us of an attack and we are very disappointed it has not come off. I fancy the Germans have rather a difficulty in getting old man Turk to face us. Intelligence said it was a certainty, and it is very sickening as we (the misprint was caused by my ducking at a shell that did not burst) should have given them a good handling. There's 3 more. It's a lively spot and I am now writing squatting right under the wall of our dugout. There's another! I won't put in any more as it reads rather theatrically, but the old man is fairly out for our blood this morning—2 more, I have climbed off my box and am now sitting in an undignified position on the floor, but they are good shells and much too near to be pleasant, the best one was within 15 yards. I shall give up counting, they seem annoyed with us this morning and are fairly letting us have it. I got another parcel from you last night, thank you. Tongue, cake and sardines, also John's cigars.

1.30 p.m. We had the most unmerciful shelling all this morning for no reason that we know of. No damage done.

1/8/15.

I have been very busy these last two days as Gen. Lawrence has been sent back and I have been handing over, etc., etc. He had finished his other job, so I am no longer a Brig.-Gen.

We are all very glad to get him back again. I rejoin the Battn. up in the trenches to-morrow.

Gen. Lawrence seems to think he may be recalled, and the funny part is, if he is, one of the dugout C.O.s is my senior, so if Gen. Lawrence goes, the Brigade will be handed over to him. It is a funny war. I am very well and have been all round the trenches these last 2 days. The Bombers (Turk) had quite got the better of K.'s army and killed several, but we have already got the old man back in his place again.

VI.—BATTLE OF 6/7TH AUGUST AT HELLES

3/8/15.

I am still very well. It seems funny to be so close to the 12th, but I fancy I shall be celebrating it in another way this time with old man Turk doing the grouse act.

We had a funny celebration two or three days ago when we heard of the Bagdad victory. A *feu de joie* was arranged for 5 p.m. Everything was very hot and quiet just before time and then suddenly the rip started up with the French and ran right along the fire trenches until brought up by the Aegean Sea. It sounded like someone tearing an enormous piece of canvas right across the Peninsula. Old man Turk woke up out of his dose and continued the *feu de joie* with every rifle and machine-gun he possessed for about 20 minutes, much to the amusement of our men, who sat in their trenches and roared. I expect the Turk thinks we are quite mad.

You keep talking of our going to Egypt! I don't see any chance. If we were to finish off here this Autumn, and I don't see why not, it would not surprise me if the 29th and 42nd Divisions were sent back to England to fill up and reorganize and rest before going to France.

This is only my idea, but after all, we have done the worst part of the job and shall have had a combination of unpleasant circumstances which would be hard to beat.

Aug. 5th.

I have been very busy all day and shall post to-night. If you don't get a letter from me for the next few days don't be surprised!

I am very well again.

'Bn. H.Q. in duplicate fire trench just W of Krithia Nullah.
E. Fletcher, HCD, J.M.B. Sanders.'
Major E. Fletcher, HCD and Captain J.M.B. Sanders.

'Fletcher, F. Hayes, 127th Bde. M.G. officer, Sanders.'
Major E. Fletcher, Lieut. F. Hayes and Captain J.M.B. Sanders.
Photographs taken at battalion headquarters in the 'duplicate fire trench'
probably in the days leading up to The Battle of 6/7 August.

VI.—BATTLE OF 6/7TH AUGUST

Sunday, 8/8/15.

When I last wrote I said you might not hear from me for a day or two as I had orders for a show.

The 29th Div. had been ordered to attack a Turk trench to our left and we (5th Man.) had to attack 2 trenches [H11a and H11b] to join up, probably the most awkward 2 trenches on the Peninsula.

So on Friday, after an artillery preparation the Worcesters[1] and 250 of our men went over the parapet.

The attack failed and was wiped out owing to our bombardment having been useless, the Turk shrapnel, and the fact that their trenches were bulging with Turks. The Worcesters lost about 800 out of 950, and we lost about 200 out of 250. Yesterday we were ordered to attack again after another artillery preparation which was not very successful, in conjunction with the rest of our Brigade and the Fusilier Brigade. The Fusiliers[2] took their trenches, which were fairly straightforward, but our Brigade never arrived, the attack was pretty well wiped out, although luckily there were a good many men kept out of the attack.

Our Brigade losses were about 700 and we have about 700 effectives left. Thirteen officers were outed in my battalion. I am afraid C. Ainscough is killed, he is missing, and one of our wounded who crawled in last night says he is dead.

Jack Sanders was slightly wounded, a scratch on the arm which is already healed. He got it from a piece of shell that came into our dugout. The Turk shelling was tremendous and was largely concentrated on our trenches, especially the trench our H.Q. are in. How we lived comfortably the two days I can't imagine, but one escapes in an extraordinary way. We got heavily shelled by our own guns by mistake, who killed and wounded some of the men, which does not help an attack altogether.

However, I am still very well and unhit, altho' it sounds selfish to say so. Our casualties during the 2 days as far as I can tell were about 240, so we are down to a low ebb again, especially in officers.

Poor Cyril [Ainscough] only arrived back the day before he was killed (from hospital).

---

1 4th Worcestershire Regiment.
2 Lancashire Fusiliers (Territorials).

LETTERS FROM HELLES

I don't think you know any of the other officers, some K.'s attached and the rest our new draft, Winterbottom was killed.[1] Young Allen rejoined to-day and has already been slightly wounded in the leg. So has Bryham, but neither are bad enough even to go to hospital. The attack was costly, but it succeeded in its object, viz., keeping the best Turk troops here whilst other operations went on elsewhere!!

We are still in the fire trenches. Division ordered another attack for last night, but it never came off as the Brigade had been so badly handled the men were not fit for it.

'Bryham.'
Captain Arthur Longsdale Bryham, 2ic,
'D' Company, 1/5th Manchesters.

---

1 Officer casualties: 9 killed, 3 wounded.

VI.—BATTLE OF 6/7TH AUGUST

10th Aug./15. 5.15.

We are just back in the Redoubt line from the fire trenches and are glad to get back after 5 days there and two days' severe fighting. Both officers and men are pretty well done up and want a rest, such as it is. Yesterday we had what is called a "combined hate," our machine-guns and snipers and the gunner officer in charge of 3 trench mortars, a most infernal machine which throws an enormous bomb of 100 lbs. full of high explosive. The Turks have a trench in the nullah which we enfilade and which is below us only we can't get at them because it is very cleverly and heavily traversed.

The trench we wanted to strafe is called G11.H [G11A]. The mortars' first bomb burst on the trench end nearest to us and all the Turks ran up to the other end. We then burst one in the far end and back they came. Then we put several right in the middle parts, blowing several Turks sky high. Of course this took some time, as we had to shepherd them a bit by heading them off when they tried to bolt, we blew in their communication trenches and also all their traverses and then of course they were like rats in a trap. As soon as the traverses were down we turned on our snipers and our machine guns and strafed them until they came out into the open and ran like rabbits, we then chased them into the nullah and bombed that. The trouble was it fetched the Turk artillery on to our trenches at once and we had the most unholy shelling all day.

The trench mortars were buried at mid-day by a shell from Annie and Co. We knocked off for a bit. We started again later on and were promptly knocked out again, so had to stop permanently.

However, the mortars are being moved to-day. They were not pleasant neighbours, as old man Turk could not find them. At any rate he must have used about 300 shells and our total casualties (our men unfortunately) were, 2 killed, 4 wounded. We blew G11.H. [G11A] to smithereens and must have bagged a fair number of Turks.

We have got their best troops (Adrianople)[1] against us here and they are extraordinarily plucky. Time after time they came back and tried to repair the damage and got killed and bombed out. Then last night

---

[1] A piece of Intelligence I am unable to verify.

we got rifles fixed on the trench to stop them working at night but they had built two traverses by this morning in spite of it. However, it really was a good hate and must have annoyed the old man and the Turk H.Q., too, judging by the amount of shells the gunners were allowed to shoot at us and they *must be short* (altho' you would not have thought so on Aug. 6th and 7th. I never imagined such a shelling as we got). I think we must arrange another hate with O.C. Mortars for August 12th, if we are up there again by then. Our men enjoyed it thoroughly. It reminded me of ferreting the steep places down the streams at Slaidburn—bar the shelling!

11/8/15. 3.30 p.m.

There is a big hate going on now by the French guns ably assisted by our big ones. They chucked hundreds of the most appalling Johnsons on to the Turk trenches away on our right. It is the most extraordinary sight and how old man Turk sticks it I can't imagine. Our guns had 3 ten minute hates during last night to tie the Turks down here, but they did not even wake me up! I was very tired and slept like a log. I spent a good deal of the nights after our attacks up in the fire trenches, as we had been warned to stand by for a Turk counter attack. We are told now that the Turk had arranged to attack us on the night of Aug. 6th, so his trenches were all double manned and that is why our attacks were wiped out. I am very well and quite rested again and Sanders and I think of going up to-morrow to the fire trenches to celebrate the 12th by sniping a Turk or so with *periscopic* rifles. I don't think we shall be sent over the parapet again for some time now unless the necessity arises as our Brigade is now at the point where we must do some reorganization.

We were not shelled yesterday or to-day except for a few odd ones. It makes us wonder if the old man has taken away some of his guns elsewhere.

VII.—MORE TRENCH LIFE

13/8/15.

I am waiting for breakfast, fried eggs and bacon, fried toast, bread and jam and no butter. I *should* like a lump of hard cold butter. We had a most restful day yesterday up to a point, very little rifle fire and only an odd shell now and then. Suddenly at 7 p.m. old man Turk started a hate, he turned on about 2 batteries firing as hard as they could and all his rifles in G.

We got a pretty fair shelling, as he is quite a conjurer with his field guns and serves them very rapidly. We are in the Redoubt line and in Brigade reserve, altho' only about 600 yards from the Turk trenches, so we had our dinner at 8 as usual, when the flies had died down. It was pretty noisy as our guns had chipped in by then. The old man then proceeded to attack some Turk trenches we captured last week in the Vineyard, but got the knock.

He stopped his guns about 9 p.m., but the rifle fire went on all night. We all got ready for a quick move, then went to sleep.

I slept all night pretty well and things are quieter this morning except for an occasional shell. This is how he celebrated the 12th for us, altho' it is also a Mohammedan festival at the end of Ramadan, so it cuts both ways.

The Division is being relieved to-day, I am glad to say by the Scotties (52),[1] and we go back to bivouac and a much needed rest, after a pretty bad week up here.

We hear now for certain that the Turk was about to attack us on the evening of the 6th and that explains why his trenches were all double manned and why our attacks were so badly handled on the 6th and 7th. That's a near shell! Also in spite of all our attacks, except on the Vineyard trenches, failing, we did what was required, that is, kept his best (Adrianople) troops here whilst the landing elsewhere was brought off.

---

1 52nd Division.

It was costly for us, but I suppose worth it, and someone had to suffer against this stone wall.

I went up to the fir wood near here yesterday with my glasses to have a look at the battlefield, and it is a sight, our Brigade and the Worcesters' dead are lying about in whole platoons and there are heaps of Turk dead too.

The dead can't be touched even if only just over the parapet, the trenches are so close together you could not put a finger up.

They are shelling these trenches again now: I hope it will be over by the time breakfast is ready, and I'm quite ready for that.

I think we are only a side show here now, and I had hoped for a quiet time; but the side show, so far, has been the hottest time I've had since I landed.

There's no doubt about it, the troops opposite us now are magnificent fighters and very brave. However, I hope we shall mop up this place fairly shortly, as we have had quite a good deal stuffed into 3 months, and of course on this narrow frontage you must be in every show even if you are in rest dugouts! We all could do with a week or two of peace. Some of our old nerveless veterans are feeling the strain and duck at shells. I always did and always shall.

I have finished breakfast, quite good, too. We had it without a shell after all. It is most awfully hot to-day, and I am sitting in my shirt sleeves, no vest nowadays, and perspiring. The wind will, I hope, get up soon and make it better.

It is very kind of Mr. Hirst[1] to send cigarettes for the men, but they have not turned up yet. They are priceless here, and if you can get any more for the battalion, send as many along as you can get given you. The issue is very small and the men deserve them if ever men did. It's one thing they are short of, also sweets, which they love.

Since the last sentence the Turks have tried again for the Vineyard but were rebuffed. I watched them with great interest running back shepherded by our shrapnel.

It did not seem much of an attack.

I am very well.

---

1 T.J. Hirst of Meltham Hall, Huddersfield, my father-in-law.

VII.—MORE TRENCH LIFE

P.S.—The only officers of the old lot who have not been on some list as killed, wounded or sick are Self, Ernest Fletcher, Cronshaw, Cunningham and Lund.[1]

Out of the two drafts and K.'s army attached there is only one left.

14/8/15.

We are relieved at last (yesterday) and are right back within 50 yards of the sea, simply ripping, you can stroll about and we have not been shelled so far.

I had a ripping bathe before breakfast off a lighter into deep water and such lovely warm water too, and now (3 p.m.) I am lying out on my valise in the sun, it is quite cool as there is a cool breeze off the sea. I feel very fit and the change down here has bucked us all up.

There is no news.

18/8/15.

I am very well and we are still back resting. My only drawback is an inevitable one, one's skin here cuts very easily, and if you knock your hand you get a sore place, which takes a long time to heal. I have 3 now! but I get them properly dressed every day, so it does not matter. I am very fit and find that a dose of salts about every 10 days keeps me all right.

Gen. Lawrence, when he saw I had what we used to call veldt sores in Africa, was keen that I should go on a Hospital ship for a week or so for a rest, but I am so well I refused.

Sanders has gone for a bit of a rest on to a Hospital ship. He got bronchitis and was threatened with fever, so I got him sacked straight off. It is very extraordinary that I should be one of the 4 survivors of the originals, who have not been on any list, but I take great care of myself. It is quite easy to get to Alexandria if you are a bit seedy and they say very difficult to get back. Talbot Woods (Staff Captain) is there now. Cronshaw and Cunningham are both seedy to-day.

I have had my first inoculation against cholera, altho' there is none on the Peninsular. In fact the health of the troops is extraordinary.

I am glad to hear all the Turks have been inoculated against cholera, too.

---

1 Lieut. Lund.

'X Beach. HCD, Cunningham, E. Fletcher.'
Bathing party: HCD, Capt. H.H.B. Cunningham, R.A.M.C., and Major E. Fletcher.

'Lighter, X Beach.'

'Dug-outs at X Beach. E.F. asleep. My dug-out (with trousers).'
Major E. Fletcher sleeping, right. Probably taken in
the 'Torres Lines' between 14–19 August 1915.

'My dug-out near X Beach.'
Probably taken in the 'Torres Lines' between 14–19 August 1915.

If anybody wants to send anything they can send cigars, I don't care what sort or how cheap. They are invaluable and more appreciated than anything.

There is nothing doing here and we are having quite a good rest and very occasional shells. I think you had better send me some thicker underclothing now, in case we are here for winter. I also want a clothes line and a pair of long rubber boots and 4 pairs of arctic socks.

I don't want felt-lined boots as *you can't dry them.*

One must prepare for the winter in case the show goes on. Personally I am afraid it will, altho' the next few weeks will decide, as things are moving, altho' slowly.

I have been sitting on the cliffs this afternoon watching a Turk Howitzer from behind Achi Baba shell Gully Beach about half a mile away.

It was extraordinarily good shooting, the cliff is nearly perpendicular and the beach only about 40 yards wide and they were dropping them just between the beach and sea, mostly into the water.

The beach was crowded and probably 50 men were bathing, but no one was hit and the bathers did not even trouble to come out of the water.[1] We are all pretty used to it here, but personally the first shell sends me to cover, or more often the first four, as they generally send down 4 at a time.

My writing is bad as my hands have just been dressed. I have 3 dressings on and am wrapped around with that stuff we stick creepers up with, also iodine on raw places is uncomfortable. However, I don't care. They are very small sores and will go in a week or so with luck.

We are all like Lazarus on this Peninsular. Gen. Douglas inspected us yesterday and as usual kept saying, "They *are* fine men, Darlington, and I should like to see them get into the Turks." He spoke to several and one conversation tickled him immensely and did for me altogether.

Gen. D.: "Have you ever bayoneted a Turk?"

Ruffian: "Yes, Sir."

Gen. D.: "Did he stay in the trench?"

R. "He *did* that! He were half-dead and I thowt I'd best finish him."

---

1 On hearing the screech of a shell the bathers to a man disappeared under water, and no doubt felt very safe.

VII.—MORE TRENCH LIFE

I think Gen. D. always had suspicions that our men are ruffians and don't take many. He roared and said something about one's duty to take prisoners, but as he could hardly speak, it had not the desired effect.

20/8/15.

We are again up in the fire trenches and came in on a sudden order to relieve "somebody else"! It is a new spot and the best we have been in yet, bar the extreme proximity of old man Turk, whose trenches are only 30 yards away and in some places closer.

We are right up "farthest North" due west of Krithia with our left flank on the sea shore, where we have a barricade. The 6th and 5th are working together as we are so small and we share a H.Q. in a ravine which runs from the top of the cliffs very steeply to the sea. It is a ripping place, our dugouts are cut out in the side of the ravine with steps up and down. My dugout and our dining-room (with table) are on a sort of terrace right over the sea and as I write I can see the shore and the sea and the sun beginning to go down behind Imbros.

It is safe from shells, too, as the ravine is so steep, altho' they plaster the opposite bank of it now and then with shrapnel. The large trench mortars are holding a private hate again near here with the usual beastly results. Already both the 6th and ourselves have had casualties from shells; they are trying to find Syers[1] and his mortars. He is a tophole chap, but I wish he would not follow us about. He has just fired one of his beastly mortars again, and the Turk guns are at it, too.

The Turk does not seem to have as many guns as he had, but he does enough damage with these. I hear several of our men have been hit up in the fire trench. The evenings are getting cool again and I am quite glad to put a woolly on now and my lined Burberry a bit later.

It is very pleasant like this, but will soon get cold enough for anyone. Sanders is not back yet and I have not heard from him lately.

---

1 Capt. Syers, officer i/c Trench Mortars.

'Bn. HQ dining room, Border Ravine.'
Taken late August or early September 1915.

'Bn. HQ dining room, Border Ravine.'
Taken late August or early September 1915.

'Bn. H.Q., Gully Ravine.'
Incorrectly captioned by HCD—photo shows 1/5th Manchesters Bn. HQ in
Border Ravine. Taken late August or early September 1915.

'My dug-out, Border Ravine.'
HCD outside his dug-out in Border Ravine (note bandaged hands).
Taken late August or early September 1915.

LETTERS FROM HELLES

Gen. Lawrence has gone again on another job and the Brigade is being taken charge of by an ex-regular, who is senior in the Brigade and who commands the ———. He is a very nice old gentleman. General ——— is exercising supervision over the whole firing line! so you can see how fatuous the whole position is.

Our little Willie would rather do that than have what he calls "a civilian" commanding the Brigade.

It is very pleasant to sit here and watch the cruiser and a destroyer taking on the Turk guns who try to hit the ships, without much success, at intervals during the day. It is very pleasant too to look at the shore and the sea, but it is annoying to be so near and yet so far from the most lovely looking sands and the clearest of clear seas; you can't set a foot on the shore and you therefore can't bathe. The Turk snipers see to that with the utmost precision. It annoys us greatly as we simply revel in the bathe before breakfast down in the bivouac, altho' there the water is rather spoilt by so many people and horses living along the cliffs and throwing all their refuse into the sea.[1]

My hands are no better and no worse and I am exceedingly fit.

The mails, &c., have been hung up owing to troop movements, but I did get to-day 4 parcels which were greeted with shouts from about 5 or 6 staff and gave us an excellent lunch when we had nothing to eat but bread and jam!

21st. 10 a.m.

I will write you before I go round the fire trenches. It is a perfect morning and I'd give anything to be able to go and bathe. The worst of it is there is no water[2] at all up here and we have to bring every drop up in fanatis on mules. It comes nearly 2 miles. You can't even have a decent wash, only a rub in a cupful at the bottom of a bucket.

Old man Turk has been very quiet since we came and has not thrown a single bomb, altho' the people we relieved said he was very energetic and threw bombs all day and night. The things I hate are his little mountain guns which he suddenly opens with, and which are exceedingly dangerous if you are moving about. We had a very good dinner last night, soup, stew (fresh meat, onions and potatoes), your

---

[1] The refuse in this tideless sea made a disgusting fringe round the shore.
[2] The Navy supplied us with water.

VII.—MORE TRENCH LIFE

plum pudding with cold cream sauce well whipped up with brandy, whiskey and coffee.

When you send sausages, which we revel in, send several tins or at any rate enough for one breakfast for 4 people!

I am not at all concerned about Russia, she is playing the game which suits her best, altho' it is forced on her and I don't consider Germany has achieved her object. Warsaw is only a lump of brick and mortar, except perhaps as regards neutrals. After all even neutrals are not damned fools and so long as Germany does not destroy the Russian armies, she must lose in the end, altho' I am afraid it will be a long job.

Do you imagine it ever enters our heads here that the Turks are going to lick us, good fighters as they are, and I suppose it is the same in France.

We are bound to win, altho' it may take a year or two. I am talking from the military point of view. I know nothing about the financial side and don't believe anyone else does.

I am afraid you are all pessimists in England, and I believe a short course of brother Turk at close range would cheer you all up considerably.

Everyone who writes to us from England, bar you, writes dismally, whereas you never hear a dismal word of any sort on this Peninsular. If we can't kill them outright we can wear them down in time and that's what is going to happen. There is always the chance of clearing things up here suddenly, but I don't think there is in France.

I went this morning up to a trench about 650 yards behind our firing line and about 700 yards from our old friend[1] in order to look for a place for a M.G. on the top of a bluff. I could not see down the slope, so I very carefully crawled over the parapet and went on my stomach in the furze bushes, just like medium-sized heather. I looked over and was back in the trench within 15 seconds, but some old devil found time to get 3 in at me before I dropped in. I shan't try it again! They are tophole snipers and very watchful. He was much too quick and close to be pleasant. Old Brute; but one can't help respecting them and nearly liking them, they play so fair at any rate on this Peninsular.

---

1 The Turk.

There is a very heavy and distant gunning going on the whole time as I write, so I suppose they are hard at it "elsewhere."[1] I am very glad to be a side show for a time.

23/8/15.

We came out of the fire trenches up on Fusilier Bluff yesterday and are now back in Border Ravine for our three days out (in Brigade Reserve). It is a very nice place running down to the sea, only very dusty. We are joining our Mess just at present with the 6th. You can bathe here altho' it is very stoney, and I bathed at 7 this morning. You can't go out more than 4 or 5 yards or you come into view of the Turk trenches, so it is impossible to get a good swim.

Sanders I hear has gone to Alexandria or Malta on a Hospital ship, so we shan't see him back for some weeks. F. James has been acting adjutant since he came back from hospital, but I have had to send him to command D. Company as Arthur Bryham is now ill and has to go to hospital and we shan't see him again for weeks. So I have no adjutant at all. The Coys. are now as follows:—*A*, 2nd Lt. E.J. Burrows. *B*, Capt. J.H. Allen (9th Lincolns), Lt. G. Allen. *C*, Major A.E. Cronshaw. *D*, Capt. F. James. *M.G.* Lieut. Lund. *Battalion H.Q.*, Self, Major E. Fletcher, Capt. H.H.B. Cunningham, R.A.M.C., 2nd Lieut. Taylor, Q.M.

A draft turned up yesterday of 118 with two 2nd Lieuts. [J. P. Y. Dickey and P. W. Batten], so that's our full complement.

Somehow drafts seem mere bullet food nowadays after our experience here. There is not a single officer left of the first 2 drafts and 2 only are alive (wounded) so far as we know and over 500 of the men are killed, wounded or missing. There is no doubt that up to now a man has very little chance of coming through, and the Coy. Officer still less.

I am very well and enjoying the 3 days out.

It is a lovely spot up in these cliff fire trenches, but you are too close to the Turks (30 yards only between trenches) and there is a lot of bombing goes on, not to mention grenades fired by a rifle, which the

---

[1] Suvla Bay. The attack on Scimitar Hall and Hill 60, with the Anzac cooperation.

VII.—MORE TRENCH LIFE

old man fires promiscuously into our trenches. They do very little harm, but are wearisome after about 3 days.

My hands are better a bit, one sore has healed up, but the other two go on for ever. I think the sea bathing does them good, but they are a beastly nuisance. I catch them on everything and can't get things out of my trouser pockets! However, I am extremely fit in spite of my age!!

It's getting on for 4 months now since we landed and I suppose taking things generally it has been one of the stiffest campaigns there has ever been. However, we keep going and are quite happy when we can get a bathe before breakfast and the food is A1, including parcels of course.

Anyway, the Turk seems a Gent, which is a good deal, altho' much too good a bomber for complete comfort. We have a bombing school[1] now away back, and the pupils after a few days, complete their education by coming up to the barricades in the fire trenches and practising on poor old man Turk, under an instructor!! I fancy old man Turk will complete their education and everything else for them. He knows a bit about it himself.

You may get me home stellenbosched at any moment, and bar leaving the 5th I really should not care, altho' I want to have one look at the other side of Achi Baba before I leave this place. Our last draft look a real good lot of pit rats, but not much smartness about them, of course, it is hard to judge that. I inspected them last night during hate time at the bottom of the ravine. A few shells pitched up on the top, but it was a fairly safe place bar an accident.

One does not notice shells at all now unless they come close and some of the recruities were very surprised when the Sgt.-Major told them to stand still and look to their front.

Syers of the Demoiselles (Big Trench Mortars) was also holding a hate about 400 yards or so away, so there *was* a bit of noise now and then, as the Turk guns were of course searching for him! He's a hardy mariner all right. One gets a friendly feeling for the Navy up here. The destroyer *Scorpion* patrols our left flank and generally looks after us.

She lights up the ground in front of us at night with her searchlight and pounds the Turk trenches now and then to keep them amused.

---

[1] C.O. Lt.-Col. A. E. F. Fawcus, D.S.O., M.C., 7th Manchester Regt.

We keep in touch with her by signal, so she fires at anything we want pounding. She comes in very close now and then, and the old man can't resist turning his guns on her. I fancy she has orders to try and make him waste ammunition.[1] He's probably pretty short nowadays.

I don't know a bit how things are going up north,[2] so can't defy the Censor, but I can't help feeling, taking all things into consideration, that it's about an even chance of the old man collapsing suddenly.

He's had a rough time, is probably short of ammunition and when he does cave in will go to pieces utterly. However, he has surprised us considerably several times before, but I think anyhow it's even money, if we have enough troops up there. That of course I can't tell.

The evening hate has just commenced. First shell 6.35 p.m.

26/8/15.

Here we are back again in the firing fine. We have got the sector next but one to the sea held by the 6th last time we were here, so we have all the unpleasant mess of very close Turks, bombs and rifle grenades. The weather is gradually changing and during the last day or two we have had lovely cloudy weather, coldish at nights, a gale from Asia which made life beastly for two days with clouds of filthy dust and a few spots of rain.

We are wondering whether the old man is gradually thinning out here. So last night I arranged a strafe to try and draw him. I allowed very little sniping up to 10 p.m. and then at 10 I blew loudly on my whistle and the whole of my line, with fixed bayonets, which glinted in the moonlight, gave the old man 2 rounds rapid. It drew him all right, very quickly, and we judged frightened the life out of him, as we so rarely do it. He opened on us with rifle fire, which we judged pretty thin, and also with 2 M.G.s, which was a grave error on his part, as I was able to locate their direction and may find their emplacements to-day. He will very likely move them now, but it won't do any harm to get our guns, assisted by our old friend the *Scorpion* to knock his emplacements to blazes. It will cheer him up and probably add to

---

1 Wishing to draw the fire of a Turk battery in order to locate it, *Scorpion* drifted slowly in towards the shore with a party on deck doing physical jerks in white duck. The Oracle worked and I never saw a squad dismiss quicker.
2 At Suvla and Anzac.

VII.—MORE TRENCH LIFE

the bag. Old Cronshaw got a bump on the head during our strafe last night, but no damage done. I think it was a bit of stone off the parapet, as the M.G. knocked our sandbags to pieces just where he and I were standing. He is a perfect marvel and is doing the most excellent work. I only hope the old Turk won't bag him. On Aug. 7th he climbed out of our trench in the attempted attack on H.11B. and was promptly blown in again by a shell! It did not seem to worry him at all and all he suffered from was a bit of stiffness, we pull his leg about it, as you can imagine.

I am very well and my two veldt sores are slowly healing, altho' they are very sore and I still have my hands bandaged, which is a nuisance.

I think I told you that Bryham had gone to hospital, sick, and I had to send F. James to command D. Co., so I have no adjutant now. However, Ernest Fletcher and I do the work between us. I hear Brig.-Gen. Baldwin is killed up North, but I hope it is not true. (It is.) I told you about him before and also Gen. Lawrence is coming back to the Brigade, which is tophole news. At present we have no brigade commander as ——— seems to rely on me if anything crops up outside his usual routine of more or less brackish chits.

27th.

Gen. Lawrence is back and Gen. Baldwin is dead, I am sorry to hear. I was up in the fire trenches yesterday and saw quite a bevy of Turks digging about 300 yards away and getting out of cover in the most impudent manner! The position of affairs there is curious. I took the trench over two days ago, and it has no loopholes whatever, the Turk trench is about 35 yards away and he has some first-class snipers there very well hidden.

The result is he is absolutely top dog and we could not even use periscopes, but had to use small pieces of looking-glass at the back of the trench, and if you move one of these it is broken immediately.

It is, of course, certain death to peep over, so we were quite impotent to deal with the brazen diggers, as they could only be seen from this particular bit of trench, about 10 yards long. I got hold of the forward observing artillery officers and showed them the digging parties and they telephoned the batteries; one Major said his battery was not on duty and would not fire, and the other Major consented, after I had got tired of hanging around, to fire 2 rounds, which certainly did discourage the diggers to some extent. I then got hold of one of the gunner subs (Lee), and we concocted a message to the Destroyer which we signalled off. She said she could not see the target, so she failed us, too. The funny part is I believe the sub with whom I was trying to arrange the strafe was Violet Ingham's brother.

In the middle of all this James went and stuck up his periscope. I had just opened my mouth to strafe him, but the Turk was quicker with his rifle than I was with my tongue. He smashed the top glass to pieces and I got 3 pieces as a reminder, none of them luckily did any damage, but I got one on the cheek, one on the arm and one on the knee, which stung most abominably. There are limits and we can't snipe back, so I determined to teach the Turk to mind his own business. Cronshaw, Lee and I got a rifle and rifle grenades and two of our men, and between us, none of us knowing in the least how to use the beastly thing, we loosed off some grenades. By sheer fluking, we got our second and third bombs right bang in the Turk trench, apparently clean in the lair of the sniper.

We trust we blew him up, but at any rate the sniping there is not so confident as it was, as we followed it up with a shower of bombs from the small trench mortars. You have to keep the old man under and chastise him when he is naughty. I am now making loopholes in order to teach the diggers discretion.

We go down to Y Ravine again to-morrow for our 3 days, and shall get some bathing, thank goodness.

Yesterday and to-day we have had our first days of cold since we left England, altho' it is hot again now (2.45 p.m.), and probably you would have been very hot when I was wearing a woolly and lined mackintosh.

It rained, too, last night, the third rain shower I have seen since we left Alexandria!

I did not get much wet and slept very well through it.

I think it is as well to assume we are here for a winter campaign, so you can act accordingly in sending the things.

Trench diagram, left and centre sectors, included in first edition endpapers.

28/8/15. 7.10 p.m.

I will write a line before dinner. We are back again in Y Ravine, Gurkha Bluff, for our 3 days' easy.

We were relieved this afternoon and just as I was coming down the communication trench to tea, I got a frantic message from Brigade to say that the 8th Corps reported that there was great activity in the Turk trenches opposite us, that they had cut through their parapets and were removing their barbed wire, and would I at once send an officer up to observe and report and that the forward observing officer had reported it to the Corps and *that all batteries had been informed*!!

As I had been in the trenches for 3 days, I merely thirsted for the blood of the Artillery Officer.

However, duty called so I gave up all ideas of tea and went up to see these frolickings for myself.

I got hold of the artillery officer, whom I found to be an elderly subaltern of a pessimistic turn of mind, and told him to show me the activities at once.

I looked very hard, but could not see anything dangerous or unusual, and I am thoroughly glad to say old man Turk smashed the pessimist's expensive telescopic periscope to atoms the first shot, altho' I got a nasty drive of powdered glass all over my face, for the second day running. I then met Gen. Lawrence hurrying up and he seemed quite relieved when I told him it was all rot, so he went home.

The next arrival was Lee,[1] very hot and with orders to range on the gaps! He is V. Ingham's brother. It's curious we should be in the same sector and arranging combined strafes together.

25th. 6.45 a.m.

I am now writing before I get up to have a swim. It has been quite a chilly night, but I have had some hot tea and a cigarette and shall go and plunge into the sea very soon. I say "plunge," but if you go out into deeper water than about 3 feet, you get sniped at once. I have been thinking you had better send me out at once some kind of a small bivouac tent. The wet weather will be here in another month and

---

[1] Lieut. Lee, R.A., afterwards killed, a brother of Mrs. Lister Ingham of Wighill Park, Tadcaster.

VII.—MORE TRENCH LIFE

R.E. stores are like all other necessities, bar food, in this campaign—there are none.

It wants to be just big enough for me to sleep in and quite low and it must be waterproof and strong, not gimcrack because of the gales. It will have to be put up in dugouts, on cliffs, &c., so that is why it must not be too big.

The fresh butter arrived very well and we simply revel in it. In fact we could eat 2 lbs. a week with gusto!! We all miss butter very much. Toffee is a very good thing to send and *do* send some seedcakes.

By the way let people know when writing *NOT* to put 127 Brigade, 42 Div., on the envelope. 1/5 Manchesters, Med. Exp. Force, is enough and anything more is forbidden and merely attracts the Censor's eye.

31/8/15.

My writing will be curious as my hand is tied up again.

My sores healed up two days ago and I took the bandages off, but they promptly started again, especially my right thumb. However, it is much better to-day as I am having hot fomentations on. I am very fit indeed otherwise. I had my second cholera inoculation, but it has no effect on anybody except a stiff arm for a short time.

We are going up to the fire trenches to-day for 2 days, and then the whole Brigade is going back on to Gully Beach for a week or so of rest.

I had a lovely bathe this morning, the water was perfectly calm and as clear as crystal.

1/9/15.

We are up again in the fire trenches and have been warned to expect a general attack in the next day or two.

The weather is gradually altering, yesterday was blazing hot, but this morning it was quite cold and I wore my lined Burberry and a woolly till 9 o'clock and even now I have got a tunic on.

We are in the fire trench that runs from Fusilier Bluff to the sea again, so if the Turks attack and break in our line further South we shall be in the soup! The last draft from the home battalion are quite a good stamp of man with a few notable exceptions, but the difference between them and our old hands in looks, bearing, smartness and soldierly qualities is very marked. It makes us realize more than we had ever done before what a fine battalion [1] we brought into this God-forsaken place. Of course, we realize that the officers who joined after the war are in many cases good officers, but you can't turn civilians into good *training* officers after war breaks out. I don't think even first-class instructors can do it. It takes years of experience and training to teach.

One feels at times rather bitter against the man who slacked in peace time, but I suppose it was not his fault, but the fault of the system and the fault of the parents in many cases whose invariable answer to the question, "How is your son getting on?" was, "well, thank you, he is earning £— a year."

You CAN'T (in red letters) make an army after war starts.

You *can* make a man who will go over the parapet and take, or not take, a trench (once or twice), but he won't hang on when the counter attack comes.

It makes me think a long war is inevitable, we can't break through modern positions, even with plenty of high explosive now that our old regular army is done in, but we *can* hold a modern position, and in time wear the devils down. I'm not a pessimist and I don't feel downhearted. We shall win, there's no doubt about that, but it will be a long job I fear, and some of the slackers will be planted with much lack of ceremony in a foreign country before the job is through. That's comforting anyhow!

I have just been round the fire trenches. There is nothing doing except the usual sniping and bomb throwing. I used my new periscope; I used it all along and never got sniped. I don't think they spot it, the top is so small.

It looks more and more like a winter campaign here, in fact I see no alternative now unless tons of troops are sent here at once.

---

[1] Our old hands are quite undefeatable. Whilst in the front line one moonlight night by myself, a jackal in no-man's land started howling to the moon. It was the only time I have really felt the hair on my scalp rise and stand up. I moved down the trench for company and found one of my old sweats on sentry go lounging on the parapet and quite unmoved. "Did you hear that dreadful noise?" I enquired, "Yes, sir," he said. "He always does it on moonlight nights, it's yon Imam saying his prayers."

VII.—MORE TRENCH LIFE

Whether our Division will be left here or not I don't know.

We have borne the brunt now for 4 months with the exception of the landing and the last fighting up North. We are a very patchwork crowd now with very few officers and we have been 12 months in a hot climate, which is inclined to take the kick out of troops, and that without any rest or leave.

If it turns into a winter campaign, the sensible thing would be to take us out for further training and reorganization.

We should be as good as new in 2 or 3 months and a valuable fighting force, whereas now as a Division we are not much use.

3/9/15.

My writing will be bad as my right thumb is painful, altho' better and on the heal, but I am waiting patiently to have it dressed when it will be more easy, as at present it is badly stuck to the dressings.

Otherwise I am very fit and it is a good thing, as I and E. J. Burrows are the only officers properly on our feet for the moment. Ernest Fletcher is not well and is resting in his valise, Cronshaw is laid up, and I am afraid will have to go to hospital. F. James is seedy, Capt. Allan [Allen] is seedy, both our new subs are seedy and Lund went to hospital yesterday! A nice crowd. There are only 3 now unlisted of the old originals. Self, E. Fletcher, and Cronshaw, and I am very afraid there will only be 2 by this evening.

The 3 seniors, too, in fact the old birds, the fathers of many who know when to change wet clothes, not to mention the ancient art of trench crouching. However, I really am fit bar sores. I have just had my thumb dressed and feel very comfortable, but it is rather septic and the dressing was badly stuck.

I may get to Alexandria yet! Altho' I don't think. This is mere wit on my part, so don't take it seriously. Septic sores are the fashion amongst the 29th and 42nd Divisions.

LETTERS FROM HELLES

5TH BATTALION THE MANCHESTER REGIMENT CASUALTIES TO AUGUST 10TH, 1915

	Original Numbers	Killed	Wounded	Total Killed and Wounded	Sick	Total Casualties
Officers.						
Original Bat.	35	7	18	25	6	31
1st Draft	1	—	1	1	—	1
2nd Draft	5	4	1	5	—	5
Kitcheners	7	5	1	6	—	6
Totals	48	16	21	37	6	43
Other Ranks.						
Original Bat.	797	148	403	551	105	656
1st Draft	100	23	32	55	6	61
2nd Draft	20	4	2	6	1	7
Totals	917	175	437	612	112	724
Add Officers	48	16	21	37	6	43
Totals	965	191	458	649	118	767

Notes.

There are no missing and no prisoners. All were killed.

Strength on August 10th, 1915:—9 Officers, 315 Other Ranks.

Officers surviving and not included in these figures:—
    Lt.-Col. H. C. Darlington, Major E. Fletcher, Major A. E. Cronshaw, Lt. Lund, Capt. J. H. Allen (9th Lincs.).

VII.—MORE TRENCH LIFE

We came back for a rest yesterday and are now on Gully Beach.

We all, men and officers, live on ledges cut in the cliff like rows of guillemots and puffins, we have a dining room, very luxurious, with a tarpaulin to keep the sun off and a rough table and forms: immediately outside is the sand and next to that the sea. I have to sleep in a sort of sarcophagus cut in the cliff and when I step, or roll, as the case may be, out of bed, I'm in the dining room. Incidentally if I roll over once before I wake up, I am in the sea.

It is all very dusty and pretty hot and the men's rest consists of endless and apparently useless fatigue parties.

The 5th and 6th Battn. H.Q.s live together and that is very nice. I think I told you we were living together up on Fusilier Bluff and in Y Ravine.

I have been round to-day looking at the new draft ——. They may fight all right. The first two drafts went over the parapet on Aug. 6th like men, but it is not going over the parapet that wants training, it's knowing what to do and how to stick on to a captured trench when you get there. I long for 2 months at them at Cairo or elsewhere.

Our old crowd were so magnificent both physically and as soldiers. One realizes it now. I am breaking the eleventh commandment (war edition), "Thou shalt not grouse" badly, so will stop.

The 2nd lb. of fresh butter arrived safely and we thoroughly enjoyed it. It is the best thing we have.

Personally, I look forward to butter and cigars more than anything, greedy pig! I can tell you we don't throw any butter away until it is so strong that you can't taste the jam through it.

Willie Douglas has been seedy and away on a Hospital ship. I hear he is back again.

6/9/15.

I am very well and my hands are better. I felt rather seedy for a day or two after my 2nd inoculation against cholera, altho' the Medical authorities say there is no effect.

We have conclusively proved they are wrong, as such a lot of us felt seedy after it. Cunningham thinks it made my hands worse, too. I have been punctured 10 times during the war, 2 enteric, 3 smallpox, 3 bronchitis and 2 cholera! What a war.

We are still doing the puffin act and enjoying it, but shall soon go back to strafe with the Turk. I am very short of officers now and W. Douglas

'Gully Beach.'
Unidentified Manchester Regiment officer outside a
ledge shelter on the cliffs above Gully Beach.

'Allan on Gully Beach.'
Perhaps Capt. J.H. Allen, 9th Lincolns, attached 1/5th Manchesters,
or 2/Lt G.E. Allen. Taken on the Coast Road, looking north.

VII.—MORE TRENCH LIFE

has this morning sent me 131 4th East Lancs, to fill up my gaps. I don't know how long they are here for, but I should imagine it is permanent. Anyhow I have spilt them up into 16 parts, one for each platoon.

I have no officers and very few sergeants left. Ernest Fletcher and I are the only ones now left of the old lot as Cronshaw and Lund are both in hospital and Ernest is pretty seedy and mostly in his valise.

The Battn. is now as follows:—

Bttn. Staff.
1. Lt.-Col. H.C. Darlington
2. Major E. Fletcher

Company Officers.
3. Capt. J.H. Allen, 9th Lincolns, Commanding A and B Coys.
4. 2nd Lt. E.J. Burrows. C Coy.
5. Capt. F. James. D Coy.
6. Lieut. G.E. Allen.
7. 2nd Lt. Dickey.
8. 2nd Lt. Batten.

Staff.
9. Capt. Cunningham, R.A.M.C.
10. Lt. Taylor, Q.M.

We still live with the 6th Manchesters, it makes a lot of difference, altho' they are down to 2 now in their Battn. H.Q., Lt.-Col. C. Pilkington and Capt. Holberton (Adjutant).

We gave a party last night and had a tophole dinner.

Hors d'oeuvres. Sardines. (Yours.)
Soups. (Meat, vegetable.)
Roast Beef (ribs). Very juicy.
Roast potatoes.
Beans.
Plum Duff.
Fruit salad. (Yours. A1.)
Cream, whipped. (Yours. A1.)
Coffee, real.
Cigars. (John Hirst's.)

We went on afterwards to a sing-song arranged by the 5th and 6th Battalions. It was quite good and was held on a sort of terrace cut in the cliff, assisted by one candle lamp. We had no piano, but there was a distinct accompaniment, the guns up at Anzac were firing heavily all the time in the far distance, and our own *Scorpion* was flinging shells over our heads at intervals.

The hit of the evening was parts of La Tosca and Faust sung by a French soldier who is chef to Gen. Douglas and cooks very well (I dined there three nights ago), and who at home is an opera singer, and a very good one, too. He finished up by singing the Marseillaise awfully well; it was perfectly magnificent and poor old "God save the King" sounded pathetic immediately after it, so far as tune and words went. Douglas was very affable the night Pilkington and I dined there.

Postlethwaite lives next door to us and I dined with him the night before last at his Field Ambulance. They have a tent as a Mess pitched on a platform cut out of the cliff. They are very lucky and have beds and chairs and have not to move house every 3 days!

I hear we go back to the trenches on Thursday (to-day is Monday) only a week's rest again. We never get as much rest as the other Brigades.

The officers at the Bombing School fish a lot just off here.

They go out in a boat and drop 3 or 4 bombs in the water which kill the fish. The fish don't float, and they then dive for them. They made an error yesterday and laid out 3 men, one of my men being wounded.

8/9/15.

We are still on the shore, but go back again to a new part of the line on the 10th.

The 5th will be in Brigade reserve, so we shall have an easy time for the first 4 days. It is a good thing, too, as Ernest Fletcher is still seedy, and if he does not improve soon I shall sack him off on to a Hospital ship for a rest.

I have no news of Sanders or Cronshaw. I am very well and have only one sore left now, but it is quite clean again and will heal in time. I have applied for Bob How as an officer, but whether I shall get him, or even where he is, is another matter.

'Fawcus & Cawley M.P. bombing fish. Gully Beach.'
Capt. Arthur Edward Flynn Fawcus, 1/7th Manchesters and O.C. Divisional Bombing School. Capt. Harold Thomas Cawley, M.P., 1/6th Manchesters.

I was very interested in the bags of the 12th and 14th Aug., and so was Postlethwaite. We licked our lips over them and tried to remember whether the birds were killed in the usual butts and came to the conclusion they were, generally.

The weather is much cooler. In fact it was very cold last night and so cold this morning that I did not bathe altho' I did yesterday. I can't get any information about young Armitage[1] and his Division are elsewhere, so I cannot go and see any of the Hampshires, but I have written to their C.O. to ask him to write to Mrs. Armitage with any details.

I have been trying to do what I can for these boys attached to me. I have had them all washed and shaved, and their hair cut and their kit fitted and tried to teach them to know what a clean rifle is, but I really want 2 months to make them even look like soldiers. I call it damned impertinence to try and quell the Turk with the riff raff we have got here just now.

---

1 Killed at Suvla.

'Bn. H.Q., Gully Beach.'

'Gully Beach.'
Both photographs taken on the Coast Road, just north of
Gully Beach (looking south).

VII. — MORE TRENCH LIFE

I only hope we are not trying to quell the Hun with the same muck, when I see samples of soldiers and adjutants and officers, it makes me quite glad there is a war as God knows what the "Englishman" would have degenerated into in another 10 years.

Even the vaunted K.'s army have got to be taught to bite firmly and old man Turk charges very heavily for his first-class lessons. The Yeoboys are an exception. They did magnificently up North, I am told.

Gen. Douglas told me that our losses on Aug. 6 and 7 were not in vain.

We not only succeeded in keeping the best troops from Adrianople here, but actually fetched part of the reserves down to us and so made the landing up North a success. He also told me that when K.'s army were sticky and did not get the ridge when they could have, Gen. de Lisle said, "I wish to God I had the 29th and 42nd Divisions here. I'd have been on that ridge now." That says a good deal, as our Brigade is admitted to be the fighting edge of the 42nd.

I am very glad my old dog Simon did so well on the moors, and I do wish I had been there. I'd sooner shoot grouse than strafe Turks. However, there's always the off chance that someone may some day shake the dust out of their eyes and realize that the Division is not much use as at present constituted. We *may* get sent home to reorganize and return. It's the only sensible course; but that's against it, of course. On the other hand they may prefer to keep their fresh troops out of it and let the weary Willies hold on here until there are none left.

9/9/15

Yesterday afternoon when I was resting I saw a naval launch quite close to the shore and some handkerchiefs waving. I did not take much notice until one of the servants rushed in and said, "There's women in that boat, Colonel." I went out and sure enough there was a party of Australian nurses being shown round the shore to see how the wild soldier lives and sleeps. I got my glasses to see the unusual sight and much to all our Tommies' annoyance, a young nut of a staff officer with much ostentation put his arm round one of the nurses' waists, struck an attitude and waved his hand at us. We all shook our fists at him, which caused great amusement on the launch. It's curious when you think of it, they were the first women I have set eyes on since May 6th! — over 4 months.

Ernest [Fletcher] is no better. I think I shall be sole survivor of the old lot in the next two days. I am not quite fit myself to-day, but it is nothing. I am being careful, I can't afford to get sick at the present moment. It's not good enough being C.O., Second in Command, Adjutant, M.G. Officer, Transport Officer and helping short-handed and not over-well Company officers, but it's got to be done and it's not so difficult as it sounds. The attached troops are rather a trouble at this juncture, I admit, but even they are looking up and seem more like semi-soldiers and less like Dago violinists. However, so long as I keep fit I don't care a damn. I manage to do that somehow altho' we all want a rest and a change of air and diet and thought, especially thought. Even the fittest are inclined to be rather listless.

However, there's nothing for you to worry about, I'm not.

11/9/15.

I am quite all right again, altho' I felt rather seedy the day before yesterday. I took great precautions in food as I cannot afford to run any risks of going sick at present.

Ernest Fletcher went to hospital yesterday, so I am now sole survivor of the original lot and there is only Capt. Allen [1] besides out of the first 48 officers. It is pretty extraordinary that I should have seen the whole lot out, one way or another.

Much to my surprise Clement Fletcher and 3 subs walked in yesterday. I had no idea that anyone was coming at all and only wish I had Lindesay Fisher and Jack Cotham as well. Clement Fletcher [2] is acting adjutant.

I hear, but don't know for certain that Sanders has gone to England, but I can hardly believe it.

We moved up the big Ravine yesterday and are now behind the firing line in reserve for 4 days, we then go up to the fire trenches.

A lot of men are going to hospital each day, but not for any one reason. The old hands are rather played out and the new ones unacclimatized, and they are all in just the condition to get crocked in their weak spots, whatever they happen to be.

---

1 Capt. J. H. Allen, 9th Lincolns.
2 Major Lindesay Fisher, my brother-in-law, Capt. J. Walmesley-Cotham, and Capt. C. Fletcher, all of the 2/5th Manchester Regt.

'*Reserve bivouac, Geoghegan's Bluff, Gully Ravine.*'

'*Bivouac, Geoghegan's Bluff.*'
The Right Sub-Section Reserve was stationed at Geoghegan's Bluff.
Probably taken between 11–14 September 1915.

'Bde. Reserve, Bivouac, Gully Ravine.'
Geoghegan's Bluff viewed from the north-west.
Probably taken between 11–14 September 1915.

'Graveyard, Geoghegan's Bluff, Gully Ravine.'
Viewed from the north-east.
Probably taken between 11–14 September 1915.

VII.—MORE TRENCH LIFE

I keep very fit bar sores and a bit of rheumatics in the neck now and then. I am taking a lot of care. It certainly pays, altho' I must confess I sometimes rather envy the slight crock going away for a rest on a Hospital ship. I am very relieved to have some new officers and they seem quite good too. We are only 11 all told, as 3 subalterns were snitched on arrival and sent to another battalion. I'm sorry for them. A subaltern[1] in the 9th Manch. has got the V.C. We don't grudge it him, but we do think Ken Burrows deserves one even more, as his performance stands out when everyone was gallant. More of your parcels turned up to-day, one of them had butter in. It was not declared on the outside but the label was soaked with butter, so I had the parcel opened at once. It is quite good altho' just turned, but we don't mind a trifle like that. I got another 2,000 cigs, and a box of cigars from Mr. Hirst. They really are priceless here. It's getting quite cold at nights now and I am sleeping in my valise even up here, for the first time since we landed. I am afraid we shall have rain very soon and of course there are no preparations to meet it! We are beauties to wage war. All the materials seem to be used for building winter palaces for red tabs: even the cement intended for a breakwater.

I think Willie Douglas[2] and I are about the only seniors in the whole Peninsular who have come through this show unstellenbosched, unsick, un-gone-off-your-head and I am afraid unsung! Next war I shall join the Navy. It is pretty safe and you don't even have to do your own advertising.

I am going to rest now and read the "Lunatic at large."

12/9/15.

I am very fit again and on full diet. Look in the films developed by Kodak and see if there is one with only a small photo in the middle of the film. It was taken through a loophole at the southern bomb barrier and ought to show the inside of the Turk trench with dead Turk complete.[3] They have turned out awfully well, but I want some new films. No. 2 Brownie.

---

1 Lieut. Forshaw, V.C.
2 Major-General Sir William Douglas, commanding 42nd Division.
3 It came out very well. The bombers having killed the Turk asked me to take his photograph.

15/9/15.

I am waiting for breakfast, I was up early this morning as the "ploughing rain" started last night, and it is difficult to keep dry in bed without proper shelter. This show is the limit, everything is tackled too late.

There are tremendous windy pow-wows going on about shelters for the troops, but no material to make them with, comforts for the troops and meantime—it rains. On paper we shall be more or less comfortable, actually, goodness only knows when.

Mañana or little by little should be the motto of G.H.Q.

Anyhow it is a certainty for a winter campaign now, altho' it is difficult to understand. If it is as important a show as people make out, why on earth they don't race out every man from home, half the Italians and any other Dagos we can beg, borrow or steal as Allies—fancy England leaning on Allies—and finish the Turk off, irrespective of losses.

We moved up into the firing line yesterday, and it is an extraordinary place, quite a new one to me. Very crooked and tricky, very near the Turk (about 40 yards away) and bullets seem to come over from all sides, partly our own and partly the Turk.

As soon as Clement Fletcher and I arrived at Bttn. H.Q. the Gunners, God bless them, put 2 shells right into us; only one man was hit, but they nearly blew our Mess shelter up. I telephoned back and objected, and in due course a subaltern, one of K.'s worst, arrived to investigate and try and pretend it wasn't he. He talked in an airy way of a premature, the usual hot air. He said the first shell was his and was a premature, but that his last shot he had seen burst on J11, so it couldn't be his. I offered to bet him a sovereign both his last rounds were fired on the same laying, but he wouldn't take it. I also told him I'd had 29 casualties from our own guns and, if he didn't mind, I didn't want to get it above 30. He now looks upon me with suspicion, altho' I stood him a whiskey.[1]

It is 11.30 a.m. now and beautifully sunny, so one can dry things. I have just been round the fire trenches and all is quiet.

---

1 Later on in the war, one understood the good gunners' difficulties better.

'Fire trench, near Eastern Birdcage.'
The Eastern Birdcage was a British bombing station about
160 metres east of Border Barricade, Gully Ravine.

'Naval H.E. on Achi Baba, 3 miles away.'
High Explosive shell explodes on Achi Baba, left of centre.

Young Gerald Allen had spotted a Turkish cookhouse up the big nullah and stopped cooking operations with a periscopic rifle, also I could hear dogs barking in the Turk trenches, otherwise all quiet. I took Clement Fletcher his first round of the fire trenches last night. The Turk was strafing with rifle grenades, but he did not seem to mind. The Turk also chucked in some bombs from a trench mortar that went off with a huge roar and did the usual amount of damage, nil.

I got part of the bomb this morning and it is homemade, apparently out of a piece of the old man's trousers and fastened on with a nail, the shell or bomb is a fired brass shell-case filled with old nails and rubbish and high explosive. I am glad he has to invent his engines of destruction, altho' we make our own bombs out of old jam tins, but they are quite efficient.

I see the pioneers are busy putting me a roof on my dugout. Good work, as we shall be here for the next 10 days and goodness knows for how many other 10 days during the winter. One of the photos I am sending back shows one of our naval big shells bursting right on the top of Achi B. and gives you some idea of the explosion when you think it was taken at least 3 miles away.

I am very well, but my hands are bad again, and I have 3 places again, more or less painful. As soon as Ernest [Fletcher] or Cronshaw comes back, I think I shall apply for 2 days' rest and sea air on a Hospital ship and get rid of them. Gen. Lawrence advises me to and it certainly would be very pleasant to have nothing to do or think about for even 2 days.

I will post now, 6 p.m. The Taube has just been over and one of our seaplanes, like a large hearse, tried to chase it. The Taube had the top berth and we could see him firing down on the seaplane. He got away of course.

17/9/15.

I am very fit again bar my hands, but I am afraid they are not bad enough to get me home!

Poor Frank James was badly hit last night. I told you about the big Turk home-made trench mortars which he only brings up at night.

We had treated them with derision, but yesterday afternoon as a precaution I got our artillery on the job and they strafed them, much to their own satisfaction. However, I fancied the Turks removed them

VII.—MORE TRENCH LIFE

by day and told them so. The strafe failed, and promptly at 9 p.m. the Mortars started again, damaged my support trench and knocked out James.

I got the gunners to open fire and the Turks have not fired since, but I am waiting to see if they start again to-night; especially as they put one just behind my cubby hole the other night. Anyway I can get the guns on if they do, but I can't get James back.

I have had to send C. Fletcher to command D. Co., and am now without an adjutant, a 2nd in command, a M.G. officer and a transport officer and C. Fletcher and Allen are my only 2 captains.

The day before yesterday the Turks exploded a very big mine under the 7th Man. fire trench and blew in about 35 yards of it with considerable casualties. It was just a few yards clear of my left flank, but we had a bit of a time straightening up and were quite relieved that no attack came. The crater was 20 yards across and very deep. The Turk seems to have some more ammunition to-night! I told you that our greeting on arrival here was 2 of our own shells into Battn. H.Q. To-night I have had 2 more put in my fire trench, wounding one man.

It is getting cooler and has rained twice, but I have a ground sheet roof to my dugout, which looks like a dilapidated cart shed. Any Parish Council would not allow you even to keep hens in it, but I regard it as the height of luxury. I should sleep in it sounder if I had more officers.

Gen. Lawrence has gone again, we don't know for how long this time, and Canning [Lt-Colonel Albert Canning] is temporarily i/c the Brigade.

We are settling down for a winter campaign and arranging amusements and a band for the men in the Division. I attended a meeting (in the chair Willie Douglas). I am very much in favour of it, as the men love a band and offered my instruments free of charge. Douglas asked me to be President of the Amusements Committee on the spot. I refused this honour. Anyhow I am on the committee by special nomination.

I got your letters up to Sept, 1 and also a parcel with no number. I have all up to 6 so far.

The stocking puttees you sent me are the most comfortable things I have had for a long time. Do send me another pair or two.

21/9/15.

We are still in the firing line; nothing much doing except bombing, sniping, shelling and mining. The Turk has blown up two mines now. The first I told you about before, the second one was a fiasco, it blew the poor old gent's parapet in and did not touch us! The edge of the crater is only about 15 yards from my trench and as it is uphill a bit from us, I can't see into it. I expect the old fox may try and turn it into a bomb pit, so I have two bomb teams opposite it and they throw a bomb into the crater every 10 minutes during the night; the Turks have tried to bomb from there twice, but each time we flooded the place with bombs and he has now given it up. We have got another humorous game up here, which annoys the old man some, we fire rifle grenades direct at his loopholes and blow them in at nights, it gives us great amusement and causes him plenty of fatigue work repairing. The only drawback is it must keep him very fit. He throws stones and clods of clay into one bit of our trench where we are very close and it amuses some of our subs throwing them back, one sub throws about 4 lumps of clay by way of humour and then a bomb, which does not seem cricket. I wanted to test a new loophole plate the other day as against an old one, and I racked my brains as to where I could get a Turk rifle and ammunition from. I suddenly remembered a very obliging sniper opposite the N. Barricade who was a very persistent and accurate shot—I put him up the old plate during the night at a 40 yards' range and in the first hour of dawn he put 27 holes clean through it. Next night I put up a proper loophole with the new plate and let him have a couple of hours at it. He could not even dint it, so I was able to report accordingly, we were all very much obliged to him, but the unwonted spell of free sniping had made him uppish, so we fetched up the trench mortar and chased him out of his cubby hole. That struck us as not being cricket too. Wouldn't he be angry if he knew?

The Forward Observing Officer (Artillery, called the F.O.O.) here is Garnett, Territorial Artillery, he knows Slaidburn well as he stays with the King-Wilkinsons. Things seem quiet here. I must now go round the fire trenches, which reminds me, I took the last bandage off my hands yesterday, went round the fire trenches last night, knocked the healed place of course and am now in bandages again, with my trouser pocket unavailable.

'Gully Ravine.'
Note anti-sniper precautions: large screen, warning sign,
and sandbag revetment.

'Our fire trench across Gully Ravine.'
Taken immediately behind 'Half Moon Street.' The cemetery in the centre of
the image was later designated 'H21 Gully Head Cemetery' by the IWGC.

22nd. 6.50 a.m.

The Turk blew up another mine yesterday evening and again blew in part of his own parapet. Our miners think the Turk is scared about our mines and is trying to blow them up. Poor Frank James died of his wounds. I am very well and am again entirely without anyone to help me as I had to send C. Fletcher to take James' place.

25/9/15.

We are back again on the seashore in the old spot for a week's rest and we are quite glad to get out after our fortnight up, as we had a pretty thick time there.

The Turks blew up 4 mines whilst we were there and twice blew in about 30 yards of our trench where we joined the 6th Man. The casualties were only about 50, however, and very few belonged to us. The last mine was a very big blow up and made a very big crater. However, they never attacked. I went down there about 11 p.m. the night before last to see if I could do anything to help the 6th and had a very exciting half-hour.

The Turks began to throw bombs right over the crater when we were all looking at the digging, etc., operations.

I stayed about half an hour and then as all was quiet, went back to bed. During that time they banged over probably 40 or 50 bombs. Luckily for us they were using too long a fuse. You can see them coming by the fuse and they fizz on the ground long enough to let you lie down. When one dropped near us we lay down and the result was the Turk only managed to kill one R.E. officer [2nd Lieut. Raymond Brocklehurst Angus] and one man [either Pte 2619 S. R. Hall or Pte 991 R. Taylor].[1] we had great difficulty in locating the bomb pit, but eventually got the trench mortars on to it and strafed it thoroughly.

Why he did not get a big bag of us I don't know: I imagine it was because our slope of the crater [2] was very uneven and if one lay down the pieces flew over one altogether. This is chiefly the reason why I have not had time to write to you the last 2 days. They managed to kill Capt. Cawley, M.P., of the 6th Manchesters, later on after I had gone.

---

1 When this man did not get up after the burst, I asked his mate what was wrong. The reply was, "'E's all right, sir, 'e 'as fits."
2 Afterwards known as "Cawley's Crater."

'Cawley's Crater. Result of a mine exploded under our fire trench.'
Probably taken around 15/16 September 1915, looking west towards
Fusilier Bluff. Capt. Harold Thomas Cawley M.P. was shot through
the head and killed in the crater on 23 September 1915.

He is a great loss to them. If you have not already thought of it, I think you had better send me out a pair of trench boots, i.e., thick nailed ones with waterproof legs right up to the thigh, also an oilskin cap. One of our missing officers had some sent out with his trench coat. I did not know there were such things, we are so out of the way here, and, not like those in France, we don't hear of these trench inventions. I had your letters up to Sept. 7th to-day and also parcels. The marmalade was broken and had saturated everything else. They are very rough with parcels and hardly any tins arrive that are not knocked all sorts of shapes.

You must remember everything for here is probably *thrown* out of a big ship down on to the deck of a trawler. However, your parcels always arrive better than anyone else's I see. I am hoping for sausages and butter. Please send lots of sausages. Don't send any more oxo, cocoa, or lemonade, we have a stock now, also we don't need anything cooling now, but rather the other way. The sun is still hot, but we are having cold winds and the nights are very cold indeed. I am very well and my hands are better than they were.

There was a very exciting scrap two days ago between 4 Taubes and one of our fast Monoplanes. Our airman apparently tried to ram one of theirs; the Taubes of course had machine guns on board, so our man, according to custom here, was handicapped by lack of munitions. However, I could not see that any damage was done to either side and the Taubes cleared as hard as they could. They use the M.G.s now on us, as they generally start shooting at something, and our aeroplanes are hardly ever about when they come.

28/9/15.

I am slightly off colour to-day and was also yesterday. No symptoms, but just what the old hands get here, a general feeling of being off colour and slackness.

Postlethwaite, who lives next door, came in to see me this morning and says I am very slightly jaundiced. He suggested a few days on a ship, but I asked him if he would treat me here for a day or two, as it was so slight. He is doing so and I have promised if it gets no better the next day or two that I will go away for a short time. I am quite comfortable here, as I have a tent and can get plenty of milk food and beef tea. The difficulty is that there is no one here. Ernest [Fletcher], Cronshaw and Sanders are all in England. I cannot therefore leave unless it is necessary, but you need not worry. I shall go off if it does not get better soon, but it is so slight I am quite hopeful that I shall be perfectly right again in a few days.

I enclose you some chits for the album. The celebration of the French victory[1] came off all right by our guns, and the old Turk participated willy nilly—at the wrong end of the shells!

---

1 Extract from Sir Ian Hamilton's letter to the author: "our *feu de joie* or, as our men called it, the 'furious joy' was fired in celebration of the battle of Loos which more than any other single factor lost us The Peninsula. Actually it was rather pathetic that we (of all people) should be pretending (at home dictation) that this bloody defeat was a victory. The preparation for Loos was the argument used by G.H.Q. and G.Q.G. in France over and over again for holding up our supply of ammunition and issue of trench mortars, a couple of dozen of which would have blown the Anzac Turks clean off the top of the Hill."

VII.—MORE TRENCH LIFE

It is quite hot again to-day, but personally the colder weather is much pleasanter. The climate of the last few days has been about as perfect as any climate could be. Beautifully clear with a hot sun and a coldish breeze and very cold at nights.

I think the beginning of the end has arrived or rather the beginning of the middle. It looks to me as if the offensive in the W. was the sign that the Germans have reached their furthest E. The diary I enclose was issued by the 8th Army Corps with their orders, presumably to cheer up the soldiers who are perfectly cheerful in any case. I have had another squad of recruits sent to me, so the KRITHIA commando is going strong. They were met at the entrance by Capt. Allen and two barbers with clippers and were first pushed into the sea to be cleaned and then operated on by the barbers.

Later, 6 p.m.

I am no worse anyhow, so that's all right, and it is very slight. I shall post this to-morrow and let you know how I go on.

29th.

I am being treated with Calomel and am much the same, so am doing nothing. If I am not better tomorrow I expect I shall go for a bit of a rest. Do not worry, it is nothing special, but probably just the natural effects of 5 months of this game. They tell me I am very nearly the only officer on the Peninsular who has been right through.

'Hospital Ship.'

VIII.—THE WAY HOME

S.S. Nevasa. 1/10/15.

I am writing this from a Hospital ship, which I came on to last night. There is nothing much the matter with me except a very slight suspicion of jaundice. I am not even in bed, no temp., and feel a fraud. However, I am not getting better on the Peninsular, so am glad to be here. I was feeling fairly seedy two days ago, and W. Douglas heard and came to see me! He suggested I should have a fortnight's leave and go to Imbros![1] He said if I got on a Hospital ship that I should never get back again. However, yesterday morning Postlethwaite came to see me, which was good of him, and said I wanted a complete change, and that Imbros was no earthly use. He said I was slightly jaundiced and that if I went away for a week or two, I should stave it off, whereas if I hung on here it was only a matter of time before I would break down. So he ticketed me "Jaundice Base, Alexandria," and sacked me on to this ship. I am now writing on deck 10 a.m. on our way to Mudros. I shall then try and get on a ship for Alexandria, as I want very badly to get back to Gallipoli in a fortnight or at any rate under a month.

The 5th and 6th Man. are combined in my absence as one battalion under Pilkington, so that's all right. They go up to-day into the fire trenches for 14 days and then back for 14 days, so I feel I have a clear month if necessary. The trouble is, once you get away from the Peninsular it is very hard to get back, they shove you on a ship and you may find yourself anywhere, probably England! I don't want to get further than Alexandria because I can get back from there, but I shall probably have to fight like blazes to get off this ship if she happens to be going to Malta or home. I wish I could get back, one must stick to the battalion as there is no one with it and I can't leave it on Pilkington's hands indefinitely.

---

1 Imbros was merely a short cut to the cemetery.

You can't think what a relief it is after 5 months' eternal strafing to feel that you have no responsibilities and nothing to do. I am in a big ward in the next cot to Rochdale, who is, I hear, for England.

The Dr. has just seen me, says there is nothing really wrong except that I am run down and has told me to do nothing and feed up and that I shall be perfectly fit with 10 days' rest, so that's all right.

I cannot tell you how nice it is to feel I have nothing whatever to do and nothing to think about. It requires 5 months in the trenches to really appreciate it. I had fish for breakfast and slept very badly last night owing to being in a bed and wearing hospital pyjamas, but shall be all right to-night I expect. This is a very comfortable ship and my doctor is very nice, and I should like nothing better than to cruise in her for a fortnight and then rejoin, but am afraid it is impossible.

3 p.m. We are at Mudros now, so I shall know whether I stay here or go for a sail to Alex, very soon. I don't want to stay here as it is a perfectly beastly place and no change at all.

2nd Oct.

I could not post at Mudros as we have been sent straight on to Malta, so I shall get a sea voyage. I feel fairly all right now and have a very good appetite. I will post at Malta.

2/10/15.

We should arrive in Malta in a couple of days, and when there I shall have to see about getting back to Helles again. I am feeling very much better again, my appetite is A1 and my sores have healed up bar one on my face, which has very nearly gone.

I don't want to stay in Malta longer than necessary as it is sure to be hot. It seems a pity I can't take a trip to England and back, but I can't afford to take any risks of not getting back to the Peninsular in about a fortnight or so.

The Matron on this Hospital ship is a Miss Knaggs, who is a relation of the Huddersfield doctor, also up to the war she was Matron of a Nursing Home at Southport.

To-day is a regular Mediterranean day, hot, damp and foggy.

VIII.—THE WAY HOME

3/10/15.

I am feeling quite fit again, the weather has changed and is quite cool. I have no news, so I talk about myself, as you will probably want to hear all about me.

There is a staff of nurses on board, but they are very hard-worked and one does not see much of them. They seem quite nice.

I have played a game of chess or two with one of the doctors, but not very intellectually, I'm not out for work. I have been beaten once, but should have won if I had not been extremely careless. We get to Malta to-morrow.

4/10/15. Blue Sisters Hospital, Malta.

Just a line to catch the mail to say I arrived here this morning. I am feeling quite fit again now and am not in bed or under treatment. I shall try and get back in 3 or 4 days as I don't want to be away long. The doctor here asked me, when I got in, how I was and I told him I was all right and wanted to get back in a couple of days. He asked how long I had been on the Peninsular—I said 5 months. He roared with laughter and I heard him telling another doctor about it afterwards. He said, "There's a colonel man here who has been on the Peninsular 5 months and wants to go back," and then they both roared with laughter. I can see I shall have to see Lord Methuen.

5/10/15. Blue Sisters Hospital, Malta.

I have posted you two letters and sent a cable since writing the previous part of this letter.

I am feeling quite fit again, but have had slight indigestion to-day. I am a little run down, and the doctor says all I want is feeding up and a bit of a rest. I expect to be only here for about a week and then go back to Helles.

They look upon me here as a sort of miracle to have done 5 months at Helles, and I think a bit mad to want to go back. I am told that they don't let you back very easily if you have been long there!

I cabled you not to come here as you would probably miss me altogether. I know you will be glad I am having a rest, and I must say I am glad to get it, especially as there is nothing the matter with me.

I am not in bed and am having a tonic.

6/10/15.

I am feeling all right to-day and my indigestion is better again. I was vetted to-day and was finally written down for a fortnight's rest, but I shall try and get back sooner. The doctors got orders this morning to evacuate this hospital, so they informed me I was for England in the next two or 3 days. I refused to go! so after a bit of strafing they suggested booking me for a month's rest. I told them that was all rot, and finally got it down via 3 weeks to a fortnight.

Five months on the Peninsular is considered enough to crock you for life or turn you into a mental case, they can't believe one can thrive there if one is lucky. Taking it all round I have never been fitter in my life than in S. Africa and in Gallipoli.

Lord Methuen was in here to-day, but I did not speak to him. I have no news, and I have not been into the Town as I have been slacking and enjoying the amazing luxury of doing absolutely nothing. I don't find it as easy as usual! It is a great temptation to say nothing and so get back home, but as long as I am not unfit of course it is out of the question. If I was unfit I should not hesitate. However...

Going to Osborne Convalescent Home to-day.

* * *

APPENDICES

Lieutenant H.C. Darlington prior to his departure for South Africa in February 1900, wearing the sword presented by his fellow officers.

APPENDIX A.—BIOGRAPHY OF COLONEL SIR HENRY CLAYTON DARLINGTON K.C.B., C.M.G., T.D., D.L.

Henry Clayton Darlington (HCD), known within the family as Hal, was a solicitor by profession but a military man by vocation, and the true embodiment of that early twentieth century British stalwart, the volunteer citizen soldier.

He was born at Elm Bank, Wigan, Lancashire, on 27 June 1877, the first child of Henry Darlington and Edith Blanche Darlington (née Smith).[1] At the time of HCD's birth, his father Henry was working as a solicitor in the family law firm in Wigan, but he was also an enthusiastic part-time soldier, holding a commission in the 1st Volunteer Bn., The Manchester Regiment. This was a battalion that Henry senior would later rise to command. HCD was destined not only to follow his father into the family firm, but more significantly, he would also be commissioned in his father's battalion.

HCD was first educated at Rivington Grammar School, where he 'spent much of his time fighting,'[2] before attending Shrewsbury school, where he 'learnt Latin and Greek, and nothing else whatsoever except leg breaks.'[3] Suffering asthma and bronchial problems throughout his childhood, fears grew that he would become consumptive and in March 1896, his parents sent him on a voyage to Tasmania via Cape Town. He travelled first class onboard the RMS *Tainui*, a four-masted clipper-bowed steam vessel. Already a keen naturalist and photographer, he took a camera on the voyage and maintained

---

1 HCD's five siblings, in age order, were Cecil Ralph, Blanche Mary (known as May), Sydney Harriet, John St. Clair (known as Jack) and Eleanor (known as Nora).
2 Hugh Darlington, *Henry Clayton Darlington, The Wigan Volunteers, and the 5th Battalion Manchester Regiment* (unpublished) p.4.
3 Ibid, p.5.

a travelogue of his experiences. The first nine days of his amusing observations survive. Disembarking at Santa Cruz, Tenerife, he wrote:

> 'We wandered around the town attended by a dirty looking Spaniard with a huge grin and knock knees. Some of the girls are very pretty and the costumes of male and female very picturesque as regards colours in the latter and shape in the former. What struck me most was the way the tiniest children, boys, and girls, some of whom could not have been more than five, all smoked cigarettes and the more fortunate cigars.'[1]

HCD returned home later that year and having been articled previously into Messrs Darlington and Sons of Wigan, the family firm, he sat his first law examination on 14 October 1896. On 27 April 1897, he was commissioned into his father's regiment,[2] the 1st Volunteer Battalion (Wigan) The Manchester Regiment. Sometime afterwards, HCD suspended his legal studies to attend a year-long course at the Guards' School of Instruction, Chelsea. This he passed with distinctions in military history, tactics, and military law, and was promoted to lieutenant on 20 July 1898.

In early 1900, an appeal made for volunteers from Yeomanry and Volunteer units to serve in the South African War was answered by HCD. He was placed in command of the Wigan Battalion's Active Service Section, comprising one officer (HCD) and 29 other ranks. On 9 February 1900, HCD and his men joined the 1st Volunteer Service Company at the Regimental Depot at Ashton-under-Lyne. The following day, the company—comprising three officers and 113 other ranks—left for Southampton. They sailed on 14 February onboard the SS *Greek,* disembarking at Cape Town on 9 March, and re-embarked the following day on the SS *Majestic* for Durban. On 13 March, HCD and his company (soon to be redesignated 'I' Company and attached to the 1st Bn., The Manchester Regt.) disembarked and entrained onto open railway trucks, to travel to Ladysmith, via Colenso. Some of HCD's letters written to his family

---

1 Darlington, *Henry Clayton Darlington,* (unpublished) p.7.
2 His father, Henry Darlington, was awarded the Volunteer Decoration on 20 December 1892 (denoting 20 years' service) and at the time of HCD's commission held the rank of major, or possibly lieut-colonel.

A.—BIOGRAPHY OF HCD

from South Africa still exist and provide a vivid account of his experiences.

'On the 10th we embarked on the Majestic and went up to Durban. We got there on the 13th and found orders to go to Colenso. We got off the boat with great difficulty (could not even cross the bar) as there was a high sea running, drowning a kaffir on the way, he fell off the lighter, and went down within 20 yards. I think a shark must have got him; and entrained at 8.30 a.m., (this is where I lost everything except my valise). We ought to have had breakfast at Mooi River, but there was none, so I had it at Estcourt. We slept in the train. We then got orders for Ladysmith. I saw the wrecked armoured train and Lord Robert's grave. We had a walk over the Tugela at Colenso, as the bridge was wrecked, entrained again on the other side, and went off to Ladysmith. On the way we saw bully beef tins, dead horses, broken bridges, and graves, also a house riddled with bullets, got to Ladysmith about 5.30, fed on tinned rabbit and bloater paste, commandeered ladies waiting room at the station and slept there. Next day we saw the wrecked town hall, etc., and shells lying about the gutter. We got orders to join the Manchesters at Ceasar's Camp and went (4½ miles) right on the hilltop, bivouacked there for the night. I slept out for the first time and slept very well. Next morning (the 16th) reveille went at 4.00 a.m., breakfast at 5, parade at 6, started for here 6.15 over the veldts, got here at 10.30 (nine miles about) and then we pitched camp. I slept in a tent and had a wash, and also took my boots off, and here I am very well. As far as I can make out, we are 5 miles west of Ladysmith, somewhere pretty close to Dewdrop; you will see it on the map, in a rest camp, for at least three weeks, and also we are a tactical camp, being the flank of the communications lines, and supposed to be looking after Van Reevan's Pass on our left. The Manchesters look very ill and have had a very hard time; you realise it when you see their trenches and the shell holes at Caesar's Camp...'[1]

---

1 From an article published in the *Wigan Observer* (pasted into HCD's scrapbook) entitled 'Lieutenant H.C. Darlington At The Front.'

The Wigan detachment of volunteers for service in South Africa, pictured on 9 February 1900. HCD sits in the centre.

Manchester Regiment officers pictured on Signpost Ridge in April 1900. The officer on the extreme right appears to be Lieutenant H.C. Darlington. *(Manchester Regiment Image Archive)*

A. — BIOGRAPHY OF HCD

Now attached to the regulars, HCD was granted the temporary rank of lieutenant in the Army on 28 March 1900. On 6 April, his company moved to Vaal-Kranz (the scene of Spion Kop) and after a few days, on to Arcadia. On the 11th 'the whole brigade was suddenly pushed back under Wagon Hill.'[1] Two days later they moved a short distance to Signpost Ridge, 'ground which had been occupied by the Boers, and which the stench that arose from dead horses etc., was horrible.'[2] They moved again on 21 April to Surprise Hill, north-west of Ladysmith, to man the outpost line, remaining in this relatively secure section of defence until 16 May. When HCD succumbed to enteric fever, he was sent for treatment on a hospital ship moored at Durban, on 14 May. He returned to the 1st Manchesters on 11 July, who were by now at Elandslaagte, and was attached to 'A' Company (regulars).

On 12 July, the battalion moved to Tinta where it was employed on outpost duty. On the 20th, the 1st Manchesters were attached to a flying column under Brig-General Francis Howard and were moved by train to Zandspruit. They arrived on the morning of 21st, leaving the train to march the eight miles in the heat of the day, to Dublin Hill. There the battalion bivouacked for the night, under notice that they would be engaging the enemy on the following day. In a letter to his parents, written 'near Sandspruit, somewhere north of Volkarnst, Transvaal, 20 [sic] July 1900,' HCD describes his 'baptism of fire' when he encountered Boer forces at Meertzicht:

> 'We were ordered up here in a hurry last Friday and were put in a flying column under General Howard. The great thing is I have at last had my baptism of fire, and a pretty hot one too. We were told we had to go out and fight when we got to Zandspruit, and on Sunday last – nice way to spend a Sabbath – went out as third line. We did not come under heavy fire, only a few shells came our way. We turned the Boers, however out of Graspan, which is what we wanted. At 4 p.m., our Company, that is A Company, went

---

1 From an article published in the *Wigan Observer* (pasted into HCD's scrapbook) entitled 'The Volunteers in South Africa—A Review of Their Work—Interesting Chat with Lieut. Darlington.'
2 From an article published in the *Wigan Observer* — 'Interesting Chat with Lieut. Darlington.'

out as outpost on a hill about four miles away (after marching 10 miles) and I with two men went out as scouts. When I got to the top I saw some Boers about 150 yards away, so I lay down and had a look at them with my glasses; then I thought if I could get back and warn the Company, we should have them. I got up and started back, but unluckily they saw me, and 'phut' the brutes put a bullet about six inches from my feet. The next two or three were better shots, and pretty close to my head. We went up and lay down, there was no cover, and fired at each other until dark (about two hours) when reinforcements came. The Boers turned a pom-pom and a 15-pounder on to us, but they seemed poor shots. One bullet touched my helmet, and another hit the ground a yard in front of me. The man on my right was shot; he was lying about three yards away. Our casualties were only one killed and one wounded, both in our Company (A Company) and both close to me. However, we drove them off. It is all right being under fire. You don't think anything about it, and got through about 50 rounds, and was making good shooting at 200, 800, 1,000 and 1,400 yards. My best range was 1,000. Since then, we have been fighting on and off the whole time, but the Manchesters have not been in it except on that one day.'[1]

'While General Buller collected his troops before moving up the country,'[2] HCD remained with the 1st Manchesters at Meertzicht, where the battalion sent out patrols encountering the enemy on several occasions. On 7 August, the column moved again, occupying Amersfoort on the following day and on the 10th they crossed the Vaal River:

'About 300 Boers held the bridge, but they were driven off, leaving it intact, and the British bivouacked there. On the 11th they marched to Klipfontein. It was a dreadful march, and the dust was quite horrible. The Boers had burned the veldt, and what with the cold wind and the black dust caused by many fires the march was a most

---

1 From an article published in the *Wigan Observer* (pasted into HCD's scrapbook) entitled 'Lieutenant Darlington Baptism of Fire.'
2 From an article published in the *Wigan Observer* (pasted into HCD's scrapbook) entitled 'The Volunteers in South Africa—A Review of Their Work—Interesting Chat with Lieut. Darlington.'

A.—BIOGRAPHY OF HCD

trying experience. On the 12th the troops got to Ermelo, and the next day they got to a place called Botha's Rust. This was the biggest march made by the Volunteer Company; the distance covered being about 25 miles.'[1]

The Manchesters reached the Komati River by the 15 August, where they remained, until operations were resumed on the 21st. The next seven days would be the most eventful and demanding week HCD would experience during the entire campaign. He wrote to his family a few days after the battle ended:[2]

> 'Being stuck here for the last day or two I am taking the opportunity of writing, and hope to be able to send it, as we are on the railway. I can tell you I am jolly glad of a rest, and also a chance of getting [away] from the zee, zee, boom, wiz, bang, swish, we have been having for some days now. I wrote last Friday, and since then have seen more than all the rest of the campaign put together. On Saturday there was the usual sniping all day; bullets coming over us all day, especially during breakfast, and Long Tom was shelling us but did no harm. On Sunday we advanced; the Devon's led, and we were next. We were sent up pretty soon and, on their left, and came under fire immediately. Long Tom tommed us, the pom-pom pommed us, and altogether we had a jolly time. We went up the ridges, however, and Johnny Boer was on the other side. The bullets were thick; two hit the ground just in front of me, and covered me with dirt, and three went between the colour-sergeant and myself. We stayed on till dark and then entrenched ourselves during the night. I got about two hours sleep, and at two in the morning was roused by hearing the rap-rap of Mausers and bullets coming over. We had to get up, and extend our companies all along the hill, but got no more sleep. Our casualties (not during the night) were three killed, 10 wounded and one missing. One of the Wigan men was killed (Pte. F. Monroe) shot through the head.[3]

1 Ibid.
2 Later known as The Battle of Belfast, or alternately as The Battle of Bergendal. It was the last set-piece battle of the South African War, even though the war would continue for another 21 months.
3 Private Frank Monroe was killed on 26 Auguust at Waai Kraal, near Geluk.

HCD sitting in a 'Long Tom' shell hole during the
Battle of Belfast (21 to 27 August 1900).

'Next morning they started sniping with the light, and also pom pommed us beastly. We had to have breakfast before it got light. I was moved to relieve a Devon company, about 10 a.m., and went on the left of our line on the right flank. The Rifles did the attack, and they lost about 90 killed and wounded. We simply looked after their flank while they attacked the Boer flank. We shelled them all day and the Rifles attacked in the afternoon. When we got close up and fixed bayonets all the Boers fled. Then we started up with our guns and I never heard such a row in my life. It was a sight worth seeing, and I don't suppose I shall see such another. I had a good view, and the only objection was, if you showed an eyelash you got shot at, and a 12-pounder was shelling us, and the guns, also Long Tom, were trying to reach the 4.7's behind us, and could not, so the result was all his shells fell around us, and it was not much fun that. Luckily it was soft ground, and no one was touched, although two fell within twenty yards of me. Our casualties I have not heard yet, but I think about a dozen.

A.—BIOGRAPHY OF HCD

Our company was lying in a road, and it was a perfect marvel no one was hit. I got so used to it by midday that I had my lunch (potted meat and biscuit) quite comfortably. All the same Long Tom frightens you very much as you can hear him screaming for a long time, and each shell sounds as if it were going to drop right on you, also he makes such a beastly noise when he bursts and throws such a lot of earth about.

'I had my photo taken sitting in a shell hole and hope it will be a pleasing likeness. I find it helps your nerves a lot to smoke cigarettes. However, we turned the whole Machadodorp position, I hear, which is good. We are left here to look after the line. I don't know for how long, and all the other regiments have gone to Machadodorp, and I have heard guns today. I am not sorry, as we have, except to-day, been under continual fire now for five days, and the night before last we could hear Mausers going off, and the bullets coming over at night and there were none really. We had the first rains last night, and a thunderstorm, but I don't care, as I went and looted a farm, and had a comfortable tarpaulin shelter. While we were lying behind our guns I went out in front to see if the snipers had gone, and as I walked out, they did not shoot at me. I laid down behind a heap, and immediately I laid down they started; so, after I had a look, I got up and bolted back, and they sniped all the way. I went out again, towards evening, and the same thing happened, only I walked back instead of running, such was my contempt for their shooting powers; nevertheless, I can now quite sympathise with a rabbit. I am very fit and very dirty; also, my clothes are in rags.

'P.S.—We must have killed lots of Boers. I saw one literally blown to atoms with a lyddite shell.'[1]

For the remainder of the campaign HCD and the Wigan Volunteers were employed on escorting convoys, digging fortifications, and manning outposts. After calls of being sent home, which proved false, the Wigan Volunteers eventually moved to Durban in May 1901, embarking for England on the SS *Englishman*.

---

1 From an article published in the *Wigan Observer* on 6 October 1900 (pasted into HCD's scrapbook) entitled 'Lieutenant Darlington in South Africa.'

HCD, seated in the centre, with the other survivors from the Wigan detachment, photographed on their return.

Missing from the photograph taken on 9 February 1900 are Ball and Monroe. Private Kennedy Ball died in the General Hospital, Howick on 10 August 1900, from burns received while trying to save officers kit from a veldt fire on 30 July 1900 at Meerzicht. Private Frank Monroe was killed by a bullet through the head on 26 August 1900 at Waai Kraal, near Geluk.

After 14 months away, the Volunteers reached Wigan at 11pm on 23 May 1901. Despite the lateness of the hour, thousands of people assembled to welcome the men home.

Altogether, HCD's service in South Africa earned him the Queen's South Africa Medal with three clasps taking account of the operations in Natal from March to June 1900, the Transvaal east of Pretoria from July to 20 November 1900 (including the actions at Reit Vlei and Belfast) and finally in the Transvaal again, from the 30 November 1900 to 1901.

After his return to Wigan, HCD returned to work in his father's practice, and resumed his legal studies. He remained actively involved with the Wigan Volunteers and in short order was made Honorary Lieutenant in the Army on 24 June 1902 before promotion to Captain on 28 March 1903. On 8 April 1904, HCD's father, Lieut-Colonel Henry Darlington, assumed command of the Wigan Volunteers.

A.—BIOGRAPHY OF HCD

Tragically, three months later, Henry died in a shooting accident when his gun discharged prematurely. He was preparing to 'pot rabbits' in his garden. The same year, HCD qualified as a solicitor.

In 1907, HCD became engaged to Mabel Anne Hirst, the daughter of Thomas Julius Hirst, a wealthy industrialist, and his wife Esther, of Meltham Mills, Yorkshire.[1] Mabel had been a close school friend of HCD's second oldest sister, Sydney.[2] In 1909, the couple married at Meltham Hall, temporarily setting up home at Field House in Parbold. On 10 June 1910, they moved to Croasdale House, Parbold, a substantial, detached property built by Mabel's father as their wedding present. Here they lived a comfortable upper-middle class life with their cook and two maids. In September 1910 a children's nurse was appointed to care for Esther, the couple's first child. The following year, the Darlington family suffered the tragic death from appendicitis of HCD's youngest brother John who had joined the British Indian Army's 6th Jat Light Infantry after passing out at Sandhurst. Then, between 1911 and 1914, Mabel gave birth to Henry John, and Anne.

After his father's death, HCD continued to serve with the Wigan Volunteers, retaining his rank and seniority on the formation of the Territorial Force (TF) on 1 April 1908. The battalion was subsequently redesignated the 5th Bn., The Manchester Regiment.

A Territorial battalion of the time was required to have two Majors in its establishment. In 1913, the 5th Manchesters' second-in-command Major Bryan retired. Major Ernest Fletcher took over as 2ic, opening an opportunity for promotion to one of the battalion's senior captains. Both HCD and Arthur Cronshaw had served in South Africa, and Cronshaw had three months seniority over HCD. Despite this, HCD was preferred and, on 16 September 1903, he was promoted to major.

---

1. Thomas Julius Hirst was a manufacturer of cotton thread and mill owner, who lived with his family in Meltham Hall, Meltham Mills, where a butler, footman, and eight other servants attended them. Hirst owned a grouse moor at Slaidburn, on the borders of Lancashire and Yorkshire. Interestingly, in a letter written to his wife on 18 August 1915 (after being married to Mabel for six years) HCD refers to his father-in-law with formality as Mr Hirst.
2. Mabel used to stay with the Darlingtons at Birkacre House near Chorley, and Sydney would frequently stay with the Hirsts at Meltham Hall. Mabel's father was at first taken aback that his daughter would want to marry a man outside the local mill-owning fraternity, and he had enquiries made in Wigan as to HCD's suitability, which amused HCD greatly.

This was not the only occasion when HCD would compete successfully for promotion against more senior peers.

In early 1914, HCD suffered an attack of pleurisy and in March, on doctor's advice, travelled with Mabel and three of her siblings to the Canary Islands for a month's convalescence.[1]

His health restored, HCD returned to England in April, resuming duties in the family firm, and with his battalion. Six weeks later, HCD and the 5th Manchesters travelled to Carnarvon for the battalion's annual camp of two weeks of range practise, field exercises, route marches, drilling, and organised sports. It would be the battalion's last camp for six years and for many officers and men, their final one.

Two weeks after the 5th Manchesters returned to Wigan, the mobilization of Austro-Hungarian and German forces was triggered by events in Sarajevo and war in Europe became inevitable. On 3 August 1914, Germany declared war on France, sending troops across the border. When, on 4 August, German forces crossed into neutral Belgium, Britain demanded that Germany withdraw her troops by midnight. When this ultimatum was ignored, Britain declared war.

Britain had already begun to mobilise its forces—Regular, Reserve, and Territorial (including the East Lancashire Division). On 3 August 1914, all units of the division then at annual camp were recalled, and an order to mobilise the division was received at 5.30 pm on the following day.

TF officers and men were contracted for 'for home service' only, but on 10 August, Lord Kitchener invited the Territorial Divisions to volunteer for active service overseas. On 14 August the East Lancashire Division responded to Kitchener's invitation, becoming the first division to do so. Although the decision was for individuals to make, by the end of the month the great majority of HCD's officers and men had signed Army Form E. 624, agreeing 'to serve in any place outside the United Kingdom in the event of a national emergency.' On 20 August, the 5th Manchesters left Wigan and moved into camp at Littleborough near Rochdale. For two weeks rumours of moves to Ireland or France were rife, but on 5th September, orders were received confirming Egypt as the division's true destination. On 9 September 1914, the division entrained for Southampton.

---

1 The group travelled first class, at the expense of HCD's father-in-law.

Officers of the 5th Manchesters outside the Wigan Drill Hall in late August 1914. From right to left: Capt. & Adjutant J.M.B. Sanders, Capt. A. Ellis, Capt. A.L. Bryham, Capt. F.S. Brown, Lieut-Colonel W.S. France, VD, and Major H.C. Darlington.

The 5th Manchesters embarked on the SS *Caledonia* the following morning, and on 11 September the convoy carrying the division left port for Alexandria. Sometime prior to the battalion's departure it became apparent its commanding officer, Lieut-Colonel W. S. France, VD, would not be going to Egypt. Command of the battalion was passed to HCD, who was promoted to temporary lieut-colonel on 14 September, despite being junior to the battalion's 2ic, Major Ernest Fletcher. HCD had been appointed on merit, and once again he had overcome the convention of seniority.

The East Lancashire Division arrived at Alexandria on 25 September and disembarked. The 5th Manchesters, with HCD in command, remained in Alexandria, quartered in Mustapha Barracks and Camp Alexandria with the majority of the Manchester Brigade as garrison troops. For the next seven months, HCD, assisted by his Adjutant, Capt. J. M. B. Sanders, oversaw a period of intensive training; honing and hardening his men into an effective, efficient fighting force. In mid-January 1915, the 1/5th Manchesters moved to Cairo and on the 31st moved into camp at Heliopolis where training became even more demanding. The men undertook long marches, rehearsed company attacks, and took part in brigade and divisional exercises.¹ They practised digging trenches, something the Wiganers excelled at. A reporter from the *Manchester Guardian* witnessed their efforts in February, writing:

> 'Seen at work the 5th Manchesters must be awarded the palm… The Colonel told me, "my men look on it as a holiday if I take them out to dig. We are just keeping our hands in for the time we get home, they say."'

On 28 April 1915, the divisional commander received a verbal order that the division must be prepared to move to the Dardanelles at short notice. The Fusilier Brigade was the first to leave on 1 May. The Manchester Brigade followed, with the 1/5th and 1/6th Manchesters embarking on the SS *Derfflinger* on 3 May, and disembarking at 'W' Beach, Helles, on 6 May 1915. HCD continued to command the 1/5th Manchesters at Helles until 7 July, when placed in temporary command of 127th Infantry Brigade. He resumed command of the 1/5th Manchesters on the return of Brigadier General Lawrence on 1 August, until evacuated sick from the peninsula on 30 September 1915. After a short stay in hospital in Malta he was sent to complete his convalescence in England. For his service at Gallipoli, HCD was twice Mentioned in Dispatches (*London Gazette* 5 November 1915 and 13 July 1916).²

HCD remained in England until 17 February 1916, when he embarked on HMT *Olympic* for Alexandria. He arrived in Egypt on 29 February but remained at the 1/5th Manchesters' base in Mustapha Barracks until 15 March when he resumed command of the battalion at Shallufa, close to the Suez Canal. The next 5 months were spent training and strengthening canal defences. On 3 June, HCD was made Companion of the Order of St. Michael and St. George (CMG) in the 1916 Birthday Honours.

In August 1916, the 5th Manchesters, with HCD in command, took part in the Battle of Romani, and follow-up operations, as part of a Mobile Column.

---

1 By this time the second-string battalions of the division were being raised, hence the redesignation of 1/5th.
2 HCD was later told that he had been recommended for the DSO, but the ship (reputed to be carrying his citation) was sunk.

A. — BIOGRAPHY OF HCD

On 8 August, HCD's fourth child, Mary, was born. Tragically, his wife Mabel died on 14 September—HCD was granted compassionate leave and returned home on the 17th. He returned to Egypt on 9 November, when he was placed in temporary command of the 127th Brigade, remaining in command until 5 December, when he rejoined the 5th Manchesters, then at El Mazar.

In the early months of 1917, the Egyptian Expeditionary Force was 'knocking on the gates of Palestine, and the safety of the Suez Canal was assured.'[1] Fewer troops were needed in Egypt, and it was decided that the 42nd Division would join the British Expeditionary Force (BEF) in France. On 2 March 1917, HCD and the 5th Manchesters left Alexandria onboard HMT *Corsica*, disembarking at Marseilles on the 8th, where they entrained for northern France.

HCD arrived with his battalion at Pont Remy near Abbeville, and shortly afterwards moved to an area 10 miles east of Amiens to train and re-equip. After a period employed in road building and general fatigues, the 1/5th Manchesters moved up to the front on 29 April 1917, taking over a section of the support and reserve lines in in front of Le Catelet. On 3 May the 42nd Division took over a sector near Ronnsoy, southeast of Epley. Two days earlier, on the night of 1/2 May, Brig-Gen V.A. Ormsby, commander of the 127th Brigade, 'was engaged in marking out the new front line of his brigade near Catelet Copse, when the enemy suddenly opened a bombardment, and he was struck on the head by a piece of shell and killed.'[2] HCD once more assumed temporary command of the brigade until the arrival of Brig-General the Hon. A. M. Henley on 5 May, when HCD returned to his battalion.

HCD led his battalion for the remainder of 1917 (save for a month's home leave—26 June to 21 July) serving at: Havrincourt (16 May to 9 July) in the Third Army's reserve area at Acheit-le-Petit (9 July to 22 August); Poperinghe (22 to 31 August); Ypres (8 to 21 September); Nieuport (22 September to 16 November), before moving to the La Bassee sector on 16 November (where the 42nd Division remained until 21 March 1918).

1 G. Derbyshire, *A Wigan Military Chronicle, Volume II* (unpublished) p.321.
2 Frederick P. Gibbon, *The 42nd (East Lancashire) Division 1914-1918* (London: Country Life Ltd, 1920) p.90.

LETTERS FROM HELLES

On 1 August 1917, HCD was made substantive lieut-colonel (with precedence from 1 June 1916) and was again placed in command of the 127th Brigade from 13 to 20 August. He was awarded the Territorial Decoration (TD) on 11 September and was Mentioned in Dispatches on 7 November 1917 (*London Gazette* 10068, 21 December 1917).

At the end of 1917, HCD suffered an outbreak of trench boils, and was sent home on sick leave on 3 January 1918, in a 'very run down' condition.[1] He spent much of his leave at Meltham Hall, where his children were being cared for by Daisy, his late wife's younger sister. Daisy was a trained nurse, and she tended HCD's boils, dressing them with 'fermentations.' HCD attended a medical board which prolonged his sick leave, and in early spring he proposed to Daisy. Despite marriage with a deceased wife's sister being lawful, it was disapproved by the Anglican church. Daisy reflected for some time before accepting, to the approval of both families. The couple were engaged in May, after Daisy's father sent HCD a message 'telling him to hurry up!'[2]

In April 1918, HCD now declared fit for Home Service, was sent to Oswestry to prepare the 4th King's Own Royal Regiment for its move to Dublin.[3] HCD moved to Dublin with the battalion, but returned on leave to England to marry Daisy on 10 June 1918.[4] After a short honeymoon, HCD was sent to Newcastle on Tyne on 25 June to command a group of officers under medical supervision. He was finally declared fit and sent back to command the 1/5th Manchesters in France on 23 July, but was invalided back to England on 14 August, where he remained until the end of the war.[5] He received the Order of the Crown of Italy in 1918.

---

1 Daisy Darlington, Margaret Phillips (ed) *The memoirs of Daisy Darlington Volume I* (Private publication, 1987) p.25.
2 Ibid, p.26.
3 HCD's son, Henry John later served in the same regiment, reaching the rank of colonel.
4 The couple would have a long and happy marriage and go on to have five children: Margaret, Jim (who later changed his name to Leonard), Robert (who died in infancy), Thomas Ralph, and Jane.
5 Like many Gallipoli veterans, HCD's health was permanently affected by his service on the peninsula.

HCD, taken in April 1919 after his return from France.

In February 1919, HCD was sent to France to arrange the return and demobilisation of the 1/5th Manchesters. He left France with a cadre of 5 officers and 50 men, crossing on 2 April, to test the return procedures which he found woefully inadequate. HCD and his cadre reached Wigan around 5pm on 7 April and received a civic reception. He was demobilised on 10 April and shortly afterwards moved back into Croasdale House. By now HCD was financially secure and with private means. He gave up his partnership with Peace & Darlington in 1919 as, in the words of Daisy, 'he was never well with an indoor life.'

LETTERS FROM HELLES

In January 1920, HCD served on a committee chaired by Winston Churchill to discuss the post war re-organisation of the Territorial Force. On 3 May 1920, he was promoted to colonel and placed in command of the 127th Infantry Brigade, on a four-year tenure at £1,000 per annum. HCD was appointed Deputy Lieutenant for Lancashire in May 1921 and made CB in the 1921 Birthday Honours. In October 1923, HCD became a Justice of the Peace. He was knighted in the 1925 New Year's Honours list, something that came a surprise to HCD.

> 'On New Year's Day at breakfast Hal looked at the Birthday Honour's list and found his name and that he had been made a Knight Commander of the Bath! He thought it must be a mistake until congratulations poured in.'[1]

HCD went to London to receive his knighthood in the spring of 1925, accompanied by Daisy, who had to wait 'by the railings at Buckingham Palace as wives were not invited inside.'[2] HCD turned down re-appointment as brigade commander later that year; earlier he had been offered command of the division. HCD declined both posts on the grounds that 'in peacetime a regular officer should have the job, to keep in touch with the Regular Army.' He did, however, maintain close links with the TF, being appointed Vice-Chairman of the Lancashire TF Association. In 1927, HCD was made Honorary Colonel of the 5th Manchesters, something of which he was particularly proud.

In 1936, as war loomed again in Europe, HCD published *Letters from Helles*, his frank and revealing letters from 1914 and 1915 to Mabel, his first wife. Today copies of HCD's book are scarce. Longmans, his publisher, was bombed in December 1940 and their remaining stock (424 copies) was destroyed.

When war broke out, HCD once again answered the call, serving first as a company commander in Local Defence Volunteers, later commanding the 4th Lancs (South Lonsdale) Bn. of the Home Guard, and finally serving as Assistant County Cadet Commandant for North Lancs, King's Own Royal Regiment.

---

1 Daisy Darlington, Margaret Phillips (ed) *The memoirs of Daisy Darlington Volume I* (Private publication,. 1987) p.36.
2 Ibid p.36.

Officers of the 4th (South Lonsdale) Battalion, County of Lancaster, Home Guard (EL4) having lunch, probably at Crag Bank, near Morecombe. HCD sits front left. *(King's Own Royal Regiment Archive, KO2917/55)*

In 1945, HCD was made High Sheriff of the County Palatine of Lancashire, a largely ceremonial office bestowed by the monarch.

HCD died at home on 25 December, 1959, at Tanglewood, Milford on Sea, Hampshire. During his life, Henry Clayton Darlington received many awards, and earned the accolades of his officers, men, and superiors alike. Shortly after HCD's death, Major John Stanley Fox, TD, one of his former officers, wrote to Lady Darlington:

> 'I was one of those who had the good fortune to serve under him in the Middle East and later in France and during the whole of my twenty-one years Army service I never met a better commanding officer. He was competent in every way; fair and just in his dealings with officers and men and never asked a subordinate to do what he was not prepared to do himself. No officer was more worthy of the love and respect sincerely showered on him by those who served under him.'

* * *

'Derflinger. Sgt. Fowler.'
Sergeant 2032 William Fowler, 1/5th Battalion, killed in action 2 June 1915.
Commemorated in Redoubt Cemetery, Helles.

APPENDIX B.—TIMELINE 1/5TH MANCHESTER REGIMENT AT GALLIPOLI

3 May to 31 December 1915

3 May   Battalion embarks from Alexandria onboard *SS Derfflinger* (battalion transport onboard *SS Cuthbert*).

6 May   First day of The Second Battle of Krithia. Battalion arrived off Cape Helles, and at 4:45 pm began to disembark on W Beach. Bivouacked for the night above the beach.

7 May   Battalion moves to reserve dug-outs at 'Bridge Bivouac.'

8 May   Final day of The Second Battle of Krithia. At 5:45 pm, the Battalion was ordered to support the Composite Brigade, and moves to occupy reserve trenches running east to west from 'Point 200—169 (Q) 4' (these being known later as Backhouse Post trenches).

11 May   8 *p.m.*, Battalion moved into support trenches on Fir Tree Spur (probably No. 1 and No. 2 Australian Lines).

16 May   8 *p.m.*, Battalion relieves the 1/8th Lancashire Fusiliers in the firing-line (Redoubt Line) from just left of Krithia Road to Achi Baba Nullah on the right.

21 May   9 *p.m.*, Battalion relieved by 1/5th East Lancashire Regt., and moved to Reserve dug-outs at 'Shell Bivouac.'

25 May   Battalion relieves the 1/5th East Lancashire Regt. Battalion takes over the same section of the Redoubt Line vacated on the 21 May, and a new section of firing-line, 'Burnley Road' (created after the 1/5th East Lancashire Regt. and the 1/9th Manchesters made a 100-yard advance on the night of 23/24th). Relief completed by 3.10 a.m. on the 26th.

26 May   Orders issued for the redesignation of the East Lancashire Division to the 42nd (East Lancashire) Division, and its three Infantry Brigades to the 125th (Lancashire Fusiliers) Brigade, 126th (East Lancashire) Brigade, and the 127th (Manchester) Brigade.

27 May   Battalion advances by 100 yards at night (together with the 1/6th Manchester Regt., on its left).

28 May   *9.30 p.m.* Relieved by 1/7th Manchester Regt. Battalion moves back into support trenches (Redoubt Line and 'Burnley Road'). Firing-line advanced a further 50 yards by that night by 1/7th Manchesters Regt.

31 May   *7.30 p.m.*, Battalion relieves the 1/7th Manchesters Regt., in the new firing-line (200 yards from enemy firing-line) later named 'Wigan Road.'

3 June   *'Battalion moves into allotted sectors for attack. 7th Manch. on right, 8th Manch. on left. 6th Manch across KRITHIA DONGA.'* [1]

The Third Battle of Krithia — 4 June, 1915

Taken from VIII Army Corps Order No. 2

Intention

A combined attack will be made on the Turkish position by the British Army Corps and the French Expeditionary Corps.

Time of Assault

The Infantry assault will take place at 12 noon precisely. All watches will be accurately set by time signal at 8 a.m.

Objectives

(a) The objective of the French Expeditionary Corps is the line of the Kereves Dere.

(b) The first objectives of the Army Corps will be the main line of

---

1 1/5th Manchester Regt., war diary, entry for 3 June, 1915.

B.—TIMELINE, 1915

Turkish trenches in 169.D.9 - 176.Y.4. – 176.G.8. [Trenches J.11, H.11, G.11, F.11 & E.11]

(c) The second objective of the Army Corps will be the line 169.D.9. – 176.Y.1. – 176.N.7. – 176.H.4. [Trenches J.13, H.14 & F.12]

(d) These objectives, and the boundaries of each section are shown in detail in the table and diagram issued to all concerned.

Sequence of Attack

8 a.m., (a) Bombardment of certain strong-points by heavy guns and howitzers.

(b) Final registration on targets by Field Batteries.

11.05 a.m. to 11.20 a.m., Bombardment of trenches by guns and howitzers.

11.22 a.m. to 11.30 a.m., (a) All guns cease fire, except those on the enemy's approach lines.

(b) Infantry cheer, then fix bayonets, showing them above the parapets. They do not advance, but open controlled fire from the trenches.

11.30 a.m. to 12 noon, (a) Heavy bombardment by all guns and howitzers.

(b) Infantry keep under cover.

(c) Machine guns open fire and continue in bursts as target present themselves.

12 noon, (a) First line of Infantry advance to the assault of the first objectives.

(b) Batteries firing on front trenches increase range on to trenches further back.

12.15 p.m., Second line of Infantry advance to the assault of the second objectives.

* * *

LETTERS FROM HELLES

1/5TH MANCHESTERS' ROLE IN THE BATTLE

Allotted Section of Front: From the track 100 yards west of Krithia Road, running east to a point about 260 yards short of Achi Baba Nullah.

4 June

Forenoon   C & D Company (1st Advance) in Wigan Road firing-line, A & B Company (2nd Advance) in Burnley Road support line.

12 noon   C & D Company advance. 12.02 p.m., first objective taken.

12.15 p.m.   A & B Company advance, and by 12.51 p.m. had taken the Second Objective, which was found to be 'a dummy trench.'[1]

1 p.m.   Battalion holding First and Second Objectives. R.N.D. and French counter-attacked and driven back to their respective firing-lines.[2]

2.45 p.m.   Battalion's forward lines being enfiladed from the right.[3]

6 p.m.   Second objective line reported as untenable, with the enemy working around its right rear. Colonel Darlington orders his men in the second objective line *'to retire at dark if it can hang on otherwise now.'*[4]

6.40 p.m.   General Gouraud, commanding the C.E.O., informs VIII Corps HQ that *'his troops were in no position to advance and he did not intend to attack today.'*[5]

On receiving General Gourand's message, General Hunter-Weston ordered the *'42nd Division to consolidate on the line of their first objective.'*[6]

1   Appendix D, D.7.
2   Appendix D, D.8.
3   Appendix D, D.12.
4   Appendix D, D.20.
5   VIII Corps, General Staff, war diary, 4 June, 1915.
6   VIII Corps, General Staff, Summary of Operations: Report on Operations of 8th Army Corps. May 24th to June 7th.

B.—TIMELINE, 1915

6.45 p.m.	Col. Darlington issues order to Maj. Fletcher (O.C. first objective line): *'Warn line that our advanced line will retire on you at dusk or sooner* AAA *Help them with fire if you can.'*[1]
7.57 p.m.	The 127th Brigade report to division that its troops had retired to the first objective: *'First Objective held, during night against two counter-attacks.'*[2]
	'Casualties: Officers; Capt. Leech, Lt. G.S. James, 2/Lt. A.C. Brook, killed, Capt. A. Hewlett, Lt. B.L. Fletcher. C. Ainscough, A.E. Johnson, 2/Lt. C.P. Brown, & H.N. Johnson, wounded. Other ranks, 35 killed, 131 wounded.'[3]
5 June	Battalion holding its first objective line, with small groups of men still out in front. Fight continues, with the enemy in the same trench on the left and right flanks. *'Impossible to clear them out owing to lack of bombs. Trenches badly enfiladed.'*
	'Casualties, 2/Lt. J.S.A. Walker killed, Lts., E.J. Burrows, M.K. Burrows & F.C. Gordon wounded. O.R. 4 killed, 21 wounded.'[4]
6 June	Battalion holding its first objective line. *'Turks counter attacked again early morning. Repulsed. Moved to right end of sector (filling) gap left by 8 L.F., moving before we relieved them. Quiet night men tired out. Casualties, 7 killed, 10 wounded.'*[5]
7 June	*'Still in fire trench. Men frightfully tired and suffering for want of sleep. Morale excellent. Attack by 9th Manch. on our left successful, R.M.L.I. attack on their left failed. 9th Manch. had to retire losing heavily. Counter-attack expected on right. Heavy firing all night. Casualties, 6 killed, 7 wounded.'*[6]

1 Appendix D, D.21.
2 1/5th Manchester Regt., war diary, entry for 4 June, 1915.
3 Ibid.
4 1/5th Manchester Regt., war diary, entry for 5 June, 1915.
5 1/5th Manchester Regt., war diary, entry for 6 June, 1915.
6 1/5th Manchester Regt., war diary, entry for 7 June, 1915.

8 June	'Relieved by 9th Manchesters at 4.30 p.m. Went into Corps Reserve in Reserve Trenches. Shelled. Casualties, 7 wounded.'[1]

* * *

9 June	In reserve trenches (probably at Shell Bivouac).
10 June	In reserve trenches (probably at Shell Bivouac). Order received to standby to embark for reorganisation, however, embarkation delayed by high winds.
13 June	8 p.m. Left reserve trenches.
14 June	3 a.m. Embarked for Imbros. Arrived Imbros at 6 a.m., and remained on the island until 21 June.
21 June	6 p.m. Sailed for Cape Helles, arrived 10 p.m. 'Moved into dug-outs W. Divisional Hqrs' (Torres Lines, close to X Beach).
23 June	Battalion relieves 1/7th Lancashire Fusiliers in the same section of firing-line captured by the battalion on 4 June.
27 June	Battalion moves into trenches on the west of Krithia Nullah (from the nullah up to the divisional boundary) relieving the 4th K.O.S.B. (29th Division). A & D Coys. in the firing-line with 1/6th Manchesters. C Coy in support, B Coy & HQ in the Redoubt Line. 1/5th and 1/6th Manchesters to act as 'pivot' for 29th Division attack on the 28 June.
27 June – 11 July:	Battalion remains in the same section of trenches, alternating between firing-line and support line with 1/6th Manchesters every two days.
7 July	Colonel Darlington placed in temporary command of the 127th Brigade, Major Fletcher takes over command of the battalion in his absence.

---

[1] 1/5th Manchester Regt., war diary, entry for 8 June, 1915.

B.—TIMELINE, 1915

11 July	Battalion relieved by 1/5th Lancashire Fusiliers and 1/8th Manchesters, and moves into reserve trenches at Clapham Junction. 127th Brigade in Divisional Reserve until 29 July.
19 July	Battalion moves to dug-outs at Pink Farm.
21 July	Battalion moves into the Eski Line immediately west of Krithia Nullah.
29 July	Battalion relieves 1/6th East Lancashire Regt. (38th Brigade, 13th Division) in the 'Left Sub-section,' firing-line & duplicate firing-line west of Krithia Nullah.
	Battalion remains in position in readiness for its attack on 6 August.
1 August	Colonel Darlington rejoins and assumes command of the battalion.

'Clapham Jn.' Taken (looking south) just north of where Engineer Gully meets Krithia Nullah. Clapham Junction was a major logistical crossroads.

LETTERS FROM HELLES

* * *

The Battle of 6/7th August 1915

Attack of 6 August 1915

The 88th Brigade was ordered to attack the Turkish trenches H.13 – H.13a – H.12b – H.12a – H.12 and the trenches under construction about 50 yards N.E. of H.12.

The attack to be carried out with co-operation from the 1/5th Manchester Regt.

Objectives for the 1/5th Manchester Regt.
Taken from 42nd Divisional Operational Order No. 25

(a) Assault and capture the North Western half of H.11b, the traversed trench running S.W. from the T. head in H.11b, and the continuation S.W. to join our present Firing Line. Assault to commence at 15.50 exactly.[1]

(b) Send bombing parties along all approaches from our present Firing Line to H.11a, and occupy H.11a during the assault on H.11b.

(c) Connect the N.W. extremity of H.11b by a diagonal trench with the present Firing Line trench of the 29th Division.

(d) Straighten out and mine the S.E. half of H.11b, and two Turkish trenches parallel to and S.E of them, blocking them with barricades at the N.W. end.

(e) After securing H.11b, construct a trench from the centre of it to connect with H.13. The 88th Brigade has been ordered to work from the southern extremity of H.13 to meet this trench.

(f) Consolidate the position, and establish a strong Firing Line to the point of junction thus made with the 88th Brigade.

---

1 Note: by this point the 42nd Division, General Staff war diary was recording timings using the 24-hour system.

B.—TIMELINE, 1915

Sequence of Attack

Taken from 42nd Divisional Operational Order No. 25

14.20	Artillery Bombardment begins.
15.15	Long-range fire opened by the 29th Division's machine guns.
15.50	Infantry assault begins. Guns lengthen range
15.55	Cessation of fire for 3 minutes, when the whole line will cheer, and dummy heads and helmets will be hoisted above the parapet and bayonets will be shown, to lead the enemy to expect a general advance.

1/5TH MANCHESTERS' ROLE IN THE ATTACK

<u>Allotted Frontage</u>: From a point just short of Krithia Nullah, west to the divisional boundary with 29th Division (at track parallel to, and around 200 yards from the nullah).

6 August	*'Order of companys right to left, D, A, B, C, working parties and supports from D & C Coys.'*[1]
15.50	Attack begins.
16.10	Battalion reported to have captured parts of H.11a and H.11b.[2]
16.40	Battalion reported to have captured H.11b, but attack on H.11a failed.[3]
	Brig. General Lawrence sends 100 men from the 1/7th Manchesters to reinforce the 1/5th Manchesters.
17.15	Order received at 127th Brigade HQ from divisional HQ *'to hang on to H.11b, but not to persevere in attempts to capture H.11a unless can be done easily.'*[4]

---

1 1/5th Manchester Regt., war diary, entry for 6 August, 1915.
2 127th Brigade, war diary, entry for 6 August 1915.
3 Ibid.
4 Ibid.

17.35	Battalion reported *'attack on H.11a & H.11b failed and H.11b found to be a dummy trench at N.W. end and that they could not hold it owing to enfilade fire.'*[1]

The 1/5th Manchester's war diary for 6 August sums up the day's tragic events in two short and embittered sentences:

> 'Artillery preparation entirely failed, and the infantry attack against entirely unsubdued rifle & M.G. fire was practically wiped out and failed. Our artillery dropped some shells in our own trench.'

Attack of 7 August 1915

Taken from 42nd Divisional Operational Order No. 26

Intention

The 42nd Division will assault and occupy the Turkish trenches up to and Including the line F.13 – G.13a – G.13 – G.12d.

Objectives

<u>1st. Objective</u> The line F.12 – G.12 – G.12a – G.11a.

<u>2nd. Objective</u> The line F.13 – G.13a – G.13 – G.12d.

Frontage

<u>125th Brigade</u>

Right	An imaginary line drawn N.E. and S.W. through the Southern extremity of F.13.
Left	An imaginary line drawn from the junction G.11 with our Firing Line to the figure 3 of G.13.

<u>127th Brigade</u>

Right	The same boundary as the Left of the 125th Bde.
Left	The West Krithia Nullah.
	The 127th Brigade in this attack will consist of three battalions only.[2]

---

1 127th Brigade, war diary, entry for 6 August 1915.
2 These orders assumed the objectives of the previous day had been captured.

B.—TIMELINE, 1915

Sequence of Attack

07.00	Troops to be in position.
08.10	Commencement of Artillery Bombardment.
09.10	Intense Artillery Bombardment.
09.40	Commencement of First Infantry Assault.
09.50	Commencement of Second Infantry Assault.
10.00	Advance of First Supporting Line.

1/5TH MANCHESTERS' ROLE IN THE ATTACK

<u>Same allotted frontage as 6 August.</u>

09.40   Attack begins.

                100 men and two officers from the 1/9th Manchesters sent to reinforce the 1/5th Manchester's firing-line.[1]

11.00   Battalion reported they had not taken H.11a or H.11b and that H.11b was strongly held.

---

1 The 1/9th Manchesters war diary refers to this detachment:

'A reinforcement of 100 rifles of C Company under Lt. Porter with 2/Lt. Ruttenau sent up to the firing line on the extreme left of the 127th Brigade. Lt. Porter was shortly after hit in the firing trench and died of his wounds. Shortly after an attack was arranged on a Turkish Redoubt to the left of H.11b. The attack was not carried out but about 16 men of C Company led by 2/Lt. Ruttenau advanced but being unsupported had to fall back again—all these men were hit, 2/Lt. Ruttenau having 2 grazes, which hit his clothes without wounding him.'

2/Lt. Ruttenau gives a slightly different, and more detailed account in a letter to his father:

'…when we arrived at our position two officers and 100 men were called upon to support the 5th Manchesters. I and Lieut. Porter were sent, and we got into the thick of it immediately. A redoubt was carried at the point of the bayonet. Porter was on my right. Poor fellow, he was killed getting over the parapet. I was on the left. The advance, however, could not be sustained, and the order to retire was given. The enemy's fire was too hot. How many got back safely I don't know. We lost very heavily. I must have a charmed life as I went. My tunic was ripped by bullets and my water bottle shot off, and I had a bullet through my helmet.'

11.25	Brig-General Lawrence ordered the 1/5th Manchesters to endeavour to work up H.11a from South end in conjunction with 7th Manchesters who were to make a fresh effort to clear G.10 and G.11.
12 noon	'All efforts to advance had failed, and 127th Brigade was back in its original Firing Line.'
14.45	'Commanding Officers all Battalions 7.15 p.m. met Brigadier at HQs of 6th Manchesters at 2.45 p.m. After conference the Brigadier reported Brigade strength. 5th Battn.: 150, 6th Bn.: 70, 7th Bn.: 300, 8th Battn.: 180, and in addition 200 men 4th East Lancs Regt., and 200 men 9th Bn. Manchesters at his disposal, and that Brigade was unfit to undertake further offensive operations for present.'[1]
19.15	'At 7.15 p.m., Brigade took up original positions East & West of Krithia Nullah. Approximate casualties in the Brigade during 6th & 7th August, 35 Officers and 600 other ranks.'[2]

*

8/9 August	Battalion remained in same position.
10 August	Battalion relieved by 1/7th Manchesters, and went back into the Redoubt Line (west of Krithia Nullah).
11–12 August	In the Redoubt Line (west of Krithia Nullah).
13 August	42nd Division relieved by the 52nd Lowland Division. Battalion goes into bivouac in the Torres Lines.
14–18 August	Battalion in the Torres Lines, employed on fatigue duties.
19 August.	42nd Division relieved the 29th Division in the Left Section. Battalion, along with 1/6th Manchesters, relieves the 2nd Royal Fusiliers, taking over the section of firing-line and support trenches from the Aegean Sea to the 'Western Birdcage.'

1 127th Brigade, war diary, entry for 7 August 1915.
2 Ibid.

B.—TIMELINE, 1915

20–21 August	Battalion remained in position.
22 August	Battalion relieved by the 1/8th Manchesters, and moves into 'Y' Ravine, in Brigade Reserve.
23–24 August	Battalion in Brigade Reserve at 'Y' Ravine.
25 August	Battalion relieves the 1/8th Manchesters and moves back into same firing and support trenches first occupied on 19 August.
26–27 August	Battalion remained in position.
28 August	Battalion relieved by the 1/8th Manchesters. A & C Coys move into 'Y' Ravine, and B & D Coys into Trolley Ravine, as Brigade Reserve.
29–30 August	Battalion remained at 'Y' and Trolley Ravines in Brigade Reserve.
31 August	Battalion relieves the 1/8th Manchesters, and moves back into same fire and support trenches first occupied on the 19 August.
1 September	Battalion remained in position.
2 September	127th Brigade relieved by 125th Brigade. Battalion relieved by 1/5th Lancashire Fusiliers, and moved into Corps Reserve at Gully Beach.
6 September	128 other ranks from the 1/4th East Lancashire Regt., attached to the Battalion.
14 September	Battalion relieved 1/6th Manchesters and a portion of the RND's firing-line and support trenches, from Southern Barricade (exclusive) in touch with the RND on right, to the right flank of 1/7th Manchesters at a point approx. 50 yards east of the Eastern Birdcage.
24 September	The 1/5th and 1/6th Manchesters relieved by the 5th and 8th Lancs Fusiliers, and moves to Gully Beach, in Corps Reserve.

30 September	Colonel Darlington invalided off the Peninsula. Battalion amalgamated with 1/6th Manchesters, under command of Lieut-Colonel C.R. Pilkington.
1 October	Battalion moved from Corps Reserve at Gully Beach into the firing-line, from No. 8 Sap inclusive, to the sea at Fusilier Bluff. 1/6th Manchesters in support.
7 October	Battalion relieved in the firing-line by the 1/6th Manchesters, and moves back into the support line.
14 October	127th Brigade relieved by the 125th and 126th Brigades. 1/5th Manchesters move into Corps Reserve at Gully Beach.
21 October	The 1/5th and 1/6th Manchesters relieve 1/8th Manchesters in 'Y' Ravine, and take over as Divisional Reserve.
29 October	127th Brigade relieves the 125th Brigade in Left Sub-section. The 1/5th and 1/6th Manchesters move into the firing and support lines west of 'Border Barricade,' relieving the 1/5th and 1/7th Lancs Fusiliers.
7 November	127th Brigade relieved by 1/4th East Lancs and the West Kent Yeomanry. The 1/5th and 1/6th Manchesters relieve the 1/8th Lancs Fusiliers on the east side of Gully Ravine, *'in the portion of line from Sap 1 inclusive, to east end of Half Moon St.'*
12 November	1/5th and 1/6th Manchesters relieved by the 1/5th, 1/7th and 1/8th Lancs Fusiliers and move into Corps Reserve at Gully Beach.
26 November	1/5th and 1/6th Manchesters relieve the 1st Composite Bn., 126th Brigade in the same portion of trenches vacated on 7 November.
10 December	1/5th and 1/6th Manchesters relieved by the 1/5th, 1/7th & 1/8th Lancashire Fusiliers, and move to Geoghegans Bluff, in Divisional Reserve.

B.—TIMELINE, 1915

19 December — 1/5th and 1/6th Manchesters placed at the disposal of Brig-Gen. Frith, 125th Brigade, as sub-section reserve (in support of the 125th Brigade's diversionary attack at the Gridiron).

24 December — 1/5th and 1/6th Manchesters relieve the 1/5th, 1/7th and 1/8th Lancs Fusiliers in the same portion of trenches vacated on 10 December.

28 December — 1/5th and 1/6th Manchesters relieved by the 9th Bn., Worcester Regt., and move into Divisional Reserve at Geoghegans Bluff.

29 December — Battalion moves to 'V' Beach and embarked at 21.30 by the *River Clyde*.

30 December — Arrived Mudros and disembarked from *Hibernia* at 10.00. Encamped at Sarpi Camp.

31 December — Moved into marquees vacated by Australian troops.

'Trolley Ravine on Aegean.'

APPENDIX C.—EMBARKATION STATE, 3 MAY 1915, 1/5TH BATTALION THE MANCHESTER REGIMENT

Taken from their war diary.

SS *Cuthbert*

6 Other Ranks with 1st Line Transport

SS *Derfflinger*

EMBARKATION STATE.   32 Officers, 816 Other Ranks

H.Qrs.
Lieut. Colonel H.C. Darlington
Major E. Fletcher (2nd in Command)
Capt. & Adjt. J.M.B. Sanders (Leinster Regt.)
Sgt. Major S. Taylor (Act. Lt. Q.M.)
Capt. H.H. Cunningham R.A.M.C. (O. Func.)
2/Lt. E.N. Holden (Machine Gun Officer)
Revd. E. Best, M.A., 4th Class Chaplain to the Forces

'A' Coy.
Capt. F.S. Brown (Commanding)
Capt. W.T. Woods (2nd in Command)
Lieut. B. Ainscough
2/Lieut. M.K. Burrows
2/Lieut. F.C. Gordon

C.—EMBARKATION STATE

'B' Coy.	Capt. H.M. Rogers (Commanding)
	Capt. J.S.A. Walker (2nd in Command)
	Lieut. G. Hall
	2/Lieut. G.E. Allen
	2/Lieut. A.C. Brook
	2/Lieut. H.N. Johnson (Supernumerary)
'C' Coy.	Major A.E. Cronshaw (Commanding)
	Capt. A. Hewlett (2nd in Command)
	Lieut. G.S. James
	Lieut. F.A. James
	2/Lieut. C.P. Brown
	2/Lieut. E.J. Burrows
	2/Lieut. G.S. Lund
	2/Lieut. T.C. Walker
'D' Coy.	Capt. A.C. Leech (Commanding)
	Capt. A.L. Bryham (2nd in Command)
	Lieut. B.L. Fletcher
	Lieut. W.G.E. Johnson
	Lieut. A.E. Johnson
	2/Lieut. A.S. Parker

Sergeant Major	Acting Sgt. Major Morrison
Q. Master Sgt.	Q.M.R. Christy
Master Cook	Sgt. Bennett

APPENDIX D.—ORDERS AND MESSAGES, THIRD KRITHIA

[Numbered Appendix A in the first edition.]

Orders and messages issued by Lt.-Col. H. C. Darlington,
1/5th Battalion The Manchester Regiment,
during the Third Battle of Krithia, June 4th, 1915:—

D.1. Brigade—The French[1] artillery observer stationed in this trench has not yet been informed of operations this day AAA He has telephoned his group commander, Commandant Deslion, who states he has received no orders yet. O.C. 5 Man., 6.45 a.m.

D.2. Brigade—Will Lieut. Vincent report to me with torpedoes[2] AAA These torpedoes will be wanted by my first line. O.C. 5 Man., 10.26 a.m.

D.3. Brigade—Lieut. Vincent is not in our sector. O.C. 5 Man., 11.12 a.m.

D.4. Brigade—Very little Turk barbed wire destroyed by shell fire on our front so far. O.C. 5 Man. R., 11.30 a.m.

D.5. Brigade—Scout officer reports Turkish M.G. in front Turk trench where trench crosses Krithia road. O.C. 5 Man., 11.48 a.m.

D.6. Brigade—First line occupied first line main Turkish trenches 12.4 p.m. AAA Second line just left. O.C. 5 Man., 12.16 p.m.

D.7. Brigade—Please send fourth line to occupy our front trench AAA 3rd line has gone forward AAA Our second line and 7th Manchesters have gained second objective a dummy trench. O.C. 5 Man., 12.51 p.m.

---

1 The battalion was supported by the French 75's.
2 For blowing up barbed-wire entanglements.

D.—ORDERS, MESSAGES, 3RD KRITHIA

D.8. Brigade—R.N.D. and French were counter-attacked on our right and driven back. O.C. 5 Man., 1.0 p.m.

D.9. Brigade—R.N.D. driven back AAA Our most advanced line is unsupported on their right AAA If advanced line is to be held we shall want reinforcements. O.C. 5 Man., 1.55 p.m.

D.10. Brigade—There is a gap on my left and Turkish trench first objective is unheld. O.C. 5 Man., 2.25 p.m.

D.11. Brigade—Ammunition urgently needed. O.C. 5 Man., 2.30 p.m.

D.12. Brigade—My forward lines are being enfiladed from our right AAA Unable to locate, but think from trenches in front of R.N.D. AAA Can guns help. O.C. 5 Man., 2.45 p.m.

D.13. Brigade—My advanced line is 300 yards in front of 1st objective AAA Turks 150–200 yards in front of this AAA Turkish trench 1st objective is held by us and 7th Manchesters to the Donga AAA Continuation of first objective trench on my right is in Turkish hands AAA Third wave gone forward AAA Know nothing of fourth wave, was it not ordered to go up Donga AAA R.N.D. back in their original fire trench. O.C.5 Man., 2.47 p.m.

D.14. Brigade—My advanced line driven in on to first objective. No reinforcements here. O.C. 5 Man., 3.22 p.m.

D.15. Brigade—Ammunition must be sent up AAA Two companies should be sent up to make our original firing line secure. O.C. 5 Man., 3.30 p.m.

D.16 Brigade—Only small portion of my front line has fallen back AAA Remainder still holding on to second objective. O.C. 5 Man., 4.11 p.m.

D.17. Brigade—Situation on our front unchanged AAA 1 Company 8th L.F. has come into this line in support on our right. O.C. 5 Man., 5.37 p.m.

D.18. O.C. advanced line (A and B companies) 1/5th Manchester Regt.—Try and hang on till dark and then retire on first objective. If unable to hang on retire now to same place. O.C. 5 Man., 5.42 p.m.

D.19. O.C. 7th Manchesters—Let me know where your companies are AAA Can you get Machine Gun up to deal with enfilade fire from right of nullah. O.C. 5 Man.

D.20. Brigade—Our second objective is reported untenable as Turks are working round right rear AAA I have ordered it to retire at dark if it can hang on, otherwise now AAA My first objective trench is suffering heavily on the right from enfilade fire, being unsupported on its right flank on the right of Mar Tepe donga AAA I don't know where the 7th Manchesters are quite AAA Please explain situation. I want 100 men to occupy the original fire trench in place of a working party of 6th L.F. who are going forward to Turk trench 1st objective. O.C. 5 Man., 6 p.m.

D.21. Major Fletcher, first objective—warn line that our advanced line will retire on you at dusk or sooner AAA Help them if you can by fire AAA I don't know where B Co. are AAA Woods' right is on Krithia road AAA Turks have got on his right flank. O.C. 5 Man., 6.45 p.m.

D.22. Brigade—Impossible send single man from our front to-night. You must arrange parties from rear for tools and ammunition. O.C. 5 Man., 8.30 p.m.

APPENDIX E.—ORDERS AND MESSAGES, BATTLE OF 6/7TH AUGUST

Orders and messages issued by Lt.-Col. H.C. Darlington, 1/5th Battalion
The Manchester Regiment,
during the Battle of 6/7th August 1915:—

6 AUGUST

HCD 1. Brigade—Battalion in position. O.C. 5 Man., 14.09.

HCD 2. Brigade—Have captured parts of H.11a and H.11b AAA Will send details when I receive them. O.C. 5 Man., 16.10.

HCD 3. Brigade—Have captured H.11b AAA Attack on H.11a failed AAA Have not enough men left to capture H.11a AAA O.C. 5 Man., 16.40.

HCD 4. O.C. 7th Man.—Have had a M.G. tripod broken AAA Can you send one up, O.C. 5 Man., 17.00.

HCD 5. Brigade—Attack on H.11b and H.11a failed AAA H.11b was dummy trench at N.W. B M eliod [?] and owing to enfilade fire AAA Am organising garrison in our original firing line AAA Cannot get into touch with Worcesters thought to hold S.W. end of H.13 AAA Afraid our casualties heavy AAA Am putting 100 7th Manchesters into present firing line. O.C. 5 Man., 17.25.

HCD 6. Brigade—Messenger from Worcesters (88th Brigade) sent from O.C. Worcesters States reinforcements urgently required AAA We are unable to supply Adjt. Worcesters confirms this in person. O.C. 5 Man., 17.50.

HCD 7. Brigade—Remainder of battalion estimated about 200 strong 50 7th Manchesters and East Lancs garrison are holding our original firing line AAA Position is as before the attack AAA Considerable number of men missing. O.C. 5 Man., 18.15.

HCD 8. Brigade—Estimated casualties 214. O.C. 5 Man., 21.20.

7 AUGUST

HCD 9. Brigade—Patrol reports that Turk sap S.W. of B of H.12b is still in possession of Turks and that an officer of the Worcesters did not know whether or not Turks hold H.13 AAA Reference No. 7 Diagram. O.C. 5 Man., 05.15.

HCD 10. Brigade—50 East Lancs not yet reported to me. O.C. 5 Man., 07.30.

HCD 11. Brigade—Available for attack 215 including 50 E. Lancs not yet arrived AAA Have no reserves AAA Consider we need 50 more men. O.C. 5 Man., 07.58.

HCD 12. Brigade—Received [in reply to BM 8]. O.C. 5 Man., 08.25.

HCD 13. O.C. East Lancs Garrison—9.35 a.m. start moving remainder of your firing line garrison up into fire trenches. O.C. 5 Man., 08.40

HCD 14. Brigade—Have not taken H.11b or H.11a AAA H.11b strongly held. O.C. 5 Man., 10.55.

HCD 15. Brigade [assumed]—Attempted to take H.11b at 10.45 but did not succeed owing to very heavy rifle and machine gun fire AAA Have not taken H.11a AAA H.11b must be flattened by artillery fire before it can be taken AAA Would require 200 for H.11b AAA Men somewhat demoralized by shelling of our own guns AAA Afraid they are not up to another assault today. O.C. 5 Man., 11.15.

HCD 16. MRG [in reply to MRG 5]—No have not taken any trenches AAA Rifle and M.G. fire too heavy. O.C. 5 Man. [no time given].

HCD 17. Brigade—Think chance of working up H.11a from south successfully very slight AAA Redoubt in H.11a commands and is held by Turks AAA All bombers killed or wounded. O.C. 5 Man., 11.35.

E.—ORDERS, MESSAGES, 6/7 AUGUST

HCD 18. Brigade—Colonel Canning says his first assault cannot get beyond Nullah Fork owing to fire from G.11a and trenches between the Nullahs AAA He does not know position on his right and cannot get on till the two Turk trenches on his right front on E of Nullah are taken AAA I cannot see any possibility of operating against H.11a from the south. AAA I think the operation would have to be a combined one on both sides of Nullah AAA Turk trenches are very strongly held AAA G.11a seems untouched by shell fire AAA Turks seem to have at least one man per yard and M.G.s in their trenches AAA Thorough artillery preparation would be a necessity AAA Artillery preparation today & yesterday useless on my objectives AAA. O.C. 5 Man., 12.25.

HCD 19. Brigade—Situation same as before attack. AAA Turks reported reforming down nullahs. AAA Have informed artillery AAA Estimated strength 5th Man. 150, 9th Manchesters 70, total 220 AAA If Turks counter attack as appears possible we can hold our own and no more AAA Our trenches badly damaged by shell fire are being repaired. O.C. 5 Man., 12.40.

9 AUGUST

HCD 20. Brigade—Observers report Turk relief in G trenches started 1500 8th inst. AAA They estimate more troops went out than came in. O.C. 5 Man., 00.10.

HCD 21. Brigade—Effective strength now 315 casualties last 3 days 232. O.C. 5 Man., 10.10.

HCD 22. Brigade—Captain Syers trench mortars have bombarded G.11a and communication trenches at intervals during day. AAA G.11a has been practically dismantled traverses blown in. AAA M.G. and snipers were able to get at Turks bolting in the open. AAA Mortars pits were found by Turk Artillery about 1515 and pits partially blown in. AAA Mortars undamaged no casualties. AAA Please inform 29th Division D.A. and ask for instructions for Capt. Syers. O.C. 5 Man., 16.00.

HCD 23. Brigade—Cannot give any reliable estimate of garrison of G trenches. AAA Movements in Nullah been considerable all day both in and out of trenches complicated by Turks evacuating G.11a twice and reinforcing it. AAA Turks have been showing themselves more than usual. O.C. 5 Man., 21.35.

10 August

HCD 24. Brigade—G.11a repaired to some extent during night and some traverses rebuilt. AAA G.11a G.12 G.11 are held apparently not strongly. AAA Digging going on in G.12. AAA Movements in and out of G.11. AAA G.10 is not sandbagged and does not appear occupied but cannot tell for certain. O.C. 5 Man., 10.40.

APPENDIX F.—LIST OF OFFICERS, 1/5TH MANCHESTER REGIMENT, 6 MAY TO 1 OCTOBER 1915

[Numbered Appendix B in the first edition.]

List of Officers of 1/5th Battalion The Manchester Regiment between landing on May 6th, 1915, and October 1st, 1915, when Lt.-Col. H. C. Darlington was invalided from the Gallipoli Peninsular.

Original Officers.

1.	Lt.-Col. H. C. Darlington	Hospital ship for rest, but sent home	30/9/15
2.	Major E. Fletcher	Hospital	10/9/15
3.	Major A. E. Cronshaw	Hospital	2/9/15
4.	Capt. J. M. Sanders, Leinster Regt., Adjutant	Wounded Hospital, sick	6/8/15 –/8/15
5.	Capt. H. M. Rogers	Killed	May, 1915
6.	Capt. F. S. Brown	Killed	May, 1915
7.	Capt. A. C. Leech	Killed	4/6/15
8.	Capt. A. L. Bryham	Hospital	Aug., 1915
9.	Capt. W. T. Woods	Hospital rejoined Sept., Staff Captain	3/8/15
10.	Capt. A. W. W. Simpson	Hospital	May, 1915
11.	Capt. A. Hewlett	Wounded	4/6/15
12.	Capt. J. S. A. Walker	Hospital	June, 1915
13.	Lieut. J. Wall	Hospital	June, 1915
14.	Lieut. P. C. Fletcher	Wounded	June, 1915
15.	Lieut. B. L. Fletcher	Wounded	June, 1915
16.	Lieut. A. E. Johnson	Wounded	June, 1915
17.	Lieut. W. G. Johnson	Wounded	June, 1915
18.	Lieut. H. N. Johnson	Wounded	June, 1915
19.	Lieut. C. Ainscough	3 times wounded, Killed	Aug., 1915

20.	Lieut. F. C. Gordon	Wounded	June, 1915
21.	Lieut. J. N. [E. N.] Holden	Hospital	June, 1915
22.	Lieut. A. C. Brook	Killed	June, 1915
23.	Lieut. Lund	Hospital	Aug., 1915
24.	Lieut. T. C. Walker	Killed	June, 1915
25.	Lieut. M. K. Burrows	Wounded	June, 1915
26.	Lieut. E. J. Burrows	Wounded	June, 1915
		Rejoined	Aug., 1915
27.	Lieut. F. James	Wounded	July, 1915
		Killed	Sept., 1915
28.	Lieut. G. S. James	Killed	June, 1915
29.	Lieut. A. Lock, Q.M.	Hospital	Sept., 1915
30.	Lieut. S. Taylor, Q.M.	Wounded	July, 1915,
		Rejoined	Aug., 1915
31.	Capt. Cunningham, R.A.M.C.	Wounded Rejoined	May, 1915
32.	Lieut. A. S. Parker (joined at Cairo)	Wounded	June, 1915
33.	Lieut. F. Verdon (joined at Cairo)	Hospital from Cairo	
34.	Lieut. A. Slaughter	Hospital	June, 1915
35.	Lieut. C. P. Brown	Wounded	June, 1915
36.	Lieut. V. Hewlett	England from Cairo	
37.	Lieut. G. E. Allen	Wounded	Sept., 1915

1st Draft.

38.	Lieut. Clayton	Wounded	Aug., 1915

2nd Draft.

39.	Capt. D. Winterbottom	Killed	Aug., 1915
40.	Lieut. McGeorge	Killed	Aug., 1915
41.	Lieut. Dickey	Wounded	Aug., 1915
42.	Lieut. Porter	Killed	Aug., 1915
43.	Lieut. Davies [Davis]	Killed	Aug., 1915

F.—OFFICERS

Attached.

44.	Capt. J. H. Allen, 9th Lincolns.		
45.	Lieut. Skipworth, 11th W. Ridings.	Killed	Aug., 1915
46.	Lieut. Messervy, 11th W. Riding Regt.	Wounded	Aug., 1915
47.	Lieut. Box, 9th Lincoln Regt.	Killed	Aug., 1915
48.	Lieut. Cowan, 9th Lincoln Regt.	Killed	Aug., 1915
49.	Lieut. Iveson, 16th D.L.I.	Killed whilst talking to Author	Aug., 1915
50.	Lieut. Foster, 16th D.L.I.	Killed	Aug., 1915

3rd Draft.

51.	Lieut. Dickey		
52.	Lieut. Batten	Hospital	Sept., 1915
53.	Capt. C. Fletcher		

4th Draft.

54.	Lieut. Scott [Stott]		
55.	Lieut. Goward		
56.	Lieut. Pearce		
57.	Lieut. J. L. Bryan		
58.	Lieut. Charlesworth		
59.	2nd Lieut. Blair	Hospital	Sept., 1915

APPENDIX G.—CASUALTIES

1/5th Manchester Regiment, to 31 December 1915

[Numbered Appendix C in the first edition.]

OFFICERS.

	Killed	Wounded	Sick	Totals	out of
Original Officers	8	18	8	34	34
Drafts	4	2	7	13	21
Attached	4	2	1	7	13
Totals	16	22	16	54	68

CENSUS OF BATTALION (31ST DEC., 1915).

	Original Battalion	Serving 31/12/15
Original Battalion	818	152
1st Draft	100	16
2nd Draft	20	2
3rd Draft	118	27
4th Draft	23	6
5th Draft	95	32
6th Draft	5	4
Totals	1,179	239

CASUALTIES TO 31ST DEC., 1915.

	Killed	Wounded	Totals
Original Battalion	167	427	594
1st Draft	30	35	65
2nd Draft	5	4	9
3rd Draft	5	10	15
4th Draft	–	–	–
5th Draft	1	2	3
6th Draft	–	–	–
Totals	208	478	686

APPENDIX H.—BIOGRAPHIES, OFFICERS & OTHER RANKS OF THE 1/5TH MANCHESTERS

All individuals are mentioned in *Letters From Helles*.

Appointments, ranks and companies shown in the heading are those on arrival at Gallipoli. Later awards shown in brackets.

The 5th Bn., The Manchester Regt., was redesignated the 1/5th Bn., The Manchester Regt., after the creation of the 2/5th Bn. in September 1914— hence the changes in battalion designation within biographies.

Lieutenant Cyril Ainscough
'A' Company

Commissioned into the 5th Bn., The Manchester Regiment, on 9 November 1912. Promoted to lieutenant on 31 August 1914. Volunteered for overseas service end of August 1914. Embarked from Southampton onboard SS *Caledonia* with the 5th Manchesters on 10 September 1914, disembarking at Alexandria, Egypt on the 25th. Made acting captain in January 1915. Remained in Egypt until the battalion embarked for Gallipoli onboard the SS *Derfflinger* on 3 May 1915, disembarking at W Beach, Helles, on 6 May. Wounded three times; slightly on 11 May and 14 May, and more seriously on 4 June, during the Third Battle of Krithia. Returned to duty with 1/5th Manchesters shortly before being killed, aged 22, during the attack on trenches H.11a and H.11b on 7 August 1915. Commemorated on the Helles Memorial, Panel 158 to 170.

2nd Lieutenant Gerald Elliston Allen (TD)
'B' Company

Commissioned into the 5th Bn., The Manchester Regt., on 27 March 1914. Volunteered for overseas service. Embarked from Southampton onboard SS *Caledonia* with the 5th Manchesters on 10 September 1914, disembarking at Alexandria, Egypt on 25th. Remained in Egypt until the battalion embarked for Gallipoli onboard the SS *Derfflinger* on 3 May 1915. Arrived off W Beach, Helles, on 6 May, but remained onboard and returned to Alexandria suffering from jaundice. Made temporary lieutenant on 7 March 1915, and promoted to lieutenant on 1 June 1915. He rejoined the battalion at Helles on 8 August, suffering a slight wound to his leg on the same day. Continued to serve with the battalion at Helles, and, after its evacuation, in Egypt from January 1916. Promoted to captain on 16 August 1916 (with precedence from 15 August 1915). Moved with the battalion to France in March 1917. Continued to serve with the 1/5th Manchesters in France and Belgium until seconded to the Royal Flying Corps (RFC) as a photographer in September 1917. He remained with the RFC (and later the RAF) until 25 August 1919, when he rejoined the 1/5th Manchesters. Post-war, promoted to lieutenant colonel, and went on to command the 5th Manchesters. Holder of the Territorial Decoration.

Captain J. H. Allen
9th Lincolns

Commissioned into the 9th (Service) Bn., The Lincolnshire Regiment on 6 January 1915. Made temporary captain on 1 February 1915. Joined the 1/5th Manchesters at Helles on 2 July 1915. Attached to 'B' Company, becoming its senior officer by 28 August. Granted the temporary rank of major and placed temporarily in command the battalion on 1 November. May have been in command when the battalion left the peninsula on 29 December 1915. Captain Allen's onward service history is unknown, but it is likely that he survived the war.

H.—BIOGRAPHIES, 5TH MANCHESTERS

2nd Lieutenant
Percy Woodruff Batten (MC)
3rd Draft (21 August 1915)

Commissioned into the 2/5th Manchesters on 17 April 1915. Joined the 1/5th Manchesters at Helles on 21 August 1915. Invalided off the peninsula on 27 September 1915. Transferred to the Royal Sussex Regiment, and later attached to the Tank Corps (24th Bn.). Promoted to lieutenant on 21 July 1917, and later made acting captain. Awarded the Military Cross (LG: 30530, 16 February 1918 / citation 16 July 1918). His citation reads:

> "For conspicuous gallantry and devotion to duty. He led his tank in an attack on a party of enemy who were advancing on his left, and when his tank was put out of action he directed operations on foot, walking about in open direct fire from the enemy. He showed disregard of danger, and set a fine example to his men."

Promoted to captain on 13 November 1920. Batten relinquished his commission on 10 January 1922, going on to have an 'interesting' and eventful life as an author and journalist.

2nd Lieutenant
Richard Henry Blair
Arrived at Helles 10 September 1915

Commissioned into the 2/5th Manchester on 28 March 1915. Joined the 1/5th Manchesters at Helles on 10 September 1915, and was initially attached to the 1/4th East Lancashire Regt. Continued to serve with the battalion at Helles, and, after its evacuation from the peninsula, in Egypt, from January 1916. Promoted to lieutenant on 1 June 1916. Moved with the battalion to France in March 1917, and continued to serve with it in France and Belgium until the end of the war. Made acting captain on 23 September 1917. Disembodied in April 1919.

Lieutenant Philip John Murray Box
9th Lincolns

Private S/7497 Philip John Murray Box, Rifle Brigade (Ceylon resident and tea planter) was commissioned as temporary lieutenant into the 9th (Service) Bn., The Lincolnshire Regt., on 26 January 1915. Joined the 1/5th Manchesters at Helles on 2 July 1915. Killed, aged 36, in the attack on trenches H.11a & H.11b on 7 August 1915. Commemorated on the Helles Memorial, Panel 45 to 47.

2nd Lieutenant Arthur 'Archie' Charles Brook
'B' Company

Brother-in-law to Henry Clayton Darlington. Commissioned into the 5th Bn., The Manchester Regt., on 12 September 1914. Volunteered for overseas service. His medal index card indicates he joined the 1/5th Manchesters in Egypt on 5 November 1914. Made acting lieutenant in November 1914. Remained in Egypt until embarked for Gallipoli with the 1/5th Manchesters onboard the SS *Derfflinger* on 3 May 1915, disembarking at W Beach, Helles, on 6 May. Made the battalion's Machine Gun Officer in mid-May. Killed in action, aged 30, on 4 June, during the Third Battle of Krithia. Buried in the Redoubt Cemetery, Helles, Grave X. A. 20.

Captain Frederick 'Freddy' Seddon Brown
Officer Commanding (OC) 'A' Company

Commissioned into the 1st Volunteer Bn., The Manchester Regt., on 16 April 1902. Promoted to captain on 15 September 1906. He retained his rank and seniority on the formation of the Territorial Force on 1 April 1908, when the battalion was redesignated the 5th Bn., The Manchester Regt. Volunteered for overseas service end of August 1914.

H.—BIOGRAPHIES, 5TH MANCHESTERS

Embarked from Southampton on SS *Caledonia* with the 5th Manchesters on 10 September 1914, disembarking at Alexandria, Egypt on 25th. Remained in Egypt until embarked for Gallipoli as OC 'A' Company with the 1/5th Manchesters, onboard SS *Derfflinger* on 3 May 1915, disembarking at W Beach, Helles, on 6th. Knocked over, but unhurt by a burst of Turkish shrapnel around 22 May. Wounded on 25 May, 'taking his company up'[1] into the firing-line (Burnley Road). Died of wounds on 26 May, aged 31. Buried at Lancashire Landing Cemetery, Helles, Grave A.2.

Lieut. John Lindsay Bryan (MC)
Arrived at Helles 10 September 1915

Private 1674 John Lindsay Bryan, The Honourable Artillery Company, was commissioned into the 2/5th Manchesters on 20 January 1915. Joined the 1/5th Manchesters at Helles on 10 September 1915. Invalided off the peninsula sick on 27 October 1915. Probably rejoined the 2/5th Manchesters in England on his recovery, and may have travelled with that battalion when the 66th Division was deployed in France in early March 1917. Seconded to the Machine Gun Corps (MGC) on 14 March 1917. Promoted to lieutenant on 31 July 1917 (with precedence from 1 June 1916). Awarded the Military Cross (LG: 31043 / 2 December 1918). His citation reads:

> "Under heavy fire he made a skilful reconnaissance and brought his guns into positions from which he broke up a counter-attack with heavy loss, and was able to cover the subsequent advance of our infantry. He displayed great ability in the way he handled his guns, and his coolness and courage under fire set a fine example to his men."

Went on to command a company in the MGC with the rank of acting major. Ceased to be employed by the MGC on 18 March 1919, and returned to the establishment of the 1/5th Manchesters. Promoted to captain on 8 December 1920, later promoted to major.

---

1 1/5th Manchesters war diary, 25 May 1915.

LETTERS FROM HELLES

Captain Arthur Longsdale Bryham (MC)
Second in Command (2i/c) of 'D' Company

Commissioned into the 1st Volunteer Bn., The Manchester Regt., on 25 April 1900. Promoted to lieutenant on 13 July 1901, and to captain on 15 September 1906. He retained his rank and seniority on the formation of the Territorial Force on 1 April 1908, when the battalion was redesignated as the 5th Bn., The Manchester Regt. Resigned his commission sometime later but was recommissioned into the 5th Manchesters on 26 August 1914.

Volunteered for overseas service end of August 1914. Embarked from Southampton onboard SS *Caledonia* with the 5th Manchesters on 10 September 1914, disembarking at Alexandria, Egypt on 25th. Remained in Egypt until embarked for Gallipoli, as 2i/c 'D' Company, onboard SS *Derfflinger* on 3 May 1915, disembarking at W Beach, Helles, on 6th. Slightly wounded around 6 to 8 August. Went to hospital sick about 23 August, and invalided off the peninsula. Returned to duty at Helles on 6 October. Continued to serve with the battalion at Helles, and, after its evacuation, in Egypt from January 1916.

Moved with the battalion to France in March 1917, and continued to serve with it in France and Belgium until the end of the war. Awarded the Military Cross (LG: 30111/4 June 1917). Mentioned in Despatches (LG: 6 July 1917). Made acting Major on 31 May 1917. Survived the war. Brother of Captain Morris Bryham.

H.—BIOGRAPHIES, 5TH MANCHESTERS

2nd Lieutenant Eric John Burrows (MC)
'C' Company and 'A' Company

Commissioned into the 5th Bn., The Manchester Regt., on 2 September 1914. Volunteered for overseas service. Embarked from Southampton onboard SS *Caledonia* with the 5th Manchesters on 10 September 1914, disembarking at Alexandria, Egypt on 25th. Remained in Egypt until the battalion embarked for Gallipoli on SS *Derfflinger* on 3 May 1915, disembarking at W Beach, Helles, on 6th. Wounded on 5 June, and evacuated off the peninsula. Made temporary lieutenant on 31 July 1915 (later substantive with precedence from 30 June 1915). Rejoined the battalion at Helles in August, and placed in command of 'A' Company. Made temporary captain on 23 September 1915. Continued to serve with the battalion at Helles, and, after its evacuation, in Egypt from January 1916, until posted to the 3/5th Manchesters in England June/July 1916.

Promoted to captain on 1 June 1916. Attached to the 6th Bn., Gloucestershire Regt., in July 1916, and to the 2/6th Bn., Gloucestershire Regt., in August/September 1917. Attached to the 9th Bn., Royal Sussex Regt., in May/June 1918, and was serving with that battalion when the war ended. Awarded the Military Cross (LG: 21366 / 2 April 1918 and 31680 / 10 December 1919—citation). His citation reads:

> "Capt. Eric John Burrows, 5th Bn., Manch. R., T.F., attd. 9th Bn., R. Suss. R. For marked gallantry and good leadership of his company in the attack on Wargnies-le-Grand, on 4th November, 1918. He received orders in the middle of the night to attack at 6 a.m. with his company on a front previously allotted to a whole battalion. He advanced in the leading line, and kept perfect control throughout the attack, dealing with each enemy post in a most able manner. His company captured seven machine guns (three heavy), sixty prisoners, and three trench mortars."

2nd Lieutenant Miles Kenneth Burrows (MC)
'A' Company

Commissioned into the 2/5th Manchesters on 12 September 1914. Volunteered for overseas service. Probably joined the 1/5th Manchesters in Egypt, late 1914. Remained in Egypt until the battalion embarked for Gallipoli onboard the SS *Derfflinger* on 3 May 1915, disembarking at W Beach, Helles on 6th. Wounded on 5 June 1915, and evacuated off the peninsula. Attached to the 3/5th Manchesters in England in Oct/Nov 1915. Mentioned in Despatches, and awarded the Military Cross (LG: 29357 / 8 November 1915) for his actions on the 4 June 1915. Described by Colonel Darlington in his letter of 14/15 June 1915 as:

> "... climbing out of a trench under heavy fire from the Turks and from our own artillery and holding up a red screen to show our guns they were firing on his Company. How he escaped I don't know."

Promoted to lieutenant on 31 October 1915. Rejoined the 1/5th Manchesters at Helles on 8 December 1915. Continued to serve with the battalion at Helles, and, after its evacuation, in Egypt from January 1916. Promoted to captain on 1 June 1916. Appointed adjutant in January/February 1917. Moved with the battalion to France in March 1917, and continued to serve as adjutant in France and Belgium until the end of the war. Resigned his commission on 20 December 1920.

Private 1921 George Carr

Born in Wigan, Lancashire. A coal miner in civilian life, Carr's low service number indicates he was a pre-war Territorial. Volunteered for overseas service at the beginning of September 1914. Embarked from Southampton onboard SS *Caledonia* with the 5th Manchesters on 10 September 1914, disembarking at Alexandria, Egypt on 25th. Remained in Egypt until the battalion embarked for Gallipoli onboard the SS *Derfflinger* on 3 May 1915, disembarking at W Beach, Helles, on the 6th. During the Third Battle of Krithia he went forward alone to check if a trench was occupied by the enemy (which it was) or by Lancashire Fusiliers (as related by Colonel Darlington in his letter of 9 June 1915). Killed, aged 35, in the attacks on trenches H.11a and H.11b on 7 August 1915. Buried in the Redoubt Cemetery Helles, Grave I.E.7

2nd Lieutenant John Charlesworth
Arrived at Helles 10 September 1915

Commissioned into the 2/5th Manchesters on 24 April 1915. Joined the 1/5th Manchesters at Helles on 10 September 1915, and was attached at various times to the 1/4th East Lancs Regt., and the 1/10th Manchesters. Probably continued to serve with the battalion at Helles, and, after its evacuation, in Egypt from January 1916. Posted to the 3/5th Manchesters in England in May/June 1916. Made temporary lieutenant on 21 July 1915 (later made substantive, with precedence from 1 June 1916). Attached to the 6th Bn., Gloucestershire Regt., in July 1916. Attached to the 20th Manchesters in February/March 1917, and remained with that battalion until Oct/Nov 1918, after which he may have returned to the establishment of the 1/5th Manchesters.

Lieutenant Percy Charles Clayton
1st Draft (22 June 1915)

Commissioned into the 2/5th Manchesters on 30 September 1914. Made temporary lieutenant on 18 November 1914. Joined the 1/5th Manchesters, then at Imbros Island, with a draft of 89 other ranks from the 2/5th Manchesters on 22 June 1915. Wounded on 7 August, and probably evacuated off the peninsula and back to England. Mentioned in Hamilton's Despatch of 11 December 1915. Attached to the 3/5th Manchesters in Jan/Feb 1916. Seconded to the Royal Engineers (Clayton was a mining engineer in civilian life) in May/June 1916. Promoted to lieutenant on 1 July 1916, and to captain on 1 August 1917 (with precedence from 1 July 1916). Remained seconded to the Royal Engineers until 14 February 1919, when he returned to the establishment of the 1/5th Manchesters.

Lieutenant Basil Terence Reilly Cowan
9th Lincolns

Private S/7565 Basil Terence Reilly Cowan, The Rifle Brigade, was commissioned as lieutenant into the 9th (Service) Bn., The Lincolnshire Regt., on 26 January 1915. Joined the 1/5th Manchesters at Helles on 2 July 1915. Reported missing on the 6 August (later confirmed killed) after the first attack on trenches H11a and H11b. Commemorated on the Helles Memorial, Panel 45 to 47.

Major Arthur Edwin Cronshaw (DSO, TD)
Officer Commanding (OC) 'C' Company

Commissioned into the 1st Volunteer Bn., The Manchester Regt., in the 1890s. Promoted to lieutenant on 28 July 1897. Served in South Africa with the 3rd Volunteer Service Company, earning the Queen's South African Medal with four clasps. Made honorary lieutenant in the Army on 26 July 1902. Promoted to captain on 7 January 1903. He retained his rank and seniority on the formation of the Territorial Force on 1 April 1908, when the battalion was redesignated as the 5th Bn., The Manchester Regiment. Made temporary major on 31 August 1914. Volunteered for overseas service end of August 1914. Embarked from Southampton onboard SS *Caledonia* with the 5th Manchesters on 10 September 1914, disembarking at Alexandria, Egypt on 25th. Remained in Egypt until embarked for Gallipoli as OC 'C' Company, onboard SS *Derfflinger* on 3 May 1915, disembarking at W Beach, Helles, on 6th. Went to hospital sick on 2 September, and evacuated off the peninsula, and back to England. Attached to the 3/5th Manchesters in England in Feb/Mar 1916. Rejoined the 1/5th Manchesters in Egypt in April/May 1916. Placed in command of the 1/7th Manchesters (in Egypt) and made temporary lieutenant-colonel. Moved with the 1/7th Manchesters to France in March 1917. Promoted to major on 1 August 1917 (with precedence from 1 June 1916). Continued to command the 1/7th Manchesters in France and Belgium until he relinquished command, due to ill health, on 15 May 1918. Rejoined the 1/5th Manchesters in France around June 1918, and continued to serve with the battalion for the remainder of the war. Awarded; the Russian, Order of the White Eagle 4th Class (with Swords) on 12 February 1917, the Territorial Decoration on 7 June 1917, and Create a Companion of the Distinguished Service Order on 1 January 1918. Also Mentioned in Despatches. Promoted to lieutenant-colonel on 4 October 1921.

Captain Francis William Murray Cunningham
RAMC (Regular)—Battalion Medical Officer (MO)

Commission as Lieutenant into the Royal Army Medical Corps on 30 January 1909. Promoted to captain on 30 July 1912. Attached to the 5th Manchesters and embarked from Southampton onboard SS *Caledonia* on 10 September 1914, disembarking at Alexandria, Egypt on 25th. Remained in Egypt until the 1/5th Manchesters embarked for Gallipoli on the SS *Derfflinger* on 3 May 1915, disembarking at W Beach, Helles, on 6th. Wounded on 12 May but returned to duty two days later. Temporarily attached to the 1/1st East Lancs Field Ambulance on 22 October 1915, and may have remained attached for the rest of the campaign. Mentioned in Hamilton's Despatch of 11 December 1915. Later brevet lieutenant-colonel. Placed on the Retired Officers list on 29 July 1919.

2nd Lieutenant Leo Edwin Davis
2nd Draft (23 July 1915)

Commissioned into the 2/5th Manchesters on 23 January 1915. Joined the 1/5th Manchesters at Helles on 23 July 1915, and attached to 'A' Company. Killed in action, aged 20, during the attacks on trenches H.11a & H.11b on 7 August 1915. Commemorated on the Helles Memorial, Panel 159 to 171.

2nd Lieutenant John Porter Yates Dickey
3rd Draft (21 August 1915)

Commissioned into the 2/5th Manchesters on 23 February 1915. Joined the 1/5th Manchesters at Helles on 21 August 1915. Continued to serve with the battalion after its evacuation from Helles, and, in Egypt from January 1916. Moved with the battalion to France in March 1917. Promoted to lieutenant on 1 August 1917 (with precedence from 1 June 1916). Continued to serve with the battalion in France and Belgium until March 1918. Seconded to the Royal Flying Corps as an Observer, and made Honorary Lieutenant on 1 April 1918. Later served in the RAF. Survived the war. Brother of Robert George Alexander Dickey.

2nd Lieutenant Robert George Alexander Dickey
2nd Draft (23 July 1915)

Commissioned into the 2/5th Manchesters on 1 December 1914. Joined the 1/5th Manchesters at Helles on 23 July 1915. Wounded during the attacks on trenches H.11a and H.11b on 6 and 7 August 1915. Probably remained on the peninsula. Continued to serve with the battalion at Helles, and, after its evacuation, in Egypt from January 1916. Moved with the battalion to France in March 1917, and continued to serve with it in France and Belgium until 23 November 1917, when seconded to the Royal Engineers. Promoted to lieutenant on 1 August 1917 (with precedence from 1 June 1916) and to captain on 2 January 1918. Died of pneumonia following wounds (gas) on 14 November 1918. Buried at St. Michael and All Angels Churchyard, Foulridge, Lancashire, grave S. 20. Brother of John Porter Yates Dickey.

Lieutenant Basil Lindley Fletcher (MC)
'D' Company

Commissioned into the 5th Bn., The Manchester Regt., on 9 March 1909. Promoted to lieutenant on 29 June 1911. Volunteered for overseas service. Probably joined the 1/5th Manchesters in Egypt, late 1914.

Remained in Egypt until the battalion embarked for Gallipoli with the 1/5th Manchesters onboard the SS *Derfflinger* on 3 May 1915, disembarking at W Beach, Helles, on 6th. Made temporary captain on 26 May 1915. Wounded on 4 June 1915, and evacuated off the peninsula. Promoted to captain on 30 June 1915. Attached to the 2/5th Manchesters in England in late June 1915, and to the 3/5th Manchesters in Oct/Nov 1915. Rejoined the 1/5th Manchesters at Helles on 8 December 1915. Continued to serve with the battalion at Helles, and, after its evacuation, in Egypt from January 1916. Moved with the battalion to France in March 1917, and continued to serve with it in France and Belgium until the end of the war. Promoted to major on 24 August 1917. Awarded the Military Cross (LG:30450 / 1 January 1918). Retired from the active list having attained the age limit on 28 September 1935.

Captain Clement Fletcher (TD)
OC 'D' Company from 18 September 1915

Commissioned into the 1st Volunteer Bn., The Manchester Regt., in the late 1890s. Promoted to lieutenant on 13 July 1901, and to captain on 23 December 1905. He retained his rank and seniority on the formation of the Territorial Force on 1 April 1908, when the battalion was redesignated as the 5th Bn., The Manchester Regt. Remained at home when the 1/5th Manchesters embarked for Egypt on 10 September. Attached to the 2/5th Manchesters in England until he joined the 1/5th Manchesters at Helles on 12 September 1915. Took command of 'D' Company after Captain F.A. James *(see entry)* was mortally wounded on 16 September 1915. Continued to serve with the battalion at Helles, and, after its evacuation from the peninsula, in Egypt from January 1916. Transferred to a reserve battalion in England in Feb/Mar 1917. Awarded the Territorial Decoration on 15 July 1919. Retired from the active list having attained the age limit on 27 October 1926. Brother of Ernest Fletcher.

Major Ernest Fletcher (TD)
Second in Command (2i/c) 1/5th Manchesters

Commissioned into the 1st Volunteer Bn., The Manchester Regt., on 2 May 1896. Probably promoted to lieutenant in 1897. Promoted to captain on 3 September 1898. He retained his rank and seniority on the formation of the Territorial Force on 1 April 1908, when the battalion was redesignated as the 5th Bn., The Manchester Regt. Promoted to major on 23 June 1912. Volunteered for overseas service end of August 1914. Embarked from Southampton onboard SS *Caledonia* with the 5th Manchesters on 10 September 1914, disembarking at Alexandria, Egypt on 25th. Remained in Egypt until he embarked for Gallipoli as the battalion's 2i/c onboard SS *Derfflinger* on 3 May 1915, disembarking at W Beach, Helles, on 6th. Commanded the battalion while Colonel Darlington was in command of the 127th Brigade (6 July to 31 July). Went to hospital sick on 10 September, and was evacuated off the peninsula, and on to England. Attached to the 3/5th Manchesters in England in Jan/Feb 1916. Rejoined the 1/5th Manchesters in Egypt in July/Aug 1916. Moved with the battalion to France in March 1917, and continued to serve as the battalion's 2i/c in France and Belgium until the end of the war. Awarded the Territorial Decoration on 7 June 1917. Brother of Clement Fletcher.

2nd Lieutenant Philip Cawthorne Fletcher (MC, TD)
Battalion Signal Officer

Commissioned into the 5th Manchesters on 12 September 1914. Volunteered for overseas service. Joined the 1/5th Manchesters in Egypt around 5 November 1914. Remained in Egypt until the battalion embarked for Gallipoli onboard the SS *Derfflinger* on 3 May 1915 (although not shown on the 1/5th Manchesters Embarkation State, he may have been included on the embarkation list of the East Lancs Divisional Signal Company, which was also onboard SS *Derfflinger*). Disembarked at W Beach, Helles, on 6th. Wounded on 4 June 1915. Evacuated off the peninsula to England. Attached to the 3/5th Manchesters in England Oct/Nov 1915. Transferred to the Royal Engineers, and later to the Royal Corps of Signals. Promoted to lieutenant on 1 July 1917 (with precedence from 1 June 1916). Awarded the Military Cross (LG:31092/1 January 1918). Promoted to Major on 11 October 1921. After the war, Fletcher resumed in his post as a schoolmaster at Chartwell School, and was attached to the schools Officer Training Corps until he resigned his commission on 1 October 1937. Holder of the Territorial Decoration. Came out of retirement on 21 September 1940.

Lieutenant Lawrence Talbot Lisle Foster
16th Durham Light Infantry

Commissioned as lieutenant into the 16th (Service) Bn., The Durham Light Infantry on 21 November 1914. Joined the 1/5th Manchesters at Imbros on 17 June 1915. Killed in action, aged 30, during the attacks on trenches H.11a & H.11b on 7 August 1915. In a letter to Foster's parents Colonel Darlington wrote:

> "As an officer he was splendid, always steadily doing his duty and quite fearless. He led his men with the utmost bravery, and was killed as he would have liked to have been, at the head of his men, and without suffering. He is a great loss to the battalion and you have every right to be proud of him as we are."

Believed to be buried in Twelve Tree Copse Cemetery, Helles, and is commemorated by Special Memorial C351.

2nd Lieutenant F. C. 'Freddy' Gordon
'A' Company

Commissioned into the 2/5th Manchesters on 12 September 1914. Volunteered for overseas service. Joined the 1/5th Manchesters in Egypt around 5 November 1914. Remained in Egypt until the battalion embarked for Gallipoli onboard the SS *Derfflinger* on 3 May 1915, disembarking at W Beach, Helles, on 6th. Wounded on 5 June 1915. Evacuated off the peninsula to England. Later employed at '*Comd, Depot*' and appears to have served there for the rest of the war.

2nd Lieutenant Ernest Evelyn Goward
Arrived at Helles 10 September 1915

Cadet Ernest Evelyn Goward, Rugby School OTC, was commissioned into the 2/5th Manchesters on 13 April 1915. Joined the 1/5th Manchesters at Helles on 10 September 1915. Continued to serve with the battalion at Helles, and, after its evacuation, in Egypt from January 1916. Moved with the battalion to France in March 1917, and continued to serve with it in France and Belgium until the end of the war. Promoted to lieutenant on 1 August 1917 (with precedence from 1 June 1916). Mentioned in Despatches.

2nd Lieutenant [J.N. sic] Edgar Neill Holden
Headquarters (Machine Gun Officer)

Commissioned into the 2/5th Manchesters on 12 September 1914. Volunteered for overseas service. Joined the 1/5th Manchesters in Egypt around 5 November 1914. Remained in Egypt until the battalion embarked for Gallipoli onboard the SS *Derfflinger* on 3 May 1915, disembarking at W Beach, Helles, on 6th. Injured on 7 May, when a machine gun cart ran over his leg, and was evacuated off the peninsula. Promoted to lieutenant on 4 November 1915. Attached to the 3/5th Manchesters from Jan/Feb 1916, until Feb/March 1917, when he was attached to the 20th Manchesters. Remained with the 20th Manchesters until he rejoined the 1/5th Manchesters in Jul/Aug 1918. Promoted to captain on 1 August 1917 (with precedence from 1 June 1916). Recommissioned into the Royal Berkshire Regiment as a lieutenant on 21 March 1940. Resigned his commission on 10 October 1941 due to ill health.

Lieutenant Frank Taylor Iveson
16th Durham Light Infantry

Commissioned as lieutenant into the 16th (Service) Bn., The Durham Light Infantry on 5 October 1914. Joined the 1/5th Manchesters at Imbros, 17 June 1915. Killed by rifle fire while talking to Colonel Darlington on 30 June 1915, aged 29/30. Buried in the Redoubt Cemetery, Helles, Grave X.E.19.

H. — BIOGRAPHIES, 5TH MANCHESTERS

Lieutenant Francis 'Frank' Arthur James
'C' Company (Transport Officer)

Commissioned as lieutenant into the 5th Manchesters on 1 August 1914. Volunteered for overseas service end of August 1914. Embarked from Southampton onboard SS *Caledonia* with the 5th Manchesters on 10 September 1914, disembarking at Alexandria, Egypt on 25th. Remained in Egypt until the battalion embarked for Gallipoli onboard the SS *Derfflinger* on 3 May 1915, disembarking at W Beach, Helles, on 6th. Wounded in July, and returned to the battalion from hospital in August. Served as acting adjutant from 18 August (on Captain Sanders' evacuation) until placed in command of 'D' Company on 23rd. Wounded on 16 September, and died on 18 September, aged 29. Believed to be buried in Pink Farm Cemetery, Helles, and is commemorated by Special Memorial 156. Brother to George Sidney James. One of four brothers, all killed in the war.

Lieutenant George Sidney James
'C' Company

Commissioned into the 5th Manchesters on 15 December 1911. Promoted to lieutenant on 16 September 1913. Volunteered for overseas service end of August 1914. Embarked from Southampton onboard SS *Caledonia* with the 5th Manchesters on 10 September 1914, disembarking at Alexandria, Egypt on 25th. Remained in Egypt until the battalion embarked for Gallipoli onboard the SS *Derfflinger* on 3 May 1915, disembarking at W Beach, Helles, on 6th. Killed in action on 4 June, aged 22, when "accompanied by a corporal, was killed clearing a trench with bombs." Recommended for a gallantry award on 10 June. Buried in the Redoubt Cemetery, Helles, Grave X.E.20. Brother to Francis Arthur James. One of four brothers, all killed in the war.

Lieutenant Alfred Earlam Johnson
'D' Company

Commissioned into the 5th Manchesters on 13 November 1913 (late Cadet Serjeant Alfred Earlam Johnson, Giggleswick School OTC). Promoted to lieutenant on 31 August 1914. Volunteered for overseas service end of August 1914. Embarked from Southampton onboard SS *Caledonia* with the 5th Manchesters on 10 September 1914, disembarking at Alexandria, Egypt on 25th. Remained in Egypt until the battalion embarked for Gallipoli onboard the SS *Derfflinger* on 3 May 1915, disembarking at W Beach, Helles, on 6th. Wounded on 4 June 1915, and evacuated off the peninsula to England. Made temporary captain on 15 August 1915. Attached to the 3/5th Manchesters in England, in Nov/Dec 1915. Rejoined the 1/5th Manchesters in Egypt in May/June 1916. Returned to the 3/5th Manchesters in England in Jun/July 1916. Promoted to captain on 22 October 1916 (with precedence from 15 August 1915). Attached to 25th Bn., The Rifle Brigade (Reserve Battalion) remaining with that battalion for the rest of the war. Relinquished his commission on 9 January 1919, on account of ill health caused by wounds received. Brother of Henry Norman Earlam Johnson and William Godfrey Earlam Johnson.

2nd Lieutenant Henry Norman Earlam Johnson
'D' Company (Supernumerary)

Commissioned into the 2/5th Manchesters on 14 October 1914. Joined the 1/5th Manchesters in Egypt around 5 November 1914. Remained in Egypt until the battalion embarked for Gallipoli onboard the SS *Derfflinger* on 3 May 1915, disembarking at W Beach, Helles, on 6th. Wounded on 4 June 1915, and evacuated off the peninsula to England. Rejoined the 1/5th Manchesters (probably at the battalion's base in Alexandria). Attached to the 3/5th Manchesters in England May/June 1916, remaining with that battalion until he rejoined the 1/5th Manchesters in France in June/July 1917. Promoted to lieutenant on 29 September 1917 (with precedence from 1 June 1916). Posted missing on 2 November 1917, later confirmed dead, aged 23. Buried in the Oostende New Communal Cemetery, Grave B.4. Brother of Henry Alfred Earlam Johnson and William Godfrey Earlam Johnson.

H.—BIOGRAPHIES, 5TH MANCHESTERS

Lieutenant
William Godfrey Earlam Johnson
'D' Company

Commissioned into the 5th Manchesters on 15 December 1911. Promoted to lieutenant 31 November 1913. Volunteered for overseas service end of August 1914. Embarked from Southampton onboard SS *Caledonia* with the 5th Manchesters on 10 September 1914, disembarking at Alexandria, Egypt on 25th. Remained in Egypt until the battalion embarked for Gallipoli onboard the SS *Derfflinger* on 3 May 1915. Disembarked at W Beach, Helles, on 6th. Wounded on 27 May, and evacuated off the peninsula to England. Attached to the 3/5th Manchesters in England in Oct/Nov 1915. Promoted to captain on 4 November 1915. Rejoined the 1/5th Manchesters in Egypt in May/June 1916. Moved with the battalion to France in March 1917, and continued to serve with it in France and Belgium until wounded. Died of wounds, age 24, on 13 October 1917. Buried in Zuydcoote Military Cemetery, Grave 1.F.19. Brother of Alfred Earlam Johnson and Henry Norman Earlam Johnson.

Captain Arthur Clive Leech
Officer Commanding (OC) 'D' Company

Commissioned into the 1st Volunteer Bn., The Manchester Regt., on 2 August 1902. Promoted to lieutenant on 15 August 1903. He retained his rank and seniority on the formation of the Territorial Force on 1 April 1908, when the battalion was redesignated the 5th Bn., The Manchester Regt. Promoted to captain on 20 March 1913. Volunteered for overseas service end of August 1914. Embarked from Southampton onboard SS *Caledonia* with the 5th Manchesters on 10 September 1914, disembarking at Alexandria, Egypt on 25th. Remained in Egypt until embarked for Gallipoli as OC 'D' Company, onboard SS *Derfflinger* on 3 May 1915, disembarking at W Beach, Helles, on 6th. Killed in action, aged 31, on 4 June. Buried in the Redoubt Cemetery, Helles, Grave X.F.18.

2nd Lieutenant
Grey Sefton Lund
'C' Company

Commissioned into the 2/5th Manchesters on 26 August 1914. Volunteered for overseas service. Joined the 1/5th Manchesters in Egypt around 11 April 1915. Remained in Egypt until the battalion embarked for Gallipoli onboard the SS *Derfflinger* on 3 May 1915, disembarked at W Beach, Helles, on 6th. Appointed Machine Gun Officer in August 1915. Went to hospital sick around 6 September, and evacuated off the peninsula to England. Rejoined the 1/5th Manchesters in Egypt in May/June 1916. Promoted to lieutenant on 7 November 1916 (with precedence from 17 June 1915). Moved with the battalion to France in March 1917. Retired on 24 May 1917 due to 'ill-health contracted on active service.'

2nd Lieutenant
Thomas Leslie McGeorge
2nd Draft (23 July 1915)

Commissioned into the 2/5th Battalion, The Manchester Regt., on 28 April 1915. Joined the 1/5th Manchesters at Helles on 23 July 1915. Killed in action, aged 24, during the attacks on trenches H.11a and H.11b on 7 August 1915. Commemorated on the Helles Memorial, Panel 159 to 171.

Lieutenant
Roney Forshaw Messervy
11th Bn., The West Riding Regt.

Commissioned into The Duke of Wellington's (West Riding) Regt., on 12 September 1914. Made temporary lieutenant on 11 December 1914. Joined the 1/5th Manchesters at Helles on 1 July 1915. Wounded during the attacks on trenches H.11a and H.11b on 7 August 1915, and evacuated off the peninsula. Later seconded to the RFC and RAF. Survived the war.

H.—BIOGRAPHIES, 5TH MANCHESTERS

2nd Lieutenant Arnold Shirecliffe Parker
'D' Company

A resident of Alexandria, Egypt, Parker was commissioned in to the 1/5th Manchesters on 22 February 1915, while the battalion was stationed in Alexandria. Embarked with the battalion for Gallipoli onboard the SS *Derfflinger* on 3 May 1915, disembarking at W Beach, Helles, on 6th. Wounded on 27 May 1915, and evacuated off the peninsula to England. Attached to the 3/5th Manchesters in England in Jan/Feb 1916. Rejoined the 1/5th Manchesters in Egypt in May/June 1916. Moved with the battalion to France in March 1917. Served in France and Belgium with the battalion until seconded to the Labour Corps in Mar/April 1918. Survived the war.

2nd Lieutenant Geoffrey Owens Pearce
Arrived at Helles 10 September 1915

Private, 539, Geoffrey Owens Pearce, 28th Bn. (Artist's Rifles) The London Regt., (having already served in France) was commissioned into the 2/5th Manchesters on 29 April 1915. Joined the 1/5th Manchesters at Helles on 10 September 1915. Continued to serve with the battalion at Helles, and, after its evacuation, in Egypt from January 1916. Promoted to lieutenant on 1 July 1916. Moved with the battalion to France in March 1917. Served with the battalion in France and Belgium until the end of the war.

2nd Lieutenant Harold James Porter
2nd Draft (23 July 1915)

Commissioned into the 2/5th Manchesters on 24 December 1914. Joined the 1/5th Manchesters at Helles on 23 July 1915. Wounded during the attacks on trenches H.11a and H.11b on 7 August 1915, and evacuated off the peninsula. Died of his wounds in Alexandria on 15 August 1915, aged 20, and is buried in the Chatby Military Cemetery, Alexandria, Egypt, Grave Q.489.

Captain Henry Milward Rogers
Officer Commanding (OC) 'B' Company

Commissioned into the 1st Volunteer Bn., The Manchester Regt., on 3 August 1899. Promoted to lieutenant on 18 July 1901, and to captain on 17 March 1905. He retained his rank and seniority on the formation of the Territorial Force on 1 April 1908, when the battalion was redesignated the 5th Bn., The Manchester Regt. Volunteered for overseas service end of August 1914. Embarked from Southampton onboard SS *Caledonia* with the 5th Manchesters on 10 September 1914, disembarking at Alexandria, Egypt on 25th. Remained in Egypt until embarked for Gallipoli as OC 'B' Company, onboard SS *Derfflinger* on 3 May 1915, disembarking at W Beach, Helles, on 6th. Wounded by shellfire on 22 May (probably while at 'Shell Bivouac') and evacuated off the peninsula. Died of his wounds onboard Hospital Ship *Reindeer* on 26 May 1915, aged 35. Buried at East Mudros Military Cemetery, Lemnos, Grave I. F. 102.

Captain John Malcolm Brodie Sanders (MC)
Adjutant of the 1/5th Manchesters

Born in Remington, Warwick on 13 December 1886. Graduated from Sandhurst and commissioned into The Prince of Wales's Leinster Regiment (Royal Canadians) on 29 August 1906. Promoted to Lieutenant on 23 December 1907. He was employed with the West African Frontier Force from 2 March 1910 to 13 November 1912. Appointed adjutant to the 5th Manchesters on 1 January 1913, and promoted to captain on 12 November 1913.

Embarked from Southampton onboard SS *Caledonia* with the 5th Manchesters on 10 September 1914, disembarking at Alexandria, Egypt on 25th. Remained in Egypt until embarked for Gallipoli with the 1/5th Manchesters, onboard SS *Derfflinger* on 3 May 1915, disembarking at W Beach, Helles, on the 6th. Wounded on 6 or 7 August, and evacuated off the peninsula on the 18 August 1915. Awarded the Military Cross (LG: 29460 / 2 February 1916) for his service on Gallipoli, and

twice Mentioned in Dispatches (one in Hamilton's Despatch of 11 December 1915— LG: 1202/28 January 1916). Seconded to the DAAG's Staff, (Egyptian Expeditionary Force) No. 3 Section on the Suez Canal Defences from 10 July until 20 October 1916. Made temporary lieutenant-colonel and placed in command of the 4th Bn., Kings Own Scottish Borderers (KOSBs) on 21 October 1916, and remained in commanded to 10 May 1917. Took command of the 4th Bn., KOSBs again from 8 June to 18 September 1917. Again, made temporary lieutenant-colonel on 22 January 1919 (sub-
stantive on 18 November 1922) while employed as commandant of a Command Depot. Appointed 'Unofficial Member of the Legislative Council of the Nyasaland Protectorate' on 9 May 1929. Released from the Reserve of Officer List on 8 August 1946.

Captain Arthur William Woodman Simpson (OBE, TD)

Commissioned into the 1st Volunteer Bn., The Manchester Regt., in the 1890s. Promoted to captain on 10 January 1906. He retained his rank and seniority on the formation of the Territorial Force on 1 April 1908, when the battalion was redesignated the 5th Bn., The Manchester Regt. Volunteered for overseas service and joined the 1/5th Manchesters in Egypt in November 1914. May have disembarked with the battalion at W Beach on 6 May 1915 (although not listed on the Embarkation List). Evacuated sick back to Alexandria sometime prior to 21 June 1915 (probably while the battalion was at Imbros). Made temporary lieutenant-colonel on 24 December 1915, and seconded as commandant of a prisoners of war camp in Egypt. Remained attached to the Egyptian Expeditionary Force for the remainder of the war, and appointed Inspector of Prisoners of War Camps ('Special Appointment'). Promoted to major on 1 August 1917 (with precedence from 1 June 1916). Mentioned in Despatches three times (LG: 6769 / 6 July 1917, LG: 930 / 16 January 1918, and LG: 10195 / 11 August 1919). Appointed OBE on 1 January 1919. Made brevet lieutenant-colonel on 3 June 1919. Awarded the Order of the Nile 3rd Class on 19 January 1920. Awarded the Territorial Decoration in July 1920. Retired from the list of Reserve Officers on 26 May 1928 'having attained the age limit.'

Lieutenant Philip John Skipworth
11th Bn., The West Riding Regt.

Commissioned into the Royal West Kent Regiment on 11 October 1911. Attached to The Duke of Wellington's (West Riding) Regiment, and promoted to lieutenant on 15 February 1915. Joined the 1/5th Manchesters at Helles on 1 July 1915. Killed in action, aged 23, during the attacks on trenches H.11a and H.11b on 7 August 1915. Commemorated on the Helles Memorial, Panel 118 to 120.

Lieutenant Arthur Slaughter

Commissioned into the 5th Bn., The Manchester Regt., on 12 September 1914. Volunteered for overseas service. Embarked from Southampton onboard SS *Caledonia* with the 5th Manchesters on 10 September 1914, disembarking at Alexandria, Egypt on 25th. Made acting lieutenant in December 1914. Remained in Egypt when the battalion embarked for Gallipoli on 3 May 1915. Rejoined the battalion at Helles on 2 June 1915. Went to hospital sick on 22 June, and was evacuated off the peninsula (probably to Alexandria). Appears to have remained in Egypt for the rest of the war. Seconded for duty at a prisoners of war camp in Egypt on 1 July 1916, and remained seconded until 12 October 1919. Promoted to lieutenant on 27 January 1917 (with precedence from 5 November 1915), captain on 14 August 1917 (with precedence from 1 June 1916) and subsequently to temporary Major.

H.—BIOGRAPHIES, 5TH MANCHESTERS

Company Serjeant Major 273 Walter Spencer

Born in Burnley, Lancashire. A cotton mill worker in civilian life. A former regular in the Manchester Regt., with service in the South African war. Attested in the 5th Manchesters (or 1st Volunteer Battalion) sometime after his discharge from the Regular Army on 29 May 1901. Volunteered for overseas service at the beginning of September 1914. Embarked from Southampton onboard SS *Caledonia* with the 5th Manchesters on 10 September 1914, disembarking at Alexandria, Egypt on 25th. Remained in Egypt until the battalion embarked for Gallipoli onboard the SS *Derfflinger* on 3 May 1915, disembarking at W Beach, Helles, on 6th. Killed in action (probably during a night advance) on 28 May 1915, aged 37. Believed to be buried in the Redoubt Cemetery, Helles, and is commemorated by Special Memorial B. 26.

Lieutenant Thomas Middleton Stott
Arrived at Helles 10 September

Commissioned into the 2/5th Manchesters on 30 September 1914. Joined the 1/5th Manchesters at Helles on 10 September 1915. Continued to serve with the battalion at Helles, and, after its evacuation, in Egypt from January 1916. Moved with the battalion to France in March 1917, and continued to serve with it in France and Belgium until the end of the war. Promoted to lieutenant on 12 June 1917 (with precedence from 24 March 1917) and to captain on 29 September (with precedence from 6 March 1917). Relinquished his commission on 30 September 1921.

Private 1385 Alexander Stuart
Servant to Colonel Darlington

Born in Wigan, Lancashire. A coal miner in civilian life, he attested in the 5th Manchesters on the 22 April 1912. Volunteered for overseas service at the beginning of September 1914. Embarked from Southampton onboard SS *Caledonia* with the 5th Manchesters on 10 September 1914, disembarking at Alexandria, Egypt on 25th. Remained in Egypt until the battalion embarked for Gallipoli onboard the SS *Derfflinger* on 3 May 1915, disembarking at W Beach, Helles, on the 6th. Wounded in the right shoulder on 5 July, and evacuated off the peninsula to hospital in Malta. Rejoined the battalion on 5 October 1915, and continued to serve with it at Helles, and, after its evacuation, in Egypt from January 1916. Granted 6 weeks home furlough while in Egypt. Embarked on HMT *Minnewaska* on 27 November 1916. Survived when the ship was torpedoed, and as a result, Stuart was granted an additional 2 weeks extension of furlough "owing to delay enroute." Moved with the battalion to France in March 1917, and continued to serve with it until transferred to the Labour Corps on 5 August 1917 (new service number 346112). Demobilised on 28 February 1919.

Acting Lieutenant Q.M. Samuel Taylor (MC)
Headquarters (Q.M.)

Acting Lieutenant Q.M., acting RSM, 5131, Samuel Taylor, Manchester Regiment. Probably a regular soldier attached to the 5th Manchesters before the war as permanent staff. Embarked for Gallipoli with the 1/5th Manchesters onboard SS *Derfflinger* on 3 May 1915, disembarking at W Beach, Helles, on the 6th. Wounded around the end of May, he rejoined the battalion at Helles in August. Commissioned 2nd lieutenant (in the field) into the 4th Bn., The Worcestershire Regt., (then at Suvla) on the 2 November 1915, and remained with the Worcesters for the remainder of the war. Awarded the Military Cross (LG:29608/3 June 1916). Promoted to lieutenant on 1 July 1917. Mentioned in Despatches. Retired 2 July 1919.

H.—BIOGRAPHIES, 5TH MANCHESTERS

Captain
James Scarlett Ashcroft Walker (TD)
2nd in Command (2ic) 'B' Company

Commissioned into the 1st Volunteer Bn., The Manchester Regt., on 4 June 1906. He retained his rank and seniority on the formation of the Territorial Force on 1 April 1908, when the battalion was redesignated the 5th Bn., The Manchester Regt. Promoted to lieutenant on 25 November 1908. Appointed Instructor of Musketry on 8 February 1912. Promoted to captain on 16 September 1913. Volunteered for overseas service end of August 1914. Embarked from Southampton onboard SS *Caledonia* with the 5th Manchesters on 10 September 1914, disembarking at Alexandria, Egypt on 25th. Remained in Egypt until embarked for Gallipoli as 2ic 'B' Company, onboard SS *Derfflinger* on 3 May 1915, disembarking at W Beach, Helles, on 6th. Went to hospital suffering from neuritis on 17 June 1915. Appointed Brigade Machine Gun Officer in Aug/Sept 1915. Employed in the Ministry of Munitions from November 1915, until the end of the war. Promoted to major on 1 October 1920. Holder of the Territorial Decoration. Brother of Thomas Cartmell Walker.

2nd Lieutenant
Thomas Cartmell Walker
'C' Company

Commissioned 13 October 1914 into the 2/5th Manchesters. Joined the 1/5th Manchesters in Egypt around 5 November 1914. Remained in Egypt until the battalion embarked for Gallipoli onboard the SS *Derfflinger* on 3 May 1915, disembarking at W Beach, Helles, on 6th. Wounded slightly in the head around 10 May. Killed, aged 20, on 6 June 1915. Buried in the Redoubt Cemetery, Helles, Grave X.F.19. Brother of James Scarlett Ashcroft Walker.

Captain Dudley Dickinson Winterbottom
2nd Draft (23 July 1915)

Educated at Eton and Trinity Hall Cambridge. Commissioned into the 2/5th Manchesters on 30 September 1914. Promoted to lieutenant on 15 November 1914, and to captain on 1 March 1915. Joined the 1/5th Manchesters at Helles on 23 July 1915. Killed, aged 23, in the attacks on trenches H.11a & H.11b on 7 August 1915. Commemorated on the Helles Memorial, Panel 159 to 171.

Captain William Talbot Woods (CB, DSO, MC, TD)
2nd in Command (2i/c) 'A' Company

Commissioned 9 July 1910 into the 5th Manchesters. Promoted to lieutenant 10 August 1914. Volunteered for overseas service end of August 1914. Made temporary captain 31 August 1914. Embarked from Southampton onboard SS *Caledonia* with the 5th Manchesters on 10 September 1914, disembarking at Alexandria, Egypt on 25th. Remained in Egypt until embarked for Gallipoli as 2i/c 'A' Company, onboard SS *Derfflinger* on 3 May 1915, disembarking at W Beach, Helles, on the 6th. Played an important part in the Third Battle of Krithia (Col. Darlington wrote "'A' Co., under Talbot Woods hung on all day splendidly with the Turks on their flank and rear and suffered very much"). Sometime after the battle appointed temporary Staff Captain for the 127th Brigade (or possibly after taking part in the Battle of 6/7th August 1915). By 18 August had been evacuated sick to Alexandria. Appears not to have returned to the 1/5th Manchesters. Appointed Staff Captain to the 127th Brigade on 30 October 1915. Mentioned in Despatches on 15 November 1915. Promoted to captain on 2 May 1916 (with precedence from 4 November 1915). Awarded the Military Cross (LG: 29608/3 June 1916). Mentioned in Despatches on 13 July 1916 and again on 11 December 1917. Created Companion of the Distinguished Service Order (LG: 1 January 1918). Went on to command several Regular infantry battalions after the war, and was eventually promoted to colonel. Awarded the Territorial Decoration on 23 September 1930. Created CB on 8 June 1950.

APPENDIX I.—BIOGRAPHIES, OFFICERS FROM OTHER UNITS

Appointments, ranks and companies shown in the heading are those on arrival at Gallipoli. Later awards shown in brackets.

Brig-General Anthony Hugh Baldwin
GOC 38th Infantry Brigade, 13th Division

Born on 30 September 1863. Commissioned as lieutenant from the 3rd Militia Bn., The East Lancashire Regt., into the 1st Bn., The Manchester Regt., on 14 May 1884. Promoted to captain on 3 February 1892; major on 15 December 1900; lieutenant colonel on 17 February 1908; colonel on 13 August 1914; and brigadier-general on 24 August 1914. Served in India (1888 to 1895), in South Africa (1902), in Ireland, and at home. Given command of the 38th Infantry Brigade on 5 September 1915. Arrived with his brigade at Helles on 7 July 1915, remaining there until it moved to Lemnos on 31st. Landed at Anzac with his brigade on 3 August. Killed with his entire staff in the firing-line at the Farm plateau on 10 August 1915, aged 51. General Baldwin's body was never recovered. He is commemorated on the Helles, Memorial, Panel 17.

Captain Harold Thomas Cawley M.P.
1/6th Manchester Regiment

Born in Crumpsall on 12 June 1878. Educated at Rugby and New College Oxford. Barrister and Liberal Member of Parliament for Heywood, Lancashire. Commissioned into 2nd Volunteer Bn., The Manchester Regt., on 19 December 1903, and promoted to lieutenant in 17 February 1906. He retained his rank and seniority on the formation of the Territorial Force on 1 April 1908, when the battalion was redesignated as the 6th Bn., The Manchester Regt. Promoted to captain on 1 June 1913. Volunteered for overseas service end of August 1914. Embarked from Southhampton onboard HMT *Deseado* with divisional headquarters (as Aide de Camp to the divisional commander, Major-General William Douglas) on 10 September 1914, disembarking at Alexandria, Egypt on 24th. Remained in Egypt until embarked with divisional headquarters for Gallipoli on 5 May 1915, disembarking at Helles on 9th. Cawley became increasingly critical of the way the campaign was being conducted, and of General Douglas in particular, describing Douglas as "the most contemptible man he had ever met, always thinking of himself, his food, his promotion and his health." Cawley wrote a scathing letter to his father, shortly before he was killed:

> "My own general is disliked by all his troops, particularly his officers. He has a third-rate brain, no capacity to grasp the lie of the land and no originality or ingenuity. He has been in the trenches three times since he landed, hurried visits on which he saw next to nothing and hardly ever goes to the observation point with his field glasses. The result is that he does not understand the lie of the land on his own front. When there is an attack, he works out all the details and leaves nothing to Brigadiers and commanding officers who know the ground. The result last time was that the best Manchester battalions were sent to an impossible place which every colonel and adjutant regarded as only to be taken after some other commanding trenches had been cleared. My battalion lost every officer who charged, I believe, except Geoff Kershaw who was hit early and got back to the trench. The curse of the whole show has been the absurd optimism of the chief generals.... and the way they have underrated their opponents.... the attacks are often badly reconnoitred and ill conceived."[1]

Cawley applied to re-join to his battalion, and on the 8 September,

---

1 Now held at King's College London.

I.—BIOGRAPHIES, OTHER UNITS

he reported to the 1/6th Manchesters, then in Corps Reserve, in Gully Ravine. Three days later the battalion was holding the sub-section to the right of Border Barricade, opposite the Turkish position known as the Gridiron, with Cawley in command of the firing-line.

On 22 September, the 1/6th Manchesters were holding the same sub-section of trenches. At about 6 pm the Turks detonated a large mine close to the firing-line, destroying about 30 yards of trench, and forming a large crater the forward lip of which was "no more than 18 yards from the Turk trench."[1] Shortly after the explosion Cawley dashed out with a party of men and occupied the crater. It was evacuated shortly before first light but reoccupied the following night. Around midnight on the 23rd, Cawley was alerted by his men to the sound of Turks digging towards the crater, and went to investigate. As he peered over the rim (possibly in the act of firing his revolver) he was shot in the temple and died shortly afterwards, aged 37. The crater thereafter became known as Cawley's Crater.

Instead of using one of the numerous small cemeteries in Gully Ravine, his body was carried back six kilometres and buried in Lancashire Landing Cemetery, Grave A.76.

Lieutenant-Colonel Albert Canning (CMG)
Commanding Officer, 1/7th Manchesters

Born in Ramsbury, Wiltshire, 26 October 1861. First served in the ranks of 19th Hussars 1882–8, in the Egyptian Expedition 1882–4, the Soudan 1884 (battles of Teb and Tamai) and in the Soudan Expedition 1885 (Suakin), gaining the Bronze Star with three clasps. Commissioned into the South

---

[1] Joseph Murray was in the firing-line at the time, and the explosion entombed four of his comrades and two fatigue men from the 1/4th East Lancs Regt., who were all working in a gallery below ground (see *Gallipoli As I Saw It*, pp.124–127).

Wales Borderers in April 1888. Promoted to lieutenant on 6 March 1891, and to captain on 9 October 1895. He was appointed adjutant of the 5th Bn., The Leinster Regt., on 22 January 1898. Promoted to major on 27 May 1903, he went on to command the 3rd Bn The Leinster Regt. He retired on half pay on 12 July 1911. Recalled from the Reserve of Officers and promoted to lieutenant-colonel on 6 August 1912.

Canning arrived at Helles and was placed in command of the 1/7th Manchesters on 16 July 1915. Was still in command when the battalion left the peninsula on 29 December 1915. Commanded the 127th Brigade from 19 to 26 August; 17 to 22 September; 19 December 1915 to (?) and 17 February to 1 March 1916.

Gerald B. Hurst, chronicler of the 1/7th Manchesters, had a high opinion of Canning:

> "On the 16th July the command was passed over to Lieutenant-Colonel A. Canning, a veteran of the Egyptian War of 1882, who had previously commanded the Leinster Regiment in Cork. We could have had no greater confidence in any possible Commanding Officer, and while he acted as Brigadier of the Manchester Territorials his influence was no less inspiring. The record of our later campaign on Gallipoli is closely associated with his name and work."[1]

Mentioned in Despatches for his service at Gallipoli (LG: 13 July 1916) and later created CMG. Retired with the rank of colonel. Died in Swindon in 1960, aged 99.

Captain Peter Hubert Creagh (DSO)
Adjutant, 1/7th Manchesters

Born in Marlow, Ireland on 18 August 1882. Attended the Royal Military College in 1902, and was commissioned into the Leicestershire Regt., on 22 October 1902. Promoted to lieutenant on 10 July 1905, and to captain on 13 November 1908. Appointed adjutant of the 1/7th Manchesters on 12 June 1911.

---

1 Gerald B. Hurst, *With Manchesters in the East* (Manchester: Longmans Green & Co., 1918) p.28.

I.—BIOGRAPHIES, OTHER UNITS

Embarked from Southhampton onboard HMT *Grantully Castle* with the 7th Manchesters on 10 September 1914, disembarking at Alexandria, Egypt on 25th. Served with the battalion in Sudan and Egypt. Embarked onboard SS *Ionian* for Gallipoli with the 1/7th Manchesters, on 3 May 1915, disembarking at V Beach, Helles on 7 May. Placed in temporary command of the battalion following the death of Major Staveacre on 4 June, and remained in command until 16 July 1915. Evacuated sick on 21 September, and on recovery returned  to the Leicester Regt., serving with them in Egypt and Mesopotamia. Promoted to major on 22 October 1917, and to lieutenant-colonel on 25 July 1929, to command the 2nd Bn., Leicestershire Regt.

Gerald B. Hurst, chronicler of the 1/7th Manchesters, wrote:

> "Captain P. H. Creagh of the Leicestershire Regiment was a fine adjutant, whose ability and character were to win him recognition in wider fields." [1]

Hurst recounts that, as the 1/7th Manchesters were disembarking on V Beach, the battalion's RSM, H.C. Franklin, overheard some Indian muleteers talking in Hindustani:

> "Here is another of the regiments of shopkeepers." One pointed to Captain P. H. Creagh, our Adjutant and only Regular officer. He said: "But he is a soldier." [2]

Created a Companion of the Distinguished Service Order (LG: 8 November 1915) "For distinguished service in the field during the operations at the Dardanelles." Twice Mentioned in Despatches for his service at Gallipoli (LG: 5 November 1915 and 28 January 1916). Received a third Mention in Despatches (LG: 22 January 1919).

---

[1] Hurst, *With Manchesters in the East*, p.4.
[2] Ibid, p.53.

Major Benjamin Palin Dobson (TD)
Officer Commanding (OC) 19th (B) Battery,
3rd East Lancashire Brigade (The Bolton Artillery) RFA (TF)

Commissioned in the 9th Lancashire (Bolton) Royal Garrison Artillery (Volunteers) in the mid-1890s. Promoted to lieutenant on 29 September 1897, and later to captain. He retained his rank and seniority on the formation of the Territorial Force on 1 April 1908, when his battery was redesignated the 19th Battery, 3rd East Lancashire Brigade (The Bolton Artillery) Royal Field Artillery. Promoted to Major on 1 September 1911, and placed in command of the 19th Battery. Served in Egypt; 1914-1915; Gallipoli 1915, Egypt 1916-1917, and in France and Belgium from March 1917. Promoted to lieutenant colonel on 7 June 1917 (with precedence from 1 June 1916). Mentioned in Despatches (LG: 6172/21 June 1916). Holder of the Territorial Decoration (LG: 7 June 1916). Retired from the Reserve of Officers list on 18 February 1933.

Major-General Sir William Douglas, KCMG, CB, DSO
GOC, 42nd (East Lancashire) Division

Born on 13 August 1858 and educated at Bath. Gazetted into the 1st Bn., The Royal Scots on 30 January 1878. Promoted to lieutenant on 25 November 1878. Served as adjutant to the 1st Royal Scots from 24 March 1880 to 23 March 1887. Served in the Bechuanaland Expedition, 1884–85. Promoted to captain on 24 June 1885. Appointed adjutant to the 3rd Royal Scots (Militia) February 1888 to February 1893, and adjutant 1st Royal Scots, 20 February 1893 to 20 August 1894. Promoted to major on 24 July 1895. Attended Staff College 1896–97. Served in South Africa, 1900–02, taking part in operations in the Orange Free State (February to May 1900); the Transvaal, east of Pretoria (July to 29 November 1900); at Belfast (26 and 27 August

I.—BIOGRAPHIES, OTHER UNITS

1900) and Lydenburg (5 to 8 September 1900). Commanded the 1st Royal Scots from 24 August 1900, and commanded a column during operations in the Transvaal, from November 1900 to November 1901. Promoted to lieutenant-colonel on 5 December 1900. Mentioned in Despatches (LG: 16 April 1901), received the Queen's South Africa Medal with three clasps, the King's South Africa Medal with two clasps, and created a Companion of the Distinguished Service Order (LG: 19 April 1901). Made brevet-colonel 10 February 1904, promoted to colonel on 1 March 1906. Appointed colonel to the General Staff, 6th Division, subsequently becoming (when the title of the appointment was changed) GSO 1st Grade, 8th Division (the 6th Division having been redesignated the 8th Division) Irish Command, from 1st March 1906 to 31 October 1909. Created a CB in 1908. Commanded the 14th Infantry Brigade from 1 November 1909 to 9 November 1912. Promoted to major general on 10 August 1912.

Commanded the 42nd (East Lancashire) Division from May 1913 to 11 March 1917. Served in Egypt from 25 September 1914 to 5 May 1915, and at Gallipoli from 9 May to 30 December 1915. Placed in temporary command of VIII Army Corps on several occasions, most notably from 24 July to 8 August, when he oversaw operations during the Battle of 6/7th August 1915 (the last major battle at Helles).

Twice Mentioned in Despatches (LG: 21 September 1915 and November 1915) and created KCMG in November 1915. Later served in Sinai, 1916–17, during the battle of Romani, and the capture of El Arish. Commanded the Desert Column from 23 October 1916 to 8 December 1916. Twice Mentioned in Despatches (LG: December 1916 and July 1917) and awarded the *Croix de Guerre* with Palm (LG: 21 May 1917).

Known throughout the division as 'Little Willie' or 'Peevish Willie,' Douglas was despised by most of the officers and men in his division. Douglas' Aide de Camp, Captain Harold Cawley, MP, gave a scathing description of Douglas in a letter to his father written just before he was killed *(see entry for Cawley)*. The other ranks were no less scathing. An unnamed NCO told Chaplain Kenneth Best that "there are only two ways of General D [Douglas] getting killed—by lyddite on top of [his dugout] direct hit, or by a bullet from his own men."[1]

---

1 Gavin Royon, *A Chaplain at Gallipoli, The Great War Diaries of Kenneth Best* (London: Simon & Schuster, 2011) p.177.

Notorious for his abrasive nature, and for micro-managing his subordinates and local operations while having little understanding of the ground or firing-line conditions. Despite his outward appearance of a brusque, unemotional commander, he was however, greatly affected by the division's losses. General Sir Ian Hamilton described Douglas as a "melancholy man before whose eyes stands constantly the tragic melting away without replacement of the most beautiful of the Divisions of Northern England."[1] Relinquished command of the division on 11 March 1917 to give evidence in the Dardanelles Inquiry. Commanded the Western Reserve Centre from 1917 until his retirement on 19 August 1918. Died on 2 November 1920, aged 62.

Captain (temporary Major) Arthur Edward Flynn Fawcus (DSO, MC, TD)
Officer Commanding (OC) 'A' Company, 1/7th Manchesters

Born in Chester on 19 October 1886. Commissioned into the 4th Volunteer Bn., The Manchester Regt., around 1903/4. Promoted to lieutenant on 25 October 1905, and to captain on 1 March 1907. He retained his rank and seniority (as supernumerary) on the formation of the Territorial Force on 1 April 1908, when the battalion was redesignated as the 7th Bn., The Manchester Regiment. Moved to Kenya (while supernumerary) and served in the Marakwet Patrol. Served with the 3rd King's African Rifles from 5 August 1914 to February 1915. Resigned his appointment on 9 February 1915, and travelled to Egypt to rejoin the 1/7th Manchesters. Embarked for Gallipoli onboard SS *Ionian*, as OC 'A' Company with the 1/7th Manchesters on 3 May 1915, disembarking at W Beach, Helles on 6 May. Left the battalion shortly after the Battle of 6/7th August 1915 to establish the Divisional Bombing School at Helles.

---

1 General Sir Ian Hamilton, *Gallipoli Diary Vol. I* (London: Edward Arnold, 1920) p.337.

I.—BIOGRAPHIES, OTHER UNITS

Continued to command the bombing school at Helles until the division was evacuated at the end of December 1915. One of only two 1/7th Manchester's officers to serve "on the peninsula from start to finish."[1] Awarded the Military Cross (LG: 29886/2 Feb 1916) for leading a night attack on 6 August 1915. Made *Chevalier,* Legion of Honour (EG: 331 Sup/28 Jan 1916) for bombing work at Gallipoli, and Mentioned in Despatches (LG: 1202/28 Jan 1916 and 13 July 1916).

Moved with the 42nd Division to Egypt in January 1916. Made temporary lieutenant-colonel, and placed in command of the 1/6th Lancashire Fusiliers in February 1916. Promoted to major on 11 August 1916 (with precedence from 12 June 1916). Created a Companion of the Distinguished Service Order (LG: 3 June 1918) for commanding the 1/5th North Staffordshire Regt., and afterwards the 1/5th Sherwood Foresters (Notts and Derby Regt.) on the Western Front for 18 months. Mentioned in Despatches a third time. Continued to command 1/5th Sherwood Foresters (Notts and Derby Regt.) after the war. Holder of the Territorial Decoration. Died on 10 August 1936, aged 49.

Lieutenant (acting Capt.) William Thomas Forshaw (VC)
Officer Commanding (OC) 'A' Company, 1/9th Manchesters

Born on 20 April 1890, in Barrow-in-Furness. A teacher in civilian life, he was commissioned into the 9th Battalion, The Manchester Regt., on 13 March 1914, and promoted to lieutenant on 4 November 1914. Volunteered for overseas service end of August 1914. Embarked from Southhampton onboard HMT *Aragon* with the 9th Manchesters on 10 September 1914, disembarking at Alexandria, Egypt on the 26th. Remained in Egypt until the battalion embarked for Gallipoli onboard the HMT *Ausonia* on 5 May 1915, disembarking at V Beach, Helles on 9 May. Acted as assistant to the battalion's QM, Major M. H. Connery for the first two months, which kept Forshaw away from the firing-line. However, officer casualties suffered by the battalion in June led to Forshaw being made acting captain, and placed in command of 'A' Company.

---

1 Hurst, *With Manchesters in the East*, p.67.

LETTERS FROM HELLES

On the morning of 7 August, the 1/9th Manchesters were in reserve in the Redoubt Line, with the left half of the battalion attached to the 127th Brigade, and the right half to the 125th Brigade. 'A' Company was in the right half, and at 15:18, Forshaw, with 2nd Lieutenant C.E. Cooke, and two platoons of 'A' Company were sent to reinforce the firing-line in the Vineyard. Ordered to hold onto the north-west corner of the Vineyard, later described as 'hottest corner in Helles,' Forshaw rebuffed Turkish attacks for 41 hours before being relieved. His bravery and determination earned him an immediate recommendation for the Victoria Cross (VC) which was confirmed one month later (LG: 8971/7 September 1915). He was evacuated from the peninsula later in August, suffering from nervous exhaustion. His VC citation reads:

> "For the most conspicuous bravery and determination in the Gallipoli Peninsula from 7th to 9th August, 1915. When holding the north-west corner of the 'Vineyard,' he was attacked and heavily bombed by Turks, who advanced time after time by three trenches which converged at this point, but he held his own, not only directing his men and encouraging them by exposing himself with the utmost disregard to danger, but personally throwing bombs continuously for 41 hours. When his detachment was relieved after 24 hours he volunteered to continue the direction of operations. Three times during the night of 8th–9th August he was again heavily attacked, and once the Turks got over the barricade, but, after shooting three with his revolver, he led his men forward and recaptured it. When he rejoined his Battalion, he was choked and sickened by bomb fumes, badly bruised by a fragment of shrapnel, and could barely lift his arm from continuous throwing. It was due to his personal example, magnificent courage and endurance that this important corner was held."

Mentioned in Despatches (LG: 1203/28 January 1916). After convalescing in England, and being feted in Ashton-under-Lyne

I.—BIOGRAPHIES, OTHER UNITS

and Barrow, he was sent to serve with the East Lancashire reserve battalions in Wiltshire. Transferred to the 76th Punjabis, Indian Army in 1917, where he took part in four frontier campaigns before retiring from the Army in November 1922. In 1940, he was appointed major in the 11th City of London Home Guard. Died of a heart attack "while cutting a hedge" on 26 May 1943, aged 53. He is buried Touchen-End Churchyard, Bray, Berkshire.

General Sir Ian Standish Monteith Hamilton, GCB, GCMG, DSO
Commander-in-Chief, Mediterranean Expeditionary Force

Commanded the Mediterranean Expeditionary Force from its inception on 12 March 1915 until his recall on 17 October 1915. Initially scapegoated for the failed campaign, Hamilton's reputation was to some extent restored after the findings of the Dardanelles Commission were made public.[1]

Lieutenant-Colonel (temp. Brig.-Gen.) Thomas Walter Brand, Viscount Hampden, GCVO, KCB, K St. J
Brigade Commander, 126th Brigade

Brigade Commander, 126th (East Lancashire) Infantry Brigade at Gallipoli from 13 July to 27 December 1915.

---

[1] The Dardanelles Commission was established in 1916 by the British government to examine the origins, conduct and failure of operations in the Dardanelles and the Gallipoli Campaign. The commission delivered its final report in 1919.

LETTERS FROM HELLES

Captain Philip Vaughan Holberton
Adjutant, 1/6th Manchesters

Born in Twickenham, Middlesex, on 24 May 1879. Educated at Shrewsbury School and the Royal Military College Sandhurst, from January 1900, passing out on 29 January 1901. Won the Sword of Honour, as the best cadet in his class, which was presented to him by Queen Victoria. Commissioned into the 2nd Bn., Manchester Regt. (then serving in South Africa) on 8 January 1901, and joined his battalion at Harrismith, South Africa in mid-June 1901. Attached to the battalion's new Mounted Infantry Company in August 1901, and was involved in fighting on 12 November, when his company encountered a group of 400 Boers near Schalkie in the Orange Free State. In the action Holberton was hit by a bullet just above his heart. Fortunately, his equipment stopped most of the force and was only slightly wounded. Promoted to lieutenant on 27 November 1901. Received the Queen's South Africa Medal with five clasps. Returned to Aldershot with his battalion on 27 September 1902. Served as adjutant to the 2nd Bn., Manchester Regt., from 1 December 1903 until 30 November 1906. Attached to the West African Regt., in Sierra Leone from 12 January 1907 to 3 July 1910. Re-joined the 2nd Manchesters, then at Mullingar, County Westmeath, Ireland, in July 1910. Appointed adjutant to the 6th Manchesters on 4 November 1911, and promoted to captain on 1 December 1911. Holberton was still serving with the battalion when it was mobilised in August 1914

Embarked from Southampton onboard HMT *Corsican* with the 6th Manchesters on 10 September, disembarking at Alexandria, Egypt, on the 26th. Served in Egypt until he embarked with the 1/6th Manchesters for Gallipoli onboard the SS *Derfflinger* on 3 May 1915, disembarking at W Beach on 6 May 1915. Took command of the battalion on 12 October, after his commanding officer was admitted to hospital, but was himself evacuated from the peninsula suffering from jaundice on 20 October. Twice Mentioned in Despatches for his service at Gallipoli (LG: 5 November 1915 and 28 January 1916).

I.—BIOGRAPHIES, OTHER UNITS

Promoted to brevet-major on 8 November 1915 (substantive 8 January 1916). He re-joined the division in Egypt in 1916, and served as brigade major to the 126th Brigade from the 5 April to 19 October 1916. Placed in command of the 1/5th Lancashire Fusiliers on 19 October 1916. He moved with that battalion to France in March 1917, and was promoted to brevet lieutenant-colonel on 3 June 1917.

When the Germans launched their offensive on 21 March 1918, the 1/5th Lancs Fusiliers were sent to defend the village of Gomiecourt. On 26 March, Holberton was inspecting defences and encouraging his men. Around 2:00 a.m., he was shot through the head and died instantly. He was buried close to where he fell and his grave was identified when the area was recaptured the following September. On 18 September 1918, almost 40 officers and many other ranks from both the 1/5th Lancashire Fusiliers and the 1/6th Manchesters attended his reinternment service, held in what is now the Achiet-Le-Grand Communal Cemetery Extension (grave IV.F.8).

Mentioned in Despatches a further three times. Awarded the Serbian Order of the White Eagle (with Swords) 4th Class.

Lieutenant-General Aylmer Gould Hunter-Weston, KCB, DSO
General Officer Commanding (GOC) 29th Division.
Later, GOC VIII Army Corps

GOC, 29th Division, from March 1915 to 24 May 1915. GOC, VIII Army Corps from 24 May, to his evacuation from the peninsula suffering from heat stroke on 20 July 1915. Known alternately as 'Hunter-Bunter' or the 'Butcher of Helles.' Much has been written about this controversial general, and some have questioned why Hunter-Weston, a Royal Engineer (who had never held a field command), should have been placed in command of an infantry division,  let alone one given such a demanding task. General William Marshall offered his own explanation. "To our great regret General Shaw left us. He was succeeded in command by General Hunter-Weston;

presumably because Hunter-Weston was a fluent French scholar and we were to act in close concert with the French during this adventure."¹

An undoubtedly courageous man, described by Hamilton as a "slashing man of action," many of Hunter-Weston's contemporaries however, held a different opinion. Major-General Edgerton, GOC, 52nd Division, had many run-ins with Hunter-Weston both on his attitude towards casualties, and his tendency to micro-manage his subordinates. Egerton later described the orders issued by Hunter-Weston for the 12 July battle:

> "The most detailed orders for the battle of July 12th were issued verbatim by Hunter-Weston commanding the Corps aided by his GSO1, Street—the first a Sapper and the latter a Gunner—they were absurdly voluminous orders, in fact they were silly and ludicrous. Anyone who doubts this assertion can turn them up and see—just the sort of rubbish that the "Scientific Corps" would issue. The Div'l Commander had simply to adopt them word for word..."²

Field Marshall Haig was even more damning, describing Hunter-Weston as "a rank amateur."

Major William Arthur Hutchinson
Officer Commanding (OC) 'W' Company, 1st Royal Munster Fusiliers

Was onboard the SS *River Clyde*, as OC, 'W' Company, 1st Royal Munster Fusiliers, when the ship ran aground at V Beach on 25 April 1915. Temporarily attached to the 1/5th Manchester Regt., at Helles, from 25 May. One of four officers who accompanied Brig-General W. Marshall, 87th Brigade Commander *(see entry)*, when sent by the newly promoted Lieut-General Hunter-Weston to 127th (Manchester) Brigade headquarters in order "to assist in training them in their duties."³

---

1 William Marshall, *Memories on Four Fronts* (London: Ernest Benn Ltd., 1929) p.45.
2 David Raw, *Gallipoli: The Egerton Diaries and Papers* (Warwick: Helion & Co., 2020) p.92.
3 VIII Army Corps, General Staff war diary, 25 May, 1915.

I.—BIOGRAPHIES, OTHER UNITS

Chaplain 4th Class (later 3rd Class) Rev., Edwin Thomas Kerby (MC)[1]

Chaplain to 1/7th Manchesters and 127th (Manchester) Brigade

Born in Aston, Warwickshire on 13 August 1877. Educated at King Edward's School, Birmingham. Matriculated into Clare College, Cambridge in 1896, he graduated with his BA in 1899 and gained his MA in 1903. Ordained deacon (Coventry for Worcester) in 1901; priest (Worcester) 1902; curate of St. Basil's, Deritend, Walsall, Birmingham 1901–03; curate of Langley, Worcestershire, 1903–04; curate of St. James's, Oldham, Lancashire, 1904–10. Appointed Chaplain 4th Class (with the rank of captain) Chaplains Department, Territorial Force, and attached to the 7th Manchesters on 10 March 1914. Volunteered for overseas service in August 1914. Embarked from Southampton onboard HMT *Grantully Castle* with the 7th Manchesters on 10 September 1914, disembarking at Alexandria, Egypt on 25th. When the 1/7th Manchesters were dispatched to Cyprus and the Sudan a few days later, he remained in Egypt, to act as chaplain to the Manchester Brigade. Embarked from Alexandria with the Manchester Brigade for Gallipoli on 3 May 1915, and landed at W Beach on 6 May 1915. Served at Helles until the 42nd Division left at the end of December 1915. Gerald B. Hurst, 1/7th Manchesters, wrote of him:

> "Nor could a Brigade have had a more gallant and untiring padre than Captain E. T. Kerby. He and Captain Farrow [the battalion medical officer] both won the Military Cross. Kerby must have said the burial service over the graves of nearly a thousand Manchesters at Gallipoli."[2]

Awarded the Military Cross (LG: 29608/3 June 1916) for his service at Gallipoli, and twice Mentioned in Despatches (LG: 10999/5 November 1915 and LG: 6952/13 July 1916). Served in Egypt from January 1916 until the 42nd Division embarked for the Western Front in March 1917. Continued to serve in France and Belgium for the duration of the war. Made temporary Chaplain 3rd class on 25 June 1919, whilst acting as Senior Chaplain to the Forces at Boulogne (substantive 1 January 1923).

1 CWCG records often show Kerby misspelled as Kirby.
2 Hurst, *With Manchesters in the East,* p.58.

LETTERS FROM HELLES

Major Henry Lewkenor Knight (CMG, DSO)
Brigade Major, 127th (Manchester) Brigade

Born at Foyhill near Litchfield, Staffordshire on 24 March 1874. Attended the Royal Military College Sandhurst in 1894. Commissioned into the Royal Irish Fusiliers on 10 October 1894, and promoted to lieutenant on 3 May 1898. Appointed acting adjutant to the 2nd Bn., The Royal Irish Fusiliers on August 1895, remaining in post until August 1899. Served with his regiment in South Africa 1899–1900, as a captain (substantive captain 1 May 1902) and on staff duties with the Mounted Infantry until invalided on 15 December 1900. Received the Queen's South Africa Medal with five clasps. Mentioned in Despatches (LG: 10 September 1901). Served as adjutant to the 1st Volunteer (City of Dundee) Bn., Royal Highlanders, 17 May 1901 to 15 August 1904. Appointed adjutant to the 4th Royal Irish Fusiliers on 19 May 1905. Seconded to the General Staff on 16 April 1912. Promoted to major on 21 January 1914, and appointed as brigade major to the Manchester Brigade on 5 August 1914.

Embarked from Southampton onboard HMT *Grantully Castle* with the Manchester Brigade headquarters on 10 September 1914, disembarking at Alexandria, Egypt on 25th. He served with the brigade in Egypt until it embarked for Gallipoli onboard SS *Derfflinger* on 3 May 1915, disembarking at W Beach, Helles on 6 May. Served as brigade major at Helles until made temporary lieutenant-colonel on 20 December 1915, and temporarily attached to the 125th (Fusilier) Brigade until 25 December. Described by Gerald B. Hurst, chronicler of the 1/7th Manchesters, as "a tower of strength when on Gallipoli."[1]

After the Manchester Brigade left Gallipoli, Knight was sent to Salonika where he was appointed GSO1 to the 10th Division, holding the post from 30 December 1915 to 15 June 1917. Made brevet lieutenant-colonel on 3 June 1916 (substantive 14 March 1917). Served as brigade commander, 80th Infantry Brigade from 16 June to 24 August 1917.

1 Hurst, *With Manchesters in the East*, p.5.

I.—BIOGRAPHIES, OTHER UNITS

Made temporary brigadier general on 16 June 1917. Served on the Staff of XVI Army Corps from 25 August 1917 to 24 February 1919. Created a Companion of the Distinguished Service Order (LG: 4 June 1917). Created CMG in 1918–19. Awarded the Order of the Redeemer 3rd Class, the Greek Military Cross, and the Greek Medal for Military Merit, 2nd Class. Five times Mentioned in Despatches. Promoted to brevet colonel on 3 June 1919 (substantive 4 August 1921). Retired as honorary brigadier general on 17 May 1929. Died 28 March 1945, aged 71, at Le Court, Liss, Petersfield, Hampshire.

Photo: HCD

Brigadier-General
Hon. Herbert Alexander Lawrence, KCMG
Brigade Commander,
127th (Manchester) Brigade

Born on 8 August 1861 at Southgate, London. Fourth son of Sir John Laird Mair Lawrence, later first Baron Lawrence (1811–79), British imperial statesman and Viceroy of India, 1864-9, and his wife, Harriette Katherine (1820–1917). Educated at Harrow School and the Royal Military College, Sandhurst.

Commissioned into 17th Lancers on 10 May 1882, where he served as adjutant from 13 May 1890 to 12 May 1894. Promoted captain on 2 February 1892. Attended Staff College at Camberley, and served as a Staff Captain (Intel.) at Army headquarters (HQ) from 1 September 1897 to 23 May 1898. Appointed Deputy Assistant Adjutant General (DAAG) Intelligence, at Army HQ on 24 May 1898 until 8 October 1899, when he was posted to South Africa to carry out the same role on the Intelligence Staff of Sir John French's cavalry division from 9 October 1899 to 5 February 1901. Promoted major on 22 November 1899, and to brevet lieutenant colonel on 29 November 1900. Acted as DAAG (Intel.) and Deputy Adjutant and Quarter Master General, Intelligence, from 6 February 1901 to 7 March 1902. Twice Mentioned in Despatches (LG:4 May 1900 and 8 Feb 1901). Received the Queen's South Africa Medal with six clasps and the King's South Africa Medal with two clasps. Returned to England with the 17th  Lancers in September 1902. Resigned his commission on 13 May 1903 (having been overlooked as commanding officer to the 17th Lancers in favour of Douglas Haig, then junior in service). He took up a career in banking and in 1907, became a partner in Glyn, Mills, Currie and Co., the bank in which his father-in-law was a senior partner.

At the outbreak of war, he was recalled from the Reserve of Officers and posted as GSO1 to the 2nd Yeomanry Division. Served with that division in Egypt until June 1915, when sent to Gallipoli to command the 127th (Manchester) Brigade on 21 June. Sent to Suvla in mid-August, and placed in command of the 53rd (Welsh) Division. He returned to Helles in late August and re-assumed command of the 127th (Manchester) Brigade. Promoted to major-general and placed in command of the 52nd Division on 17 September 1915. Appointed to oversee the embarkations for the evacuation of Helles. Twice Mentioned in Dispatches for his service on Gallipoli (LG: 5 November 1915 and 13 July 1916).

Moved with the 52nd Division to Egypt in 1916. Made temporary lieut-general. Achieved great success during the battle of Romani in early August 1916. After a disagreement regarding the planning of Palestine Campaign, he was sent to command the 71st Home Forces Division in England on 23 October 1916. Given command of the 66th (2nd East Lancashire) Territorial Division on 12 February 1917, and commanded them on the Western Front at Ypres in October 1917. Field Marshal Haig's command underwent major change during the winter of 1917–18. In January 1918, Lawrence briefly replaced Brig-General John Charteris as Haig's Chief Intelligence Officer, and on

I.—BIOGRAPHIES, OTHER UNITS

24 January 1918, was made Haig's Chief of the General Staff and retained this post throughout 1918. Promoted to lieut-general on 3 June 1918, and general on 3 June 1919, he retired later that year. He was made honorary colonel of the 6th Manchesters in 1925, a title he held until 1932.

His many honours included: Commander of Legion of Honour (1916); 2nd class Serbian order of Karageorge, with Swords (1916); Knight Commander of Bath (1917); French *Croix de Guerre* (1916); Belgium Croix de Guerre (1918); the American Distinguished Service Order (1918); Grand Cross St Benedict of Aviz (1918); Grand Cross Crown of Romania (1918); Grand Officer Legion of Honour (1919); *Grand Cordon* (Crown of Belgium); 1st Class Rising Sun Japan; and Knight Grand Cross (1926). Mentioned in Despatches a further six times.

After the war he returned to Glyn Mills & Co. as managing partner and was appointed chairman in 1934. Under Lawrence's leadership Glyn Mills & Co. became Britain's largest private bank. He died on 17 January 1943, aged 81, at Woodcock, Little Berkhamsted, Hertfordshire.

Brigadier-General Noel Lee, VD

Brigade Commander, 127th (Manchester) Brigade

Born in Altrincham on 23 December 1868, third son of Sir Joseph Lee. Educated at Eton College before going into the family textile business Tootal Broadhurst Lee and Co.

Prevented from joining the regulars by his father, he was commissioned as lieutenant into the 6th Lancashire Rifle Volunteers (2nd Volunteer Bn., The Manchester Regt., from 1888) on 25 December 1886. Promoted to captain on 1 February 1890, and to major in May 1901 (substantive 2nd February 1902). Made honorary lieutenant-colonel and placed in command of the battalion on 17 May 1906. Awarded the Volunteer Officers Decoration (VD) in June 1906, and made honorary colonel in 1907. He retained his rank and seniority on the formation of the Territorial Force on 1 April 1908, when the battalion was redesignated the 6th Bn., The Manchester Regiment. Member of the Territorial Force (TF) Advisory council and the

East Lancashire TF Association. Relinquished command of the 6th Manchesters on being placed in command of the Manchester Brigade (the first territorial officer to command a brigade) in September 1911. Made substantive colonel on 10 March 1914, and temporary brigadier-general on 5 August 1914.

Volunteered for foreign service in late August 1914. Embarked from Southampton onboard HMT *Grantully Castle* with the Manchester Brigade headquarters on 10 September 1914, disembarking at Alexandria, Egypt on 25th. Remained in Egypt until he embarked with his brigade headquarters for Gallipoli onboard SS *Derfflinger* on 3 May 1915, disembarking at W Beach on 6 May 1915. Seriously wounded by a shrapnel ball while in his advanced headquarters in the Redoubt Line around noon on 4 June. Evacuated of the peninsula on 4 or 5 June, arriving at Malta around 10–11 June, his condition seemed to improve, but he suffered a haemorrhage and died, age 48, on 22 June 1915, at the Blue Sisters Hospital in St Julians. Buried in the Pieta Military Cemetery in Malta, Grave XXV.4.

Widely regarded as one of the division's best commanders, when Brig-General William Marshall *(see entry)* was sent by Hunter-Weston to 'tutor' Lee in late May 1915, and found Lee to be "a really good Brigadier—and very much liked and trusted by his officers and men." Lee's divisional commander, Major-General Douglas wrote of him:

> "He is a very great loss to the Brigade, he has done splendidly—the most gallant, hardworking, thorough leader that I had, and I don't know how I shall replace him. I am sure that I shall not be able to find his equal."

Mention in Despatches (LG: 5 November 1915).

I.—BIOGRAPHIES, OTHER UNITS

Brigadier-General Sir William Raine Marshall (GCMG, KCB, KCSI, CB)
General Officer Commanding (GOC) 87th Brigade
GOC, 42nd Division

Born 29 October 1865 in Stranton near Hartlepool, County Durham. Educated at Repton School and the Royal Military College, Sandhurst. Commissioned as lieutenant into the 1st Bn., The Sherwood Foresters (Derbyshire Regt.) on 30 January 1886. Served in India in the campaigns of Malakand and Tirah in 1897–8. Present at the storming of the Dargai Heights and the capture of the Sampagha and Arhanga Passes. Awarded the Indian Frontier Medal of 1895 with two clasps. Served in South Africa, in command of a Mounted Infantry company, then a battalion, and finally a Mounted Column (of several thousand men) from May 1900 to the end of hostilities on 31 May 1902. Twice Mentioned in Despatches (LG: 9 July and 10 September 1901) and received the Queen's South Africa Medal with three clasps, and the King's South Africa Medal with two clasps.

Promoted to brevet lieutenant-colonel on 26 June 1902, made substantive major on 7 December 1904, and brevet colonel on 26 June 1908. Promoted to substantive lieutenant colonel and given command of the 1st Sherwood Foresters on 11 February 1912. Shortly after the outbreak of war, Marshall and his battalion were recalled from India. They arrived in England on 2 October 1914 and were attached to the 8th Division, which moved to France on 5 November. Mentioned in Despatches (LG: 17 February 1915). Recalled to England in February 1915 to command the 87th Brigade, 29th Division (then at Rugby, and earmarked for operations at the Dardanelles).

LETTERS FROM HELLES

Landed at X Beach, shortly after the Royal Fusiliers on 25 April 1915. Charged with pressing the division's attack in the 1st Battle of Krithia. Commanded the 87th Brigade during the Second Battle of Krithia. Attached to the 127th (Manchester) Brigade from 25 May to 3 June 1915 to 'tutor' its commander, Brig-General Noel Lee. This he considered "a most unpleasant duty," and found Lee to be "a really good Brigadier and very much liked and trusted by his officers and men." Marshall was also impressed by "the appearance and general efficiency" of the 1/5th and 1/6th Manchesters.[1]

Although promoted to major-general mid-June, he continued to command the 87th Brigade. Placed in temporary command of the 42nd Division on 24 July, returning to his brigade on 8 August. Placed in temporary command of the 29th Division on 15 August, and moved with the division to Suvla on 19 August. After General de Lisle re-assumed command of the 29th Division on 23 August, Marshall was placed in command of the 53rd (Welsh) Division and remained in command until the division was evacuated in mid-December. Marshall, however, remained at Suvla to assist in preparations for the final evacuation. Mentioned in Dispatches thrice (LG: 5 August 1915, 5 November 1915, and 13 July 1916).

After Gallipoli, Marshall was sent to command the 27th Division at Salonika. Promoted to temporary lieutenant-general in early September 1916, and placed in command of the III (Indian) Army Corps on the Mesopotamian front. Participated in the capture of Kut-al-Amara in February 1917, and in the capture of Baghdad the following month. On General Sir Frederick Maude's death, Marshall succeeded him as Commander in Chief of the Mesopotamia Expeditionary Force, and in this capacity accepted the surrender of the Ottoman Army at Mosul on 30 October 1918. Appointed post-war to command the Southern Army in India, remaining in post until 1923. After retiring in 1924, Marshall wrote his memoir, *Memories of Four Fronts,* which was published in 1929.

---

1 Marshall, *Memories on Four Fronts*, p.78.

I.—BIOGRAPHIES, OTHER UNITS

A modest, methodical, and highly capable soldier, Marshall's self-confessed lack of military ambition had seen him sidelined for the greater part of his career. But given the opportunity to command, he showed his true worth, and in the space of six years, went from commanding a company of two hundred men, to an Army with a ration strength of nearly half a million. Marshall was rewarded with numerous British honours: KCB, KCSI, GCMG, together with the White Eagle of Serbia, 2nd Class with Swords, the *Legion d'Honneur* and the Chinese order of Wen-hu. Mentioned in Dispatches a further three times (nine times in all). He died in France on 1 June 1939, aged 73.

Captain Thomas Nevill Carleton Nevill
1/6th Manchesters
Staff Captain, 127th (Manchester) Brigade

Born on 12 November 1879, in Eastbourne, Sussex. Originally commissioned into the 4th Volunteer Bn., The Cheshire Regt., around the turn of the 19th Century. Promoted to lieutenant on 15 May 1901, he later transferred into the 6th Manchesters. Appointed Staff Captain to the Manchester Brigade, and probably embarked from Southampton onboard HMT *Grantully Castle* with the Manchester Brigade headquarters on 10 September 1914, disembarking at Alexandria, Egypt on the 25th. In November he was employed for a time "processing German prisoners on ships in port" in Alexandria.[1] Remained in Egypt until he embarked with brigade headquarters for Gallipoli onboard SS *Derfflinger* on 3 May 1915, disembarking at W Beach on 6 May. Nevill was probably with this brigade commander, Brig-General Noel Lee *(see entry)* when Lee was wounded in his forward observation position, in the Redoubt Line on 4 June 1915.[2] Still serving as Staff Captain to 127th (Manchester Brigade) when Colonel Darington was temporarily in command of the brigade in July 1915. Survived the war.

1 Niall Cherry, *I Shall not find his equal*
(Knutsford: Fleur de Lys Publishing, 2001) p.10.
2 Ibid, p.38.

LETTERS FROM HELLES

Lieutenant-Colonel Charles Raymond Pilkington, CMG

Second in Command, and later CO, 1/6th Manchesters

Born into a wealthy mining and glass manufacturing family in the Haydock area of Lancashire on 9 October 1875, Pilkington was commissioned into the 2nd Volunteer Bn., The Manchester Regiment on 12 July 1899. Served as a lieutenant with the 77th Imperial Yeomanry in the South African War, 1900–01. Took part in the relief of Mafeking, and was present during operations in the Transvaal in May and June 1900; in the Transvaal, east of Pretoria, July and August 1900; in Orange River Colony, September to 29 November 1900; and again from 30 November to January 1901. Received the Queen's South Africa medal with four clasps. Promoted to captain on 16 February 1901, and made honorary lieutenant in the Army on 19 August 1901. He retained his rank and seniority on the formation of the Territorial Force on 1 April 1908, when the battalion was redesignated the 6th Bn., The Manchester Regiment. Promoted to major on 24 July 1908, and was Second in Command of the 6th Manchesters at the outbreak of war.

Volunteered for overseas service end of August 1914. Embarked from Southhampton onboard HMT *Corsican* with the 6th Manchesters on 10 September, disembarking at Alexandria, Egypt, on the 26th. Served in Egypt until he embarked with the 1/6th Manchesters for Gallipoli onboard the SS *Derfflinger* on 3 May 1915, disembarking at W Beach on 6 May 1915. Made temporary lieutenant-colonel on 1 June 1915, and in August took command of the 6th and 8th Manchesters when the two battalions combined for their attack on the 7 August. Continued to command the 6th Manchesters until evacuated sick on 12 October 1915. Created CMG (LG: 8 November 1915) and Mentioned in Dispatches (LG: 5 November 1915). He re-joined the battalion in Egypt in 1916, and served with it throughout the rest of the war. Died on 27 October 1938, aged 63.

I.—BIOGRAPHIES, OTHER UNITS

Captain (Dr) Joseph Marshall Postlethwaite
1st East Lancashire Field Ambulance, RAMC (TF)

Commissioned as lieutenant into the 1st East Lancashire Field Ambulance, RAMC (TF) on 2 February 1910. Promoted to captain on 2 August 1913. Volunteered for overseas service end of August 1914. Embarked from Southhampton onboard SS *Atlantian* with the 1st East Lancashire Field Ambulance on 10 September 1914, disembarking at Alexandria, Egypt on 25th. Remained in Egypt until embarked for Gallipoli on 3 May 1915, disembarking at W Beach, Helles on 6th. Present when Colonel Darlington was evacuated sick on 30 September, and may have remained at Helles until the 42nd Division left at the end of December 1915. Appointed as a 'serving brother' to the Order of St. John of Jerusalem on 22 December 1933.

Lieutenant-Colonel Lord Rochdale (George Kemp)
Commanding Officer (CO) 1/6th Lancs Fusiliers. Temporary Brigade Commander 126th (East Lancs) Brigade and 127th (Manchester) Brigade

Born in Rochdale on 9 June 1866. Educated at Mill Hill and Shrewsbury schools, Balliol College Oxford, and Trinity College Cambridge. After University he entered the family business of Kelsall and Kemp (flannel manufacturers) and pursued an interest in politics. Commissioned into the Duke of Lancaster's Yeomanry on 3 October 1888, and promoted to Captain on the 18 July 1891. As the Unionist Party candidate, he was elected Member of Parliament (MP) for Heywood in the 1895 election, and retained his seat in the autumn 1900 election (while serving in South Africa 1900–1902).

Rochdale served with the Duke of Lancaster's Own Yeomanry in the South African War. Promoted to major on 20 September 1901. Placed in command of the 32nd Bn Imperial Yeomanry on 13 January 1902, and promoted to lieutenant-colonel on 22 January 1902.

Twice Mentioned in Despatches (LG: 8 February and September 1901) and received the Queen's South Africa medal with two clasps. Resigned his commission on 22 January 1904. Knighted in the King's Birthday Honours list in 1909. In 1910 was again elected MP, as Liberal candidate for North West Manchester, but resigned his seat in 1912, in protest against Liberal Party policies. Created Baronet Rochdale for services to politics in the King's Birthday Honours list in 1913.

Became chairman of the East Lancashire Territorial Association, on the creation of the Territorial Force, on 1 April 1908. Placed in command of the 6th Lancashire Fusiliers on 13 December 1909.

Volunteered for overseas service at the end of August 1914. Embarked from Southhampton onboard SS *Saturnia* with the 6th Lancashire Fusiliers on 10 September 1914, disembarking at Alexandria, Egypt on the 25th. Remained in Egypt until embarked for Gallipoli with his battalion on 2 May 1915, disembarked at Helles on 5 May 1915 (the day before the second Battle of Krithia). The following day he led his battalion in an attack across Gully Spur, displaying great personal courage as he encouraged his inexperienced troops. As one of the division's most experienced commanding officers he was chosen to command the 126th (East Lancs) Brigade from 21 May to 3 June, and the 127th (Manchester) Brigade from 4 June (relieving Colonel Heys, who had taken command of the brigade shortly after Brig.-General Lee was wounded) to 21 June 1915.

A vociferous critic of the way the campaign was being conducted, he used his House of Lords privilege (and against the advice of his superiors) to leave Helles for England in early July. On 26 July 1915 he met with the Prime Minister, Herbert Henry Asquith, the 1st

I.—BIOGRAPHIES, OTHER UNITS

Lord of the Admiralty, Arthur Balfour, and the Secretary of State for the Colonies (and leader of the opposition) Andrew Bonar Law and submitted a detailed, and highly critical report, fully aware of the damage he was doing to his own career. He returned to Gallipoli in early August and was again placed in command of the 127th (Manchester) Brigade from 19 to 26 August. He was evacuated from the peninsula on 29 September suffering from para-typhoid and phlebitis. On his recovery he was placed on the Reserve of Officers List, never again to hold an active service command.

Beloved by the men of his battalion, one of them, Private Charles Watkins, wrote:

> "Maybe it is that a Territorial Unit such as ours feel closer attachment to its Commanding Officer than does a Regular Unit, COs of regular units tend to get posted away to other units. A CO of a Territorial Unit like ours was the same CO we had in peace-time, as well as in war-time. We went abroad with him as a close-knit town unit. Our comrades were the same boys we played with as kids, grown up with, worked with and scrapped with. So it's natural that we should all feel tightly attached. And the CO himself was, as one of our chaps said, 'one of us, like—a chap from the same town.'

> "Beloved in war by his gang of boy soldiers. Beloved, too in the days before the war, by our fathers. They, these older chaps, our dads, loved him mainly because he was all that tradition said a real live lord should be—hail-fellow-well-met, flamboyant, good-hearted, 100% for King, country, and British Empire."[1]

Rochdale's representations in July ensured his significant contribution to the campaign, and many instances of personal bravery, went completely unrecognised (without even a Mention in Despatches). He died in Lingholm near Keswick, Cumberland, on 24 March 1945, aged 78.

---

[1] Charles Watkins, *Lost Endeavour* (Little Gully Publishing, 2023) p.38.

Captain Thomas Scott Syers (MC)
147th Brigade Ammunition Column, Royal Field Artillery

Born 5 January 1883. Commissioned into the Royal Artillery on 21 December 1900, and promoted to lieutenant on 26 September 1903. Transferred from the Royal Garrison Artillery to the Royal Field Artillery and made temporary captain on 14 October 1914. Placed in command of 147th Brigade, RFA, Ammunition Column, 29th Division, and landed with it at Helles around 29 April 1915. Later commanded the Dumezil Trench Mortar Battery, which was often deployed in support of 42nd Division operations. Syers set up his mortars in the 5th Manchesters forward trenches during the Battle of 6/7th August, and in the days that followed, and was awarded the Military Cross (LG: 29344 / 29 October 1915) for his actions. His citation reads:

> "For conspicuous gallantry and determination on the 9th August, 1915, in the Gallipoli Peninsula. He was in charge of some mortars, and, although heavily shelled, succeeded in totally destroying a hostile trench, and only ceased firing when he and his mortars were buried through the parapet being blown in. Again, on the 24th August, when bombarding the enemy, three shells bursting prematurely, stunned him, but when recovered, he continued to fire and demolished the enemy's trench. He was then taken to hospital suffering from severe shock."

Later wounded and evacuated off the peninsula to England. Promoted to captain on 3 November 1915, and made acting major on 5 April 1917. Attached to 157th Brigade, RFA, and placed in command of D Battery in France. He died in England, on 14 November 1918, age 35, and is buried in Hove Old Cemetery, Grave C.C.2.

Lieutenant-Colonel Arthur Wyndham Tufnell, CMG
General Staff Officer 1st Class (GSO1)
42nd (East Lancashire) Division, General Staff

Born 16 February 1872. Commissioned into The Queen's Royal West Surrey Regiment on 3 December 1891. Promoted to lieutenant

I.—BIOGRAPHIES, OTHER UNITS

on 16 March 1896. Served on the north-west frontier of India, 1897–8, including the Tirah Campaign, earning the India General Service Medal with two clasps. Served in the South Africa with his regiment from 21 October 1899, and was wounded on 15 December 1899 at Colenso. Promoted to captain on 7 May 1900. Served on the Staff of Brigadier-General E.O.F. Hamilton, CB, in South Africa, 1901–1902. Twice Mentioned in Despatches (LG: 8 February and 10 September 1901) and awarded the Queen's South Africa Medal with six clasps, and the King's South Africa Medal with two clasps. Appointed GSO2 to the East Lancashire Division Staff on 12 April 1912, GSO1 on 4 August 1914, and promoted to temporary lieutenant-colonel on the 20th.

Embarked from Southhampton onboard HMT *Deseado* with divisional headquarters on 10 September, disembarking at Alexandria, Egypt, on the 25th. Served as GSO1 in Egypt, until embarked from Alexandria with divisional headquarters onboard HT *Crispin* on 5 May 1915, disembarking at W Beach, Helles with General Douglas, around 3:30 pm on 9 May 1915. Wounded in the arm walking along a communication trench on 30 June 1915, but remained in post at Helles until he embarked with divisional headquarters for Mudros on 30 December 1915. Appointed Brigade Commander of the 126th (East Lancashire) Infantry Brigade on 10 January 1916. Commanded the brigade in Egypt from January 1916. Created CMG (LG: 1 February 1916) and made *Chevalier* of the Legion of Honour (LG: 20671 Sup / 24 February 1916). Moved with the brigade to France in March 1917, and continued to serve as brigade commander in France and Belgium until 14 September 1917. Appointed GSO1 to the 68th Division on 20 October 1917. Appointed Brigadier General, General Staff (B-GGS) to the XXIII Army Corps (Home Forces) on 15 October 1918. Mentioned in Despatches a further three times (LG: 5 November 1915, 28 January 1916 and 13 July 1916). Tufnell survived the war but was murdered while on a train to Simla, India, on 17 May 1920, age 48. He is buried at Bhowanipore Cemetery, Kolkata, Kolkata District, West Bengal, India, Plot O.J.12.

APPENDIX J.—ORDER OF BATTLE & FIELD STATE 42ND (EAST LANCASHIRE) DIVISION 2–5 MAY 1915

Showing all units that embarked for Gallipoli.

Details of personnel and appointments are taken from the 42nd Division War Diary—Appendix 37—Order of Battle 29 May 1915, with the exception of the 1/9th Manchesters' C.O., Lieutenant Colonel D.H. Wade, who had been wounded and evacuated by this date.

Divisional Headquarters

GOC, Major General William Douglas, CB, DSO
Captain H.T. Cawley, MP, ADC
Lieutenant J.W. Fry, ADC
Lieutenant Colonel A.W. Tufnell, GSO 1
Lieutenant Colonel F.A. Earle, GSO 2
Captain S.H. Kershaw, GSO 3
Colonel E.S. Herbert, AA & QMG
Captain R.S. Allen, DAA & QMG
Major R.J. Slaughter, DAQMG
Colonel J. Bentley-Mann, ADMS
Captain C.M. Drew, DADMS
Captain Briercliffe, Sanitary Officer
Lieutenant Colonel T. Marriott, ADVS
Captain J. Magill, VO
Major O.R.E. Milman, DADOS
Captain T.B. Forwood, APM

J. — 42ND DIVISION

Divisional Signal Company

Major A.W. Lawford

Divisional Artillery

Due to the lack of space for artillery at Helles, only the 5th Lancs Battery and two guns of the 6th Lancs Battery were landed, all other batteries and guns being returned to Egypt.

1/1st East Lancs Brigade RFA

    4th Lancs Battery
    5th Lancs Battery (grouped with 29th Div. Artillery)
        Major J.C. Browning

6th Lancs Battery

    1st Ammunition Column
    2nd Ammunition Column
    1/3rd East Lancs Brigade RFA
    18th Lancs Battery
    19th Lancs Battery
    20th Lancs Battery
    3rd Ammunition Column

Divisional Engineers

Lieutenant Colonel S.L. Tenant, CRE

  1/1st East Lancs Field Company
        Major J.H. Mousley

  1/2nd East Lancs Field Company
        Major L.F. Wells

125TH (LANCASHIRE FUSILIERS) INFANTRY BRIGADE

The main recruiting centre for each of the division's infantry battalions is shown in brackets.

Brigadier General H.C. Frith, CB
Brevet Major A.J. Allardyce, Brigade Major
Captain J.C. Kenyon, Staff Captain

1/5th Bn Lancashire Fusiliers (Bury)
Lieutenant Colonel J. Isherwood, VD

1/6th Bn Lancashire Fusiliers (Rochdale)
Lieutenant Colonel Lord Rochdale

1/7th Bn Lancashire Fusiliers (Salford)
Lieutenant Colonel A.F. Maclure, TD

1/8th Bn Lancashire Fusiliers (Salford)
Lieutenant Colonel J.A. Fallows, TD

126TH (EAST LANCASHIRE) INFANTRY BRIGADE

Brigadier General D.G. Prendergast, CMG
Major C.J. Hickie, Brigade Major
Captain T.C. Robinson, Staff Captain

1/4th Bn East Lancs Regt. (Blackburn)
Lieutenant Colonel F.D. Robinson, VD

1/5th Bn East Lancs Regt. (Burnley)
Lieutenant Colonel W.E. Sharples, TD

1/9th Bn Manchester Regt. (Ashton under Lyne)
Lieutenant Colonel D.H. Wade

1/10th Bn Manchester Regt. (Oldham)
Lieutenant Colonel J.B. Rye, VD

J.—42ND DIVISION

127TH (MANCHESTER) INFANTRY BRIGADE

Brigadier General Noel Lee, VD
Major H.L. Knight, Brigade Major
Captain T.C. Nevill, Staff Captain

- 1/5th Bn Manchester Regt. (Wigan)
  Lieutenant Colonel H.C. Darlington
- 1/6th Bn Manchester Regt. (Stretford—Manchester)
  Major C.R. Pilkington
- 1/7th Bn Manchester Regt. (Manchester city centre)
  Lieutenant Colonel H.E. Gresham, TD
- 1/8th Bn Manchester Regt. (Ardwick—Manchester)
  Lieutenant Colonel W.G. Heys, TD

EAST LANCS DIVISIONAL TRAIN A.S.C.

Due to lack of space at Helles only No. 2 Company was allowed to land with the division. The other three companies were then sent back to Egypt.

Major A. England

- No. 1 (Headquarters) Company
- No. 2 (Lancs Fusiliers) Company
  Major A. England
- No. 3 (East Lancs) Company
- No. 4 (Manchester) Company

DIVISIONAL ROYAL ARMY MEDICAL CORPS

Although the 1/1st and the 1/3rd Field Ambulances both landed with the division, only C Section and part of B Section of the 1/2nd Field Ambulance landed at Helles on 10 May, with the remainder landing on 17 June 1915.

- 1/1st Field Ambulance
  Lieutenant Colonel H.G. Parker
- 1/2nd Field Ambulance
- 1/3rd Field Ambulance
  Lieutenant Colonel W.M. Steinthal

Summary of Arms
on Embarkation for Gallipoli

	Officers	Other Ranks	Guns	MGs
Headquarters & Signal Coy	25	249	—	—
Artillery	57	1,257	24	—
Engineers	15	394	—	—
Infantry	386	10,830	—	24
RAMC	30	644	—	—
ASC	24	313	—	—
Total	537	13,687	24	24

Summary of Arms
for 30 September 1915

	Officers	Other Ranks	Guns	MGs
Headquarters & Signal Coy	18	220	—	—
Artillery	29	497	26	—
Engineers	17	300	—	—
Infantry	133	4,714	—	24
RAMC	19	478	—	—
ASC	8	101	—	—
Total	224	6,319	26	24

The loss in the division's field strength by 30 September is particularly significant given the above figure includes infantry reinforcements of approximately 100 officers and 3,500 other ranks. The 18th Battery RFA and the 1/2nd West Lancashire Field Company RE had also joined the division at Gallipoli.

RECOMMENDED READING

Aspinall-Oglander, C.F., and Archibald F. Becke, eds., *Military Operations, Gallipoli, History of the Great War Based on Official Documents / by Direction of the Historical Section, Committee on Imperial Defence* (London: William Heinemann, 1929–1932)

Behrend, Arthur, *Make Me a Soldier: A Platoon Commander in Gallipoli* (London: Eyre & Spottiswoode, 1961)

Best, Kenneth, and Gavin Roynon, *A Chaplain at Gallipoli: The Great War Diaries of Kenneth Best* (London: Simon & Schuster, 2011)

Bigwood, George, *The Lancashire Fighting Territorials* (London: 'Country Life' & George Newnes, 1916)

Bonner, Robert (ed.), *Great Gable to Gallipoli – The Diary of Lieutenant Colonel Claude S Worthington DSO, 5 October 1914 – 25 September 1916. 6th Battalion The Manchester Regiment* (Knutsford, Cheshire: Fleur de Lys Publishers, 2004)

Bonner, Robert, *Volunteer Infantry of Ashton-under-Lyne 1859–1971* (Knutsford: Fleur de Lys Publishers, 2005)

Campbell, Captain G.L., *The Manchesters* (London: Picture Advertising Co. Ltd, 1916)

Chambers, Stephen, *Walking Gallipoli* (Barnsley, South Yorkshire: Pen & Sword, 2019)

—, *Krithia: Gallipoli* (Barnsley, South Yorkshire: Pen & Sword, 2021)

Cherry, Niall, *I Shall Not Find His Equal: The Life of Brigadier-General Noel Lee, The Manchester Regiment* (Knutsford, Cheshire: Fleur de Lys Publishing, 2001)

Darlington, Daisy, Phillips, Margaret (ed.), *The memoirs of Daisy Darlington Volume I* (Private publication, 1987)

Darlington, Hugh, *Henry Clayton Darlington, The Wigan Volunteers, and the 5th Battalion Manchester Regiment* (unpublished)

Derbyshire, G., *A Wigan Military Chronicle, Volume II* (unpublished)

Gibbon, Frederick P., *The 42nd (East Lancashire) Division: 1914–1918* (London: Country Life, 1920)

Grundy, Jim, *Hell & Confusion: Gallipoli Day-by-Day, Vol. 1: 'Alive with Death', August 1914–April 1915* (Mosman, NSW: Little Gully Publishing, 2024)

Hamilton, General Sir Ian, *Gallipoli Diary* (London: E. Arnold, 1920)

Hart, Peter, *Gallipoli* (Oxford: Oxford University Press, 2011)

Hartley, John, *6th Battalion, the Manchester Regiment in the Great War: Not a Rotter in the Lot* (Barnsley: Pen & Sword, 2010)

Hurst, Gerald B., *With Manchesters in the East* (Manchester: The University Press, 1918)

Purdy, Martin, and Ian Dawson, *The Gallipoli Oak* (Ramsbottom, Lancashire: Moonraker Publishing, 2013)

Riley, Alec, edited by Michael Crane, Bernard de Broglio, *Egypt Diary 1914–1915* (Mosman, NSW: Little Gully Publishing, 2022)

—, *Gallipoli Diary 1915* (Mosman, NSW: Little Gully Publishing, 2021)

Snelling, Stephen, *VCs of the First World War, Gallipoli* (Stroud: The History Press, 1995)

Van Emden, Richard, and Stephen Chambers, *Gallipoli: The Dardanelles Disaster in Soldiers' Words and Photographs* (London: Bloomsbury, 2015)

Watkins, Charles, edited by Michael Crane, Bernard de Broglio, *Lost Endeavour: A survivor's account of the ill-fated Gallipoli Campaign* (Mosman, NSW: Little Gully Publishing, 2023)

Westlake, Ray, *British Regiments at Gallipoli* (Barnsley, South Yorkshire: Pen & Sword, 2004)

Westlake, Ray, *The Territorials 1908–1914* (Barnsley, South Yorkshire: Pen & Sword, 2011)

Williams, Orlo, edited by Rhys Crawley, Stephen Chambers and Ashleigh Brown, *Inside GHQ: The Gallipoli Diary of Captain Orlo Williams* (Mosman, NSW: Little Gully Publishing, 2025)

'HCD, Sanders.'
Darlington with Captain J.M.B. Sanders (right),
Adjutant of the 1/5th Manchesters.

ABBREVIATIONS AND ACRONYMS

2/ic	Second-in-command
2/Lt	Second Lieutenant
75s	French quick-firing 75 mm field guns
AAA	Used in signals to denote a full stop or separate phrases, similar to STOP in a telegram
AA & QMG	Assistant Adjutant & Quartermaster General
ADC	Aide-de-Camp
Adjt.	Adjutant
ADMS	Assistant Director of Medical Services
ADVS	Assistant Director of Veterinary Services
ANZAC	Australian and New Zealand Army Corps
APM	Assistant Provost Marshal
ASC	Army Service Corps
Bde	Brigade
BEF	British Expeditionary Force
Bn., Bttn.	Battalion
B-GGS	Brigadier-General, General Staff
CB	Companion of the Most Honourable Order of the Bath
CEO	*Corps Expéditionnaire d'Orient* (French Expeditionary Corps)
CLB	Church Lads Brigade
CMG	Companion of the Most Distinguished Order of St Michael and St George
CO	Commanding Officer
Coy., Co.	Company
CRE	Commander, Royal Engineers
CSM	Company Sergeant-Major
CWCG	Commonwealth War Graves Commission
DA	Divisional Artillery
DAA & QMG	Deputy Assistant Adjutant & Quartermaster General
DAAG	Deputy Assistant Adjutant-General
DADMS	Deputy Assistant Director of Medical Services
DADOS	Deputy Assistant Director of Ordnance Services
DAQMG	Deputy Assistant Quartermaster General

ABBREVIATIONS & ACRONYMS

DCM	Distinguished Conduct Medal
Div.	Division
DLI	Durham Light Infantry
DL	Deputy Lieutenant
DSO	Distinguished Service Order
EG	*Edinburgh Gazette*
FA	Field Ambulance
FOO	Forward Observing Officer (for artillery)
GCB	Knight Grand Cross of the Most Honourable Order of the Bath
GCMG	Knight Grand Cross of the Most Distinguished Order of St Michael and St George
GCVO	Knight Grand Cross of the Royal Victorian Order
Gen.	General
GHQ	General Headquarters
Gib	Gibraltar
GOC	General Officer Commanding
GSO1 / GSO2	General Staff Officer (1st and 2nd Grade)
HCD	Henry Clayton Darlington (author's initials)
HE	High Explosive
HMS	His Majesty's Ship
HMT	His Majesty's Transport
HQ	Headquarters
HT	Hired Transport (civilian ship hired for military use)
i/c	In command of
Inf.	Infantry
IWGC	Imperial War Graves Commission
K.'s Army	Kitchener's Army
KCB	Knight Commander of the Most Honourable Order of the Bath
KCMG	Knight Commander of the Most Distinguished Order of St Michael and St George
KCSI	Knight Commander of the Order of the Star of India
KOSB	King's Own Scottish Borderers
K St. J.	Knight of the Most Venerable Order of the Hospital of St. John of Jerusalem
Lancs	Lancashire
LG	*London Gazette*

Lieut. / Lt.	Lieutenant
Lt-Col.	Lieutenant-Colonel
Lt-Gen.	Lieutenant-General
MC	Military Cross
MG	Machine Gun
MGC	Machine Gun Corps
MO	Medical Officer
MP	Member of Parliament
MRG	Message
NCO	Non-Commissioned Officer
OBE	Officer of the Most Excellent Order of the British Empire
OC	Officer Commanding
OTC	Officers' Training Corps
Pte	Private
QM	Quartermaster
QMS	Quartermaster Sergeant
RAF	Royal Air Force
RAMC	Royal Army Medical Corps
RE	Royal Engineers
Regt.	Regiment
Rev.	Reverend
RA	Royal Artillery
RFA	Royal Field Artillery
RFC	Royal Flying Corps
RMLI	Royal Marine Light Infantry
RND	Royal Naval Division
RSM	Regimental Sergeant Major
SA	South Africa (generally referring to the Second Boer War)
SS	Steamship
T.'s	Territorial soldiers
TD	Territorial Decoration
TF	Territorial Force
VC	Victoria Cross
VD	Volunteer Officers' Decoration
VO	Veterinary Officer

MAPS

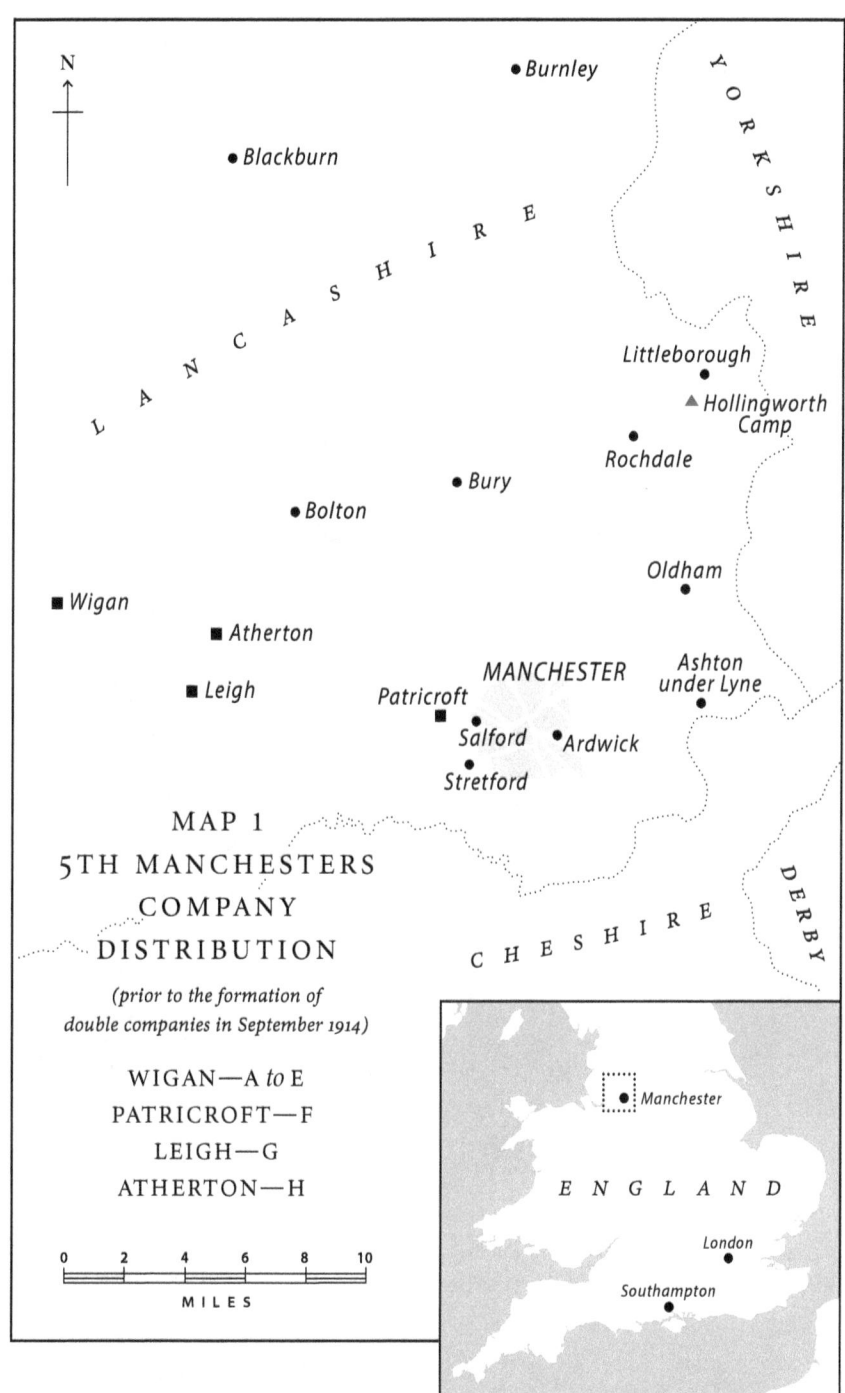

259

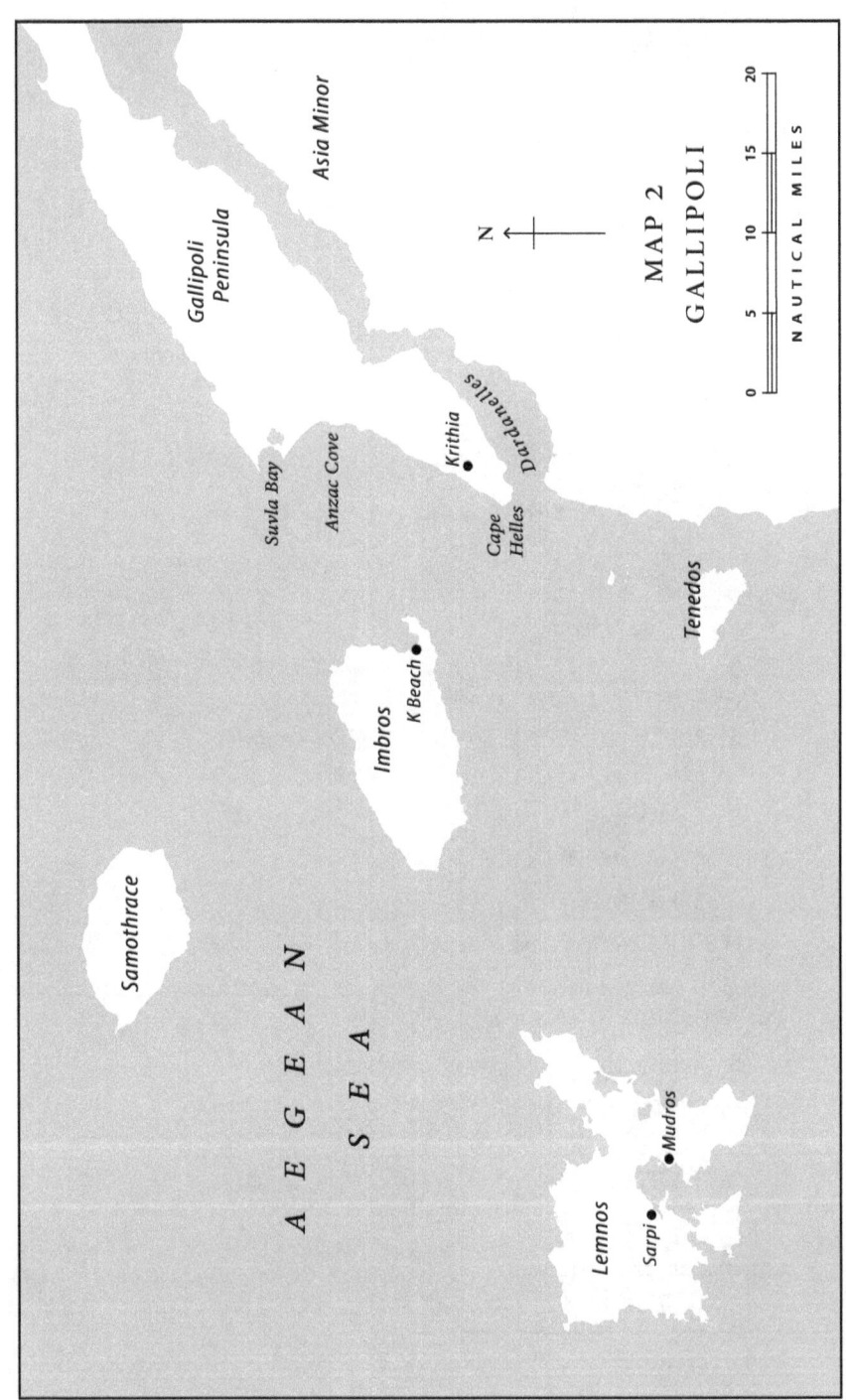

MAPS

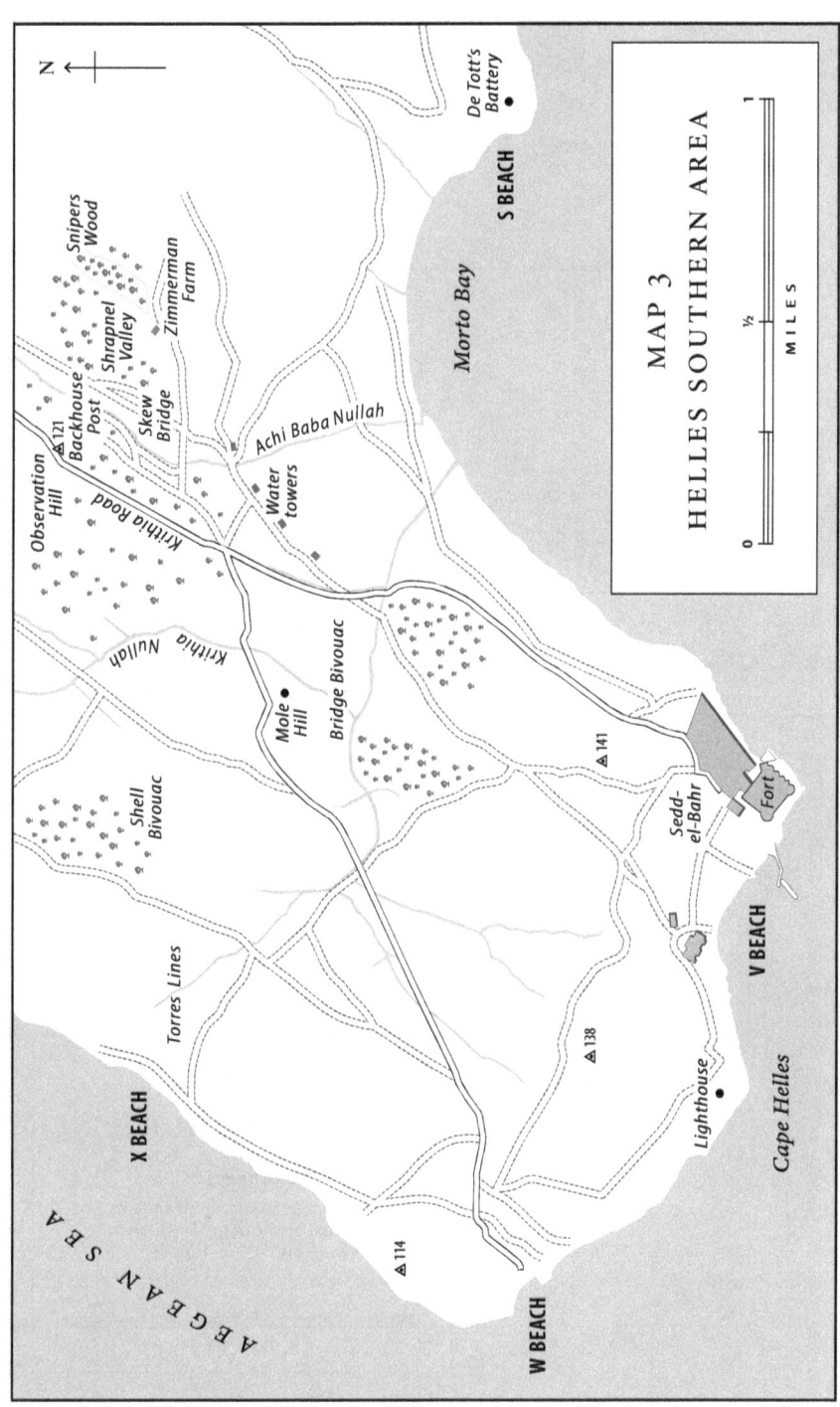

MAP 3
HELLES SOUTHERN AREA

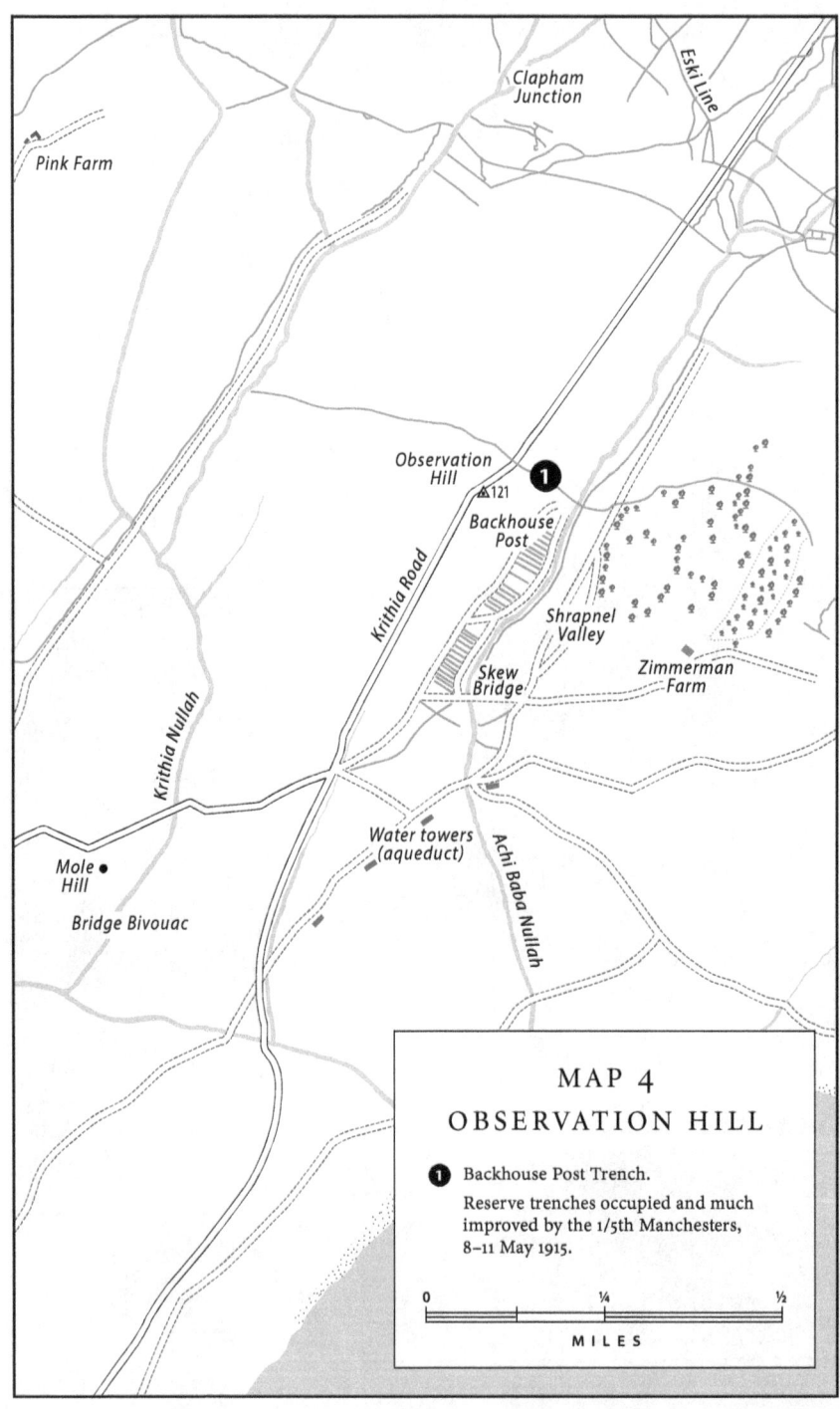

MAPS

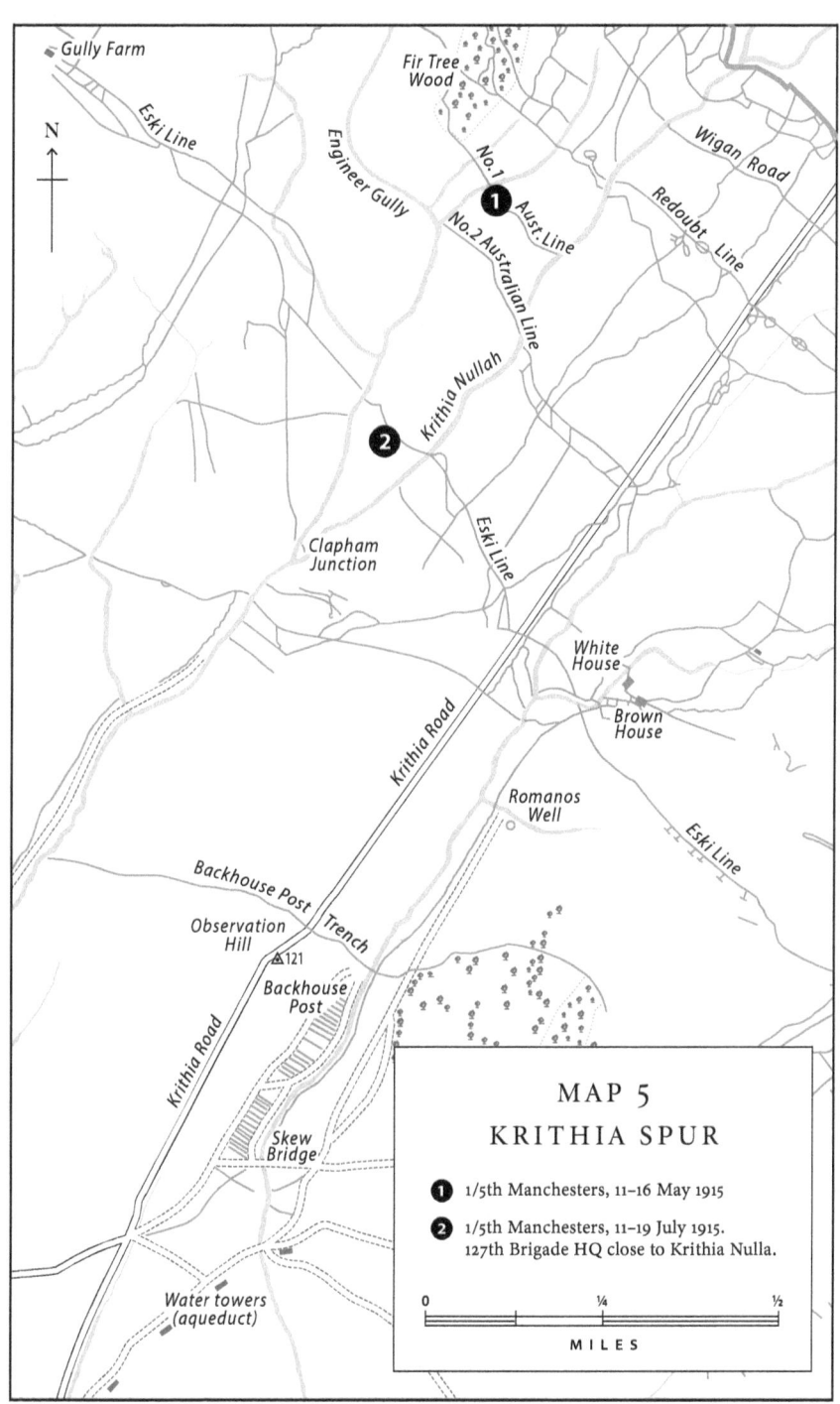

LETTERS FROM HELLES

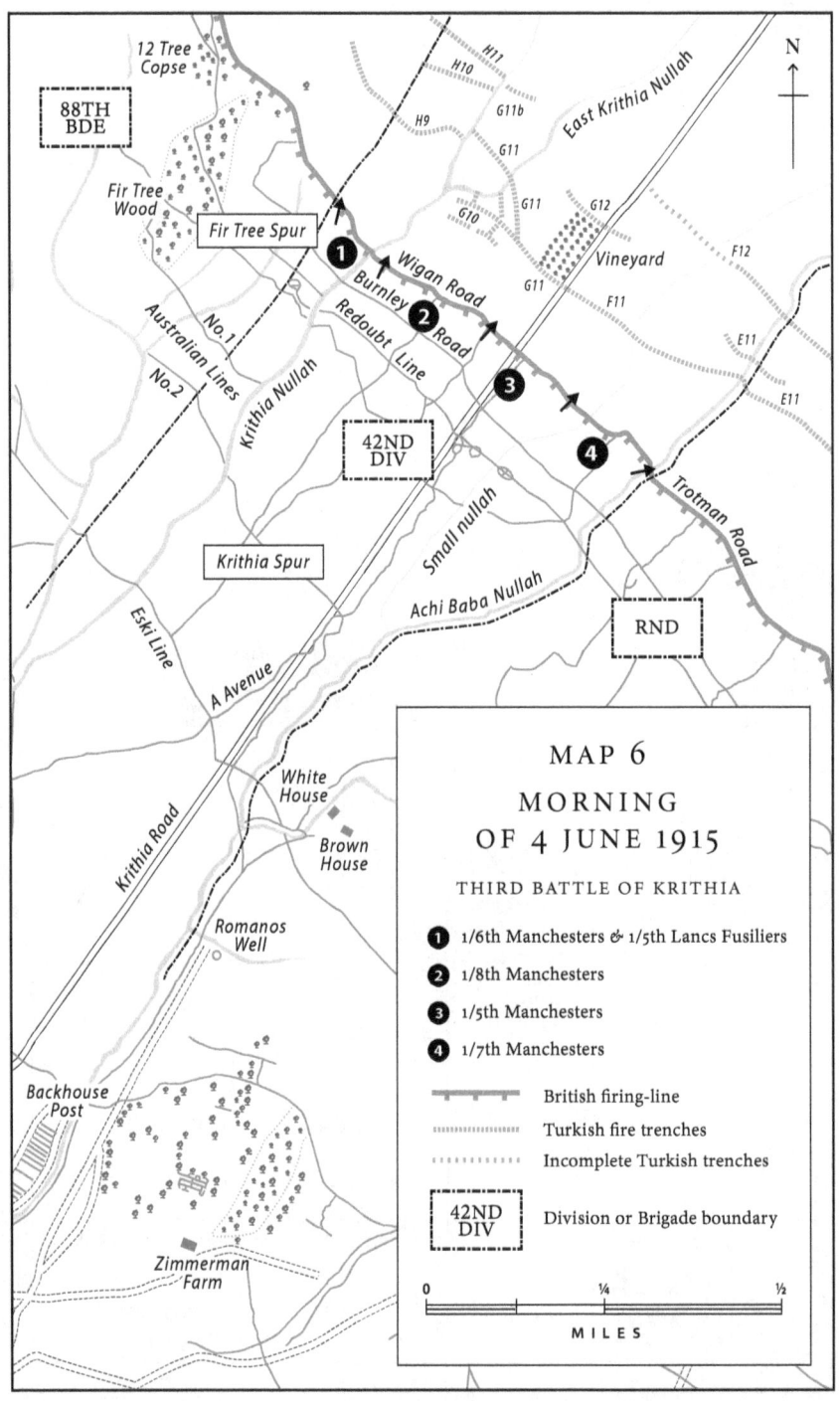

MAPS

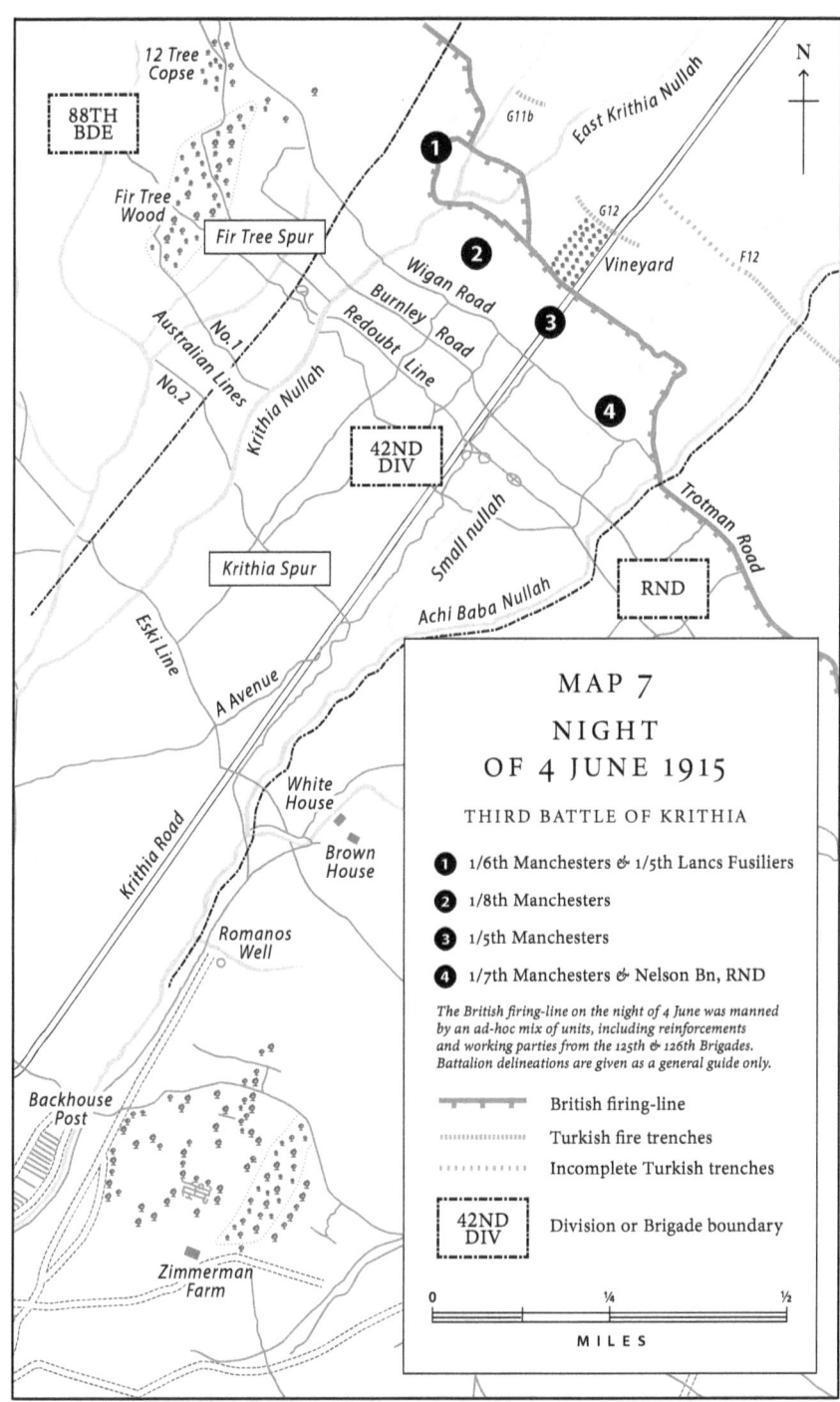

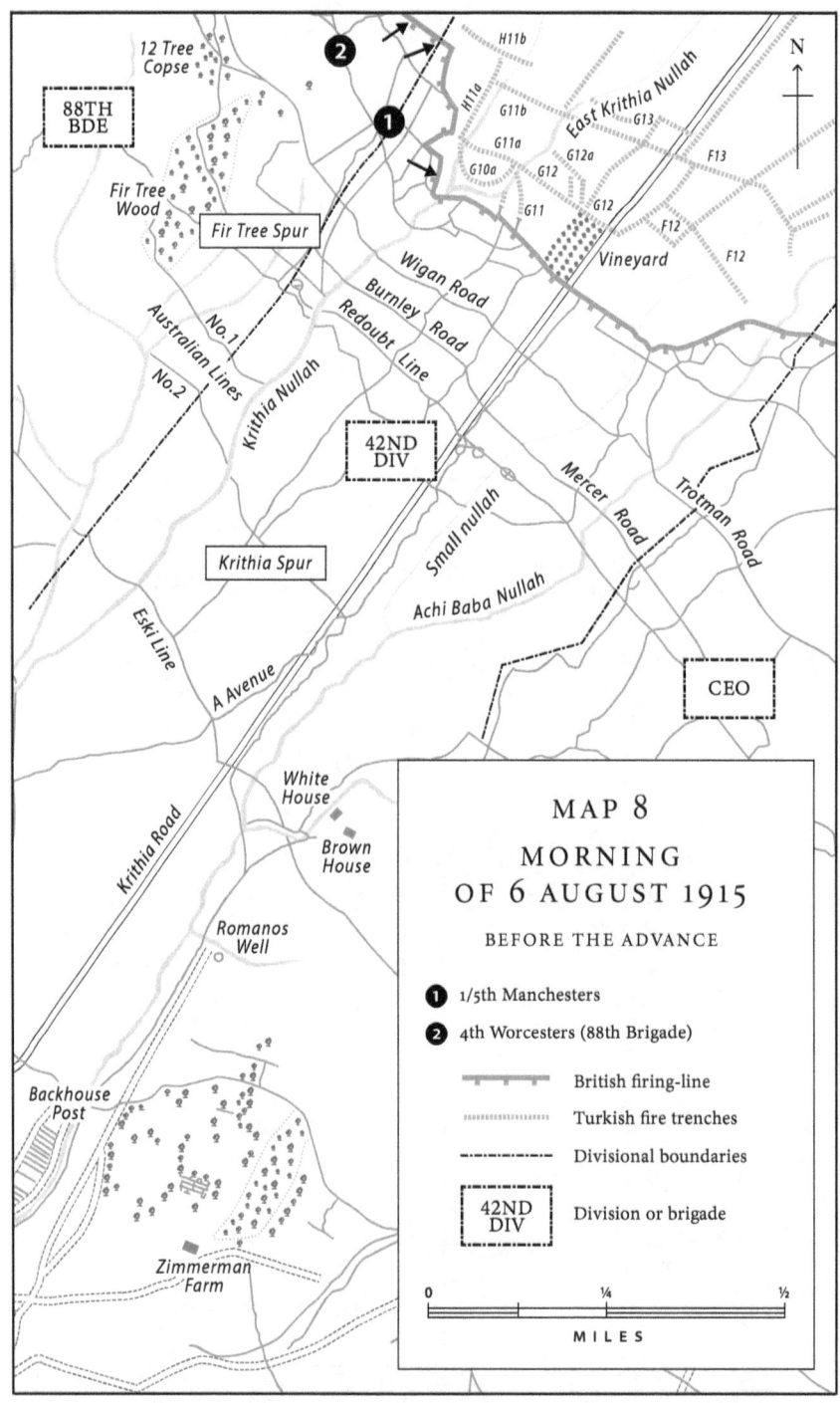

MAPS

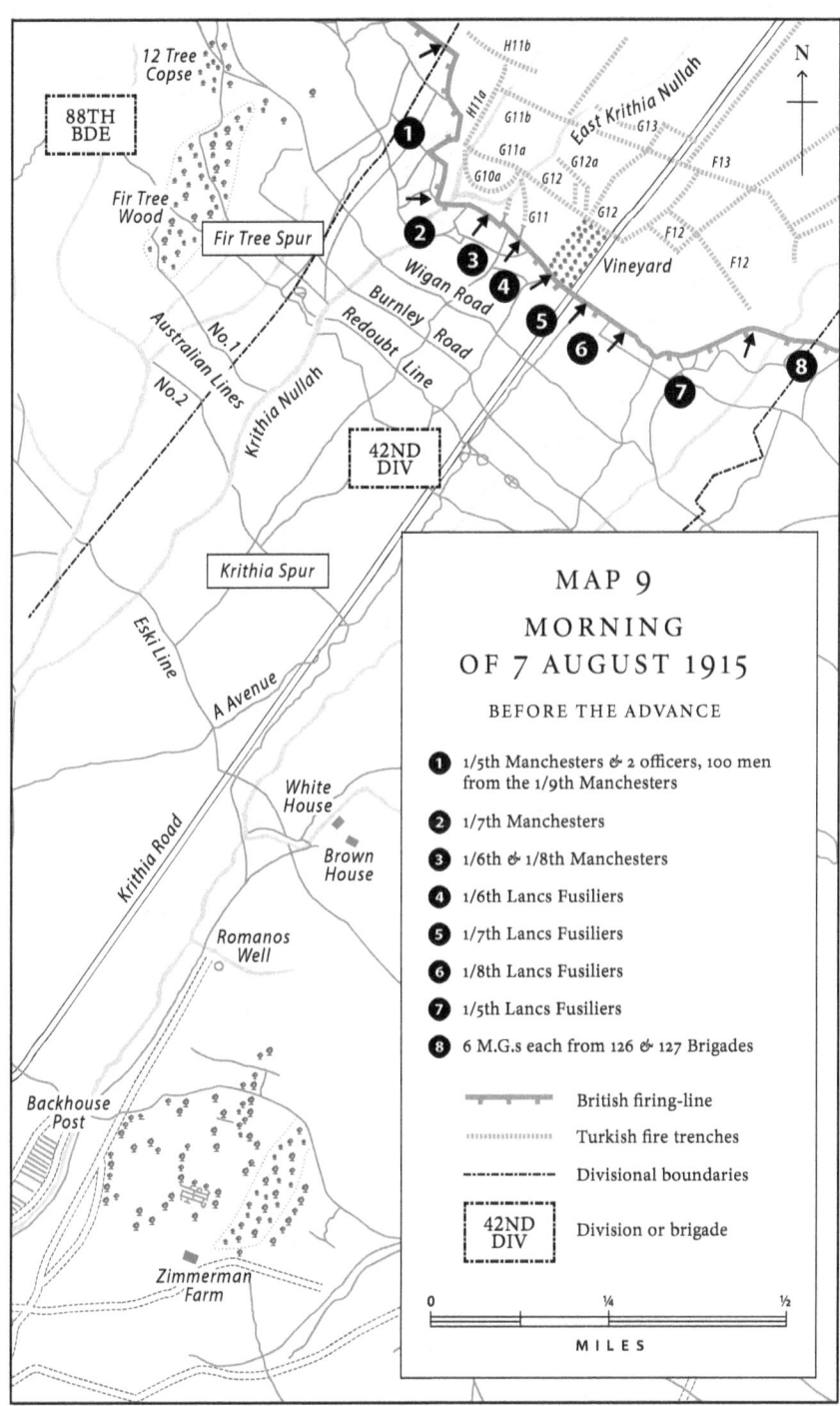

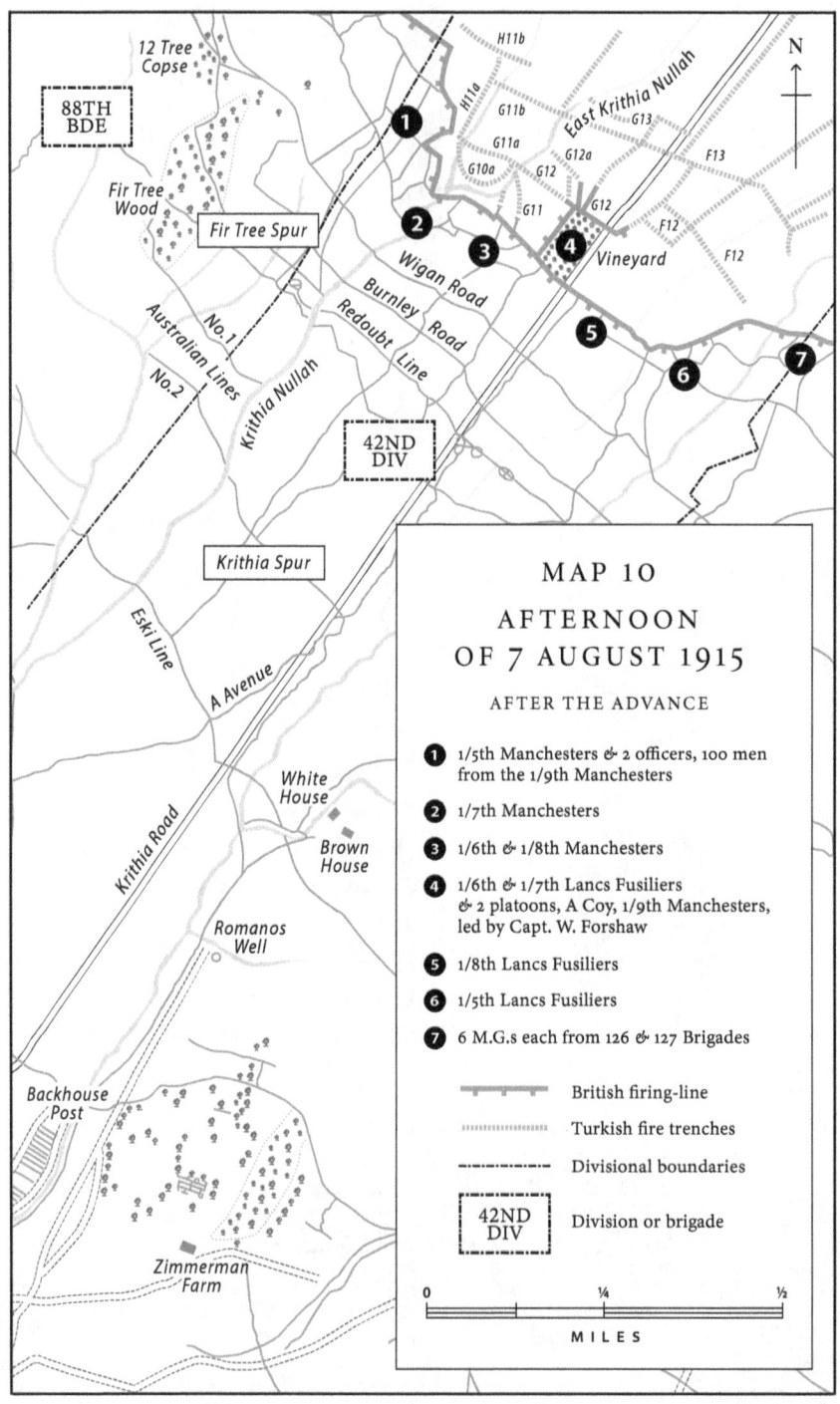

MAPS

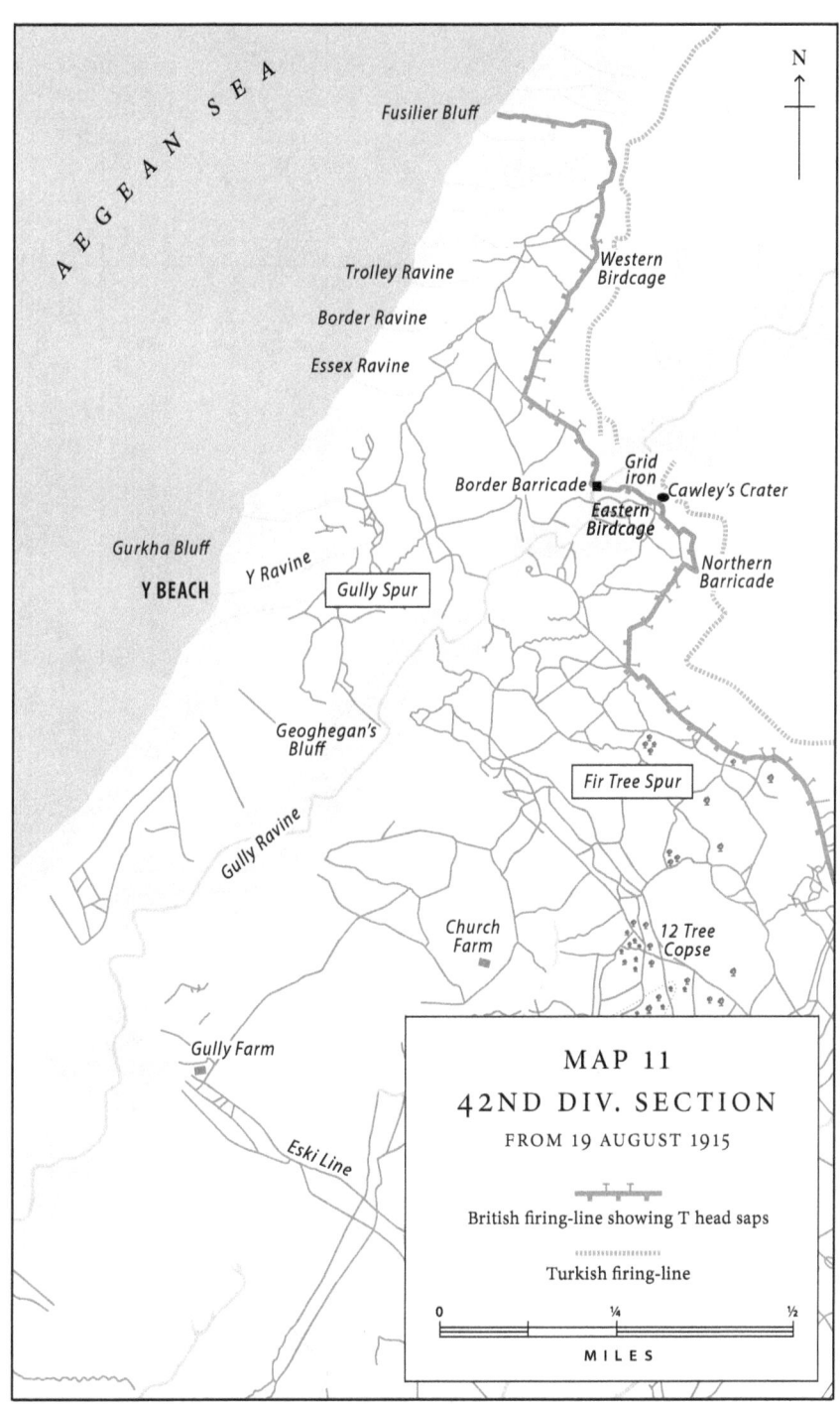

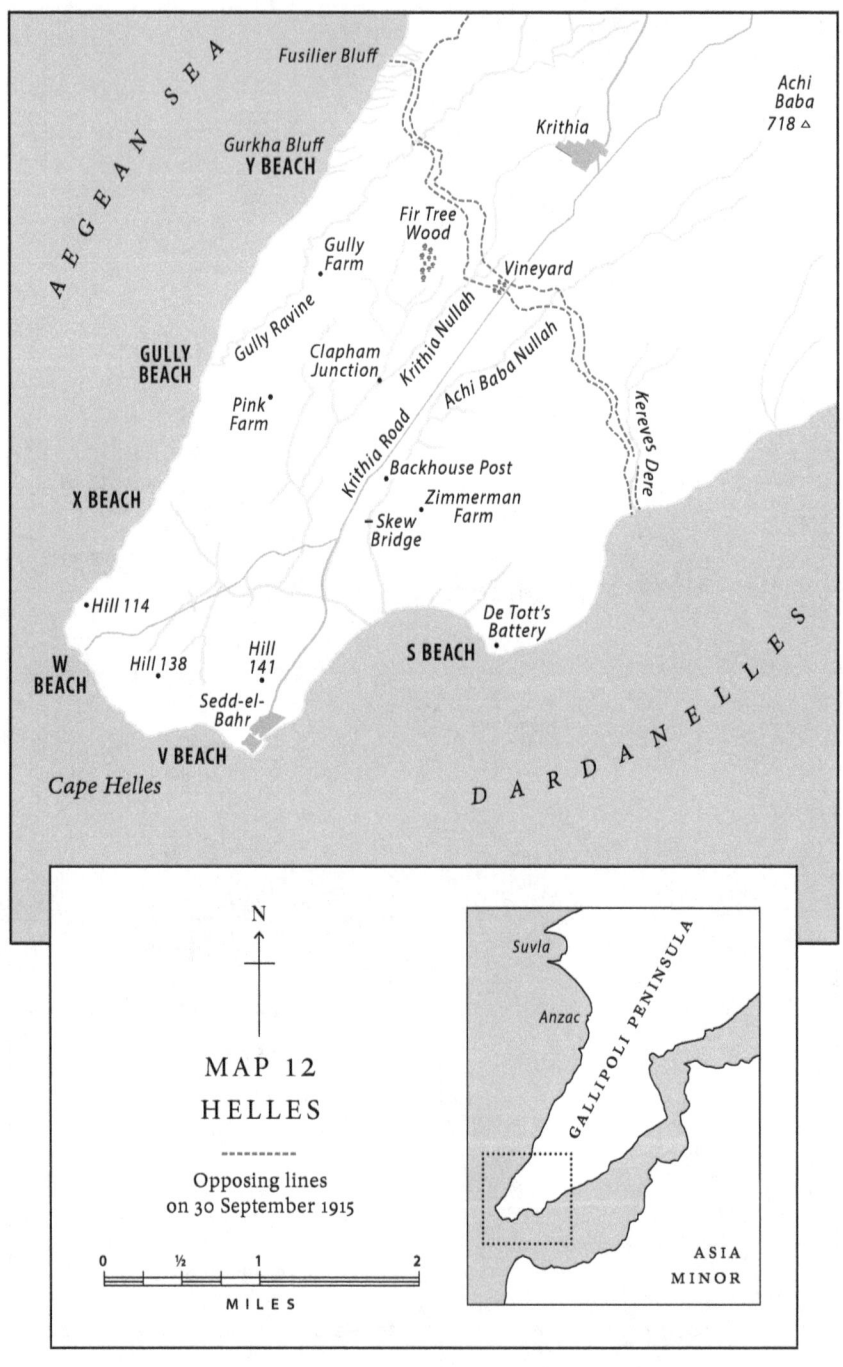

INDEX

1st Volunteer Bn., The Manchester Regiment 143, 144
29th Division
  88th Brigade 170
  Royal Fusiliers, 2nd (City of London) Bn. 174
  Worcestershire Regt, 4th Bn. 89, 94, 183, 184, 216
  Worcestershire Regt, 9th Bn. 177
42nd (East Lancashire) Division 9, 154, 157, 164, 174, 248–252
  125th (Lancs Fusiliers) Brigade 89, 164, 175, 176, 177, 250
    1/5th Lancs Fusiliers 169, 175, 176–177
    1/7th Lancs Fusiliers 168, 176–177
    1/8th Lancs Fusiliers 163, 167, 175, 176–177, 181
  126th (East Lancs) Brigade 164, 250
    1/4th East Lancs 117, 174, 175, 176
    1/5th East Lancs 163
    1/6th East Lancs 169
    1/9th Manchesters 163, 168, 173, 185
  127th (Manchester) Brigade 37, 63, 67, 68, 70, 72, 73, 74, 76, 83, 89–90, 92, 156, 157, 160, 164, 169, 174, 251
    1/5th Manchesters 10, 70, 72, 79, 137, 153, 154, 174
    1/6th Manchesters 47, 56, 59, 69, 70, 75, 84, 104, 115, 117, 118, 132, 137, 164, 168, 174, 175, 176
    1/7th Manchesters 44, 53, 129, 164, 171, 174, 175, 183
    1/8th Manchesters 53, 169, 174, 175
  Duke of Lancaster's Own Yeomanry 9
  West Kent Yeomanry 176
52nd (Lowland) Division 93, 174
  1/4th KOSB 168
Royal Naval Division 41, 44, 166, 175, 181
  Royal Marine Light Infantry 167

A

Achi Baba 72, 78, 84, 98, 105, 127, 128
Ainscough, Lt C. 23, 31, 89, 167, 178, 187, 191
air war 20–21, 23–24, 35, 52, 128, 134
  Naval flying station, Imbros 47
Allardyce, Major A.J. 250
Allen, 2/Lt G.E. 20, 21, 90, 104, 116, 117, 128, 179, 188, 192
Allen, Capt J.H. 104, 113, 114, 116, 117, 122, 129, 135, 189, 192
Allen, Capt R.S. 248
Angus, 2/Lt R.B. 132
Anzac 104, 106, 118. *See also* Australians
Armitage (Hampshire Regt, KIA Suvla) 119
Asiatic Annie. *See* Ottoman army, artillery
Atherton 9
Australians 26, 27, 33, 121, 177

B

Backhouse Post 163
Baldwin, Brig-Gen A.H. 78, 107, 219
Bankes, Capt 12
Batten, 2/Lt P.W. 104, 117, 189, 193
Battle of 6/7th August 82, 87, 89–90, 92, 93–94, 115, 121, 170–174, 183–186
Battles. *See* Second Battle of Krithia; Third Battle of Krithia; Battle of 6/7th August
Bennett, Sgt 179
Bentley-Mann, Col J. 248
Best, Rev. K. 178
Blair, 2/Lt R.H. 189, 193
Border Barricade 176, 221
Border Ravine 100, 101, 104
Box, Lt J.M. 189, 194
Brand, Brig-Gen T.W., Viscount Hampden 78, 229
Bridge Bivouac 22, 163
Briercliffe, Capt 248
Brook, Lt A.C. 12, 23, 24, 31, 38, 39, 41, 167, 179, 188, 194
Brown, 2/Lt C.P. 167, 179, 188
Brown, Capt F.S. 28, 31, 33, 35, 178, 187, 194–195
Brown, Capt W.S. 17
Browning, Major J.C. 249
Bryan, Lt J.L. 189, 195
Bryham, Capt A.L. 52, 90, 104, 107, 155, 179, 187, 196
Burnley Road 163, 164, 166, 195
Burrows, 2/Lt E.J. 104, 113, 117, 167, 179, 188, 197
Burrows, 2/Lt M.K. 31, 47, 125, 167, 178, 188, 198

C

Canning, Lt-Col A. 74, 129, 185, 221–222
Carr, Pte G. 43, 198
Cawley, Capt H.T., MP 119, 132–133, 219–221, 248
Cawley's Crater 132–133, 221
Charlesworth, 2/Lt J. 189, 199
cholera 95, 111, 115
Christy, QMS Q.M.R. 179
Church Lads Brigade 19
Clapham, Capt P.K. 16
Clapham Junction iv, 68, 169
Clayton, Lt P.C. 188, 199
Corps expéditionnaire d'Orient. *See* French forces
Cotham, Capt J. 122
Cowan, Lt B.T.R. 189, 200
Creagh, Capt P.H. 67, 68, 222–223
Cronshaw, Major A.E. 29, 52, 95, 104, 107, 108, 113, 114, 117, 118, 128, 134, 179, 187, 200
Cunningham, Capt F.W.M. 23, 48, 49, 52, 95, 96, 104, 115, 117, 178, 188, 201

D

Darlington, Daisy (second wife) 1, 2, 158
Darlington, Edith Blanche (mother) 143
Darlington, Henry (father) 143, 144, 152–153
Darlington, Henry John (son) 153, 158
Darlington, John (brother) 153

INDEX

Darlington, Lt-Col H.C.D.
  biography 143–161
  images of 22, 29, 48, 49, 60, 68, 81, 85, 88, 96, 146, 159, 178
  Letters from Helles 3, 160
  photography 33, 67, 69, 82, 84, 125, 128, 143
Darlington, Mabel (first wife) 1, 153, 154, 157, 160
Darlington, Mary (daughter) 157
Darlington, Sydney (sister) 143, 153
Davis, 2/Lt L.E. 188, 201
de Lisle, Gen 121, 240
Demoiselles. *See* trench mortars
Dickey, 2/Lt J.P.Y. 189, 202
Dickey, 2/Lt R.G.A. 104, 117, 188, 202
Dobson, Major B.P. 16, 224
Douglas, Major-Gen W. 15–16, 36, 42, 53, 54, 67, 79, 98–99, 102, 115, 118, 121, 125, 129, 137, 220, 224–226, 248
Drew, Capt C.M. 248

E

Earle, Lt-Col F.A. 248
Eastern Birdcage 127, 175
Egypt 9–10, 14–19, 155–157
England, Maj. A. 251
Eski Line 81, 169

F

Fallows, Lt-Col J.A. 250
Fawcus, Capt A.E.F. 105, 119, 226–227
Fir Tree Spur 163
Fisher, Major L. 122
Fletcher, 2/Lt P.C. 187, 204–205

Fletcher, Capt C. 122, 126, 128, 129, 132, 189, 203
Fletcher, Lt B.L. 167, 179, 187, 202–203
Fletcher, Major E. 22, 27, 29, 35, 48, 52, 54, 60, 63, 64, 67, 68, 88, 95, 96, 97, 104, 107, 113, 114, 117, 118, 122, 128, 134, 155, 168, 178, 182, 187, 204
flies 44, 54, 64, 93
food 23, 24, 27, 28, 43, 45, 47, 50, 58, 78, 80, 102–103, 105, 117, 138. *See also* parcels from home
football 16–17
Forshaw, Capt W.T. 125, 227–229
Forwood, Capt T.B. 248
Foster, Lt L.T.L. 189, 205
Fowler, Sgt W. 162
Fox, Maj. J.S. 161
France, Lieut.-Col W.S. 155
French forces 13, 32, 44, 50, 58, 64, 71, 79–80, 92, 166, 181
  chef to Gen. Douglas 118
  Deslion (artillery commander) 180
Frith, Brig-Gen H.C. 177, 250
Fry, Lt J.W. 248
Fusilier Bluff 104, 111, 115, 176

G

Garnett, artillery officer 130
gas 67, 78
Geoghegan's Bluff 123, 124, 176, 177
Gibraltar 11–12
Gordon, Lt F.C. 33, 34, 167, 178, 188, 205
Goward, 2/Lt E.E. 189, 206

Gresham, Lt-Col H.E. 251
Gridiron 177, 221
Gully Beach 35, 98, 111, 115, 116, 119, 120, 175, 176
Gully Ravine 122, 124, 131
Gurkha Bluff 110

H

Hall, Lt G. 179
Hall, Pte S.R. 132
Hamilton, Gen. Sir Ian 5–7, 19, 36, 50, 67, 79, 134, 229
Hay, CSM F. 56
Hayes, Lt F. 70, 71, 88
Henley, Brig-Gen A.M. 157
Herbert, Col E.S. 248
Hewlett, Capt A. 31, 167, 179, 187
Hewlett, Lt V. 188
Heys, Lt-Col W.G. 244, 251
Hickie, Major C.J. 250
Hirst, C.J. (Jules) 55
Hirst, E. 153
Hirst, T.J. 94, 125, 153
Holberton, Capt P.V. 56, 83, 117, 230–231
Holden, 2/Lt E.N. 52, 178, 188, 206
How, Bob 118
Hunter-Weston, Lt-Gen A.G. 42, 79, 166, 231–232
Hutchinson, Major W.A. 48, 49, 51, 53, 232

I

Imbros 45–50, 99, 137, 168
Indian troops 18
  Lahore Division 14
Ingham, Violet 108, 110

inoculation 11, 12, 95, 111, 115
Isherwood, Lt-Col J. 250
Iveson, Lt F.T. 57, 189, 206

J

James, Lt F.A. 23, 47, 48, 52, 64, 104, 107, 108, 113, 117, 128, 129, 132, 179, 188, 207
James, Lt G.S. 31, 39, 41, 167, 179, 188, 207
Johnson, 2/Lt H.N.E. 167, 179, 187, 208
Johnson, Lt A.E. 31, 167, 179, 187, 208
Johnson, Lt W.G.E. 35, 179, 187, 209

K

K Beach. *See* Imbros
Kenyon, Capt J.C. 250
Kerby, Rev E.T. 41, 233
Kershaw, Capt S.H. 248
King's Own Royal Regiment 158, 160
Kitchener's Army 50, 53, 57, 59, 75, 77, 78, 82, 86, 121
 Yeomanry 121
Knaggs, Miss, matron hospital ship 138
Knight, Major H.L. 16, 20, 83, 85, 234–235, 251
Komlosy, Rev F. 47, 54
Krithia 71
Krithia Nullah 79, 81
Krithia Road iv, 68

L

Lawford, Major A.W. 249

INDEX

Lawrence, Brig-Gen H.A. 52, 53, 59, 63, 67, 72, 86, 95, 102, 107, 110, 128, 129, 156, 171, 174, 235–237
Lee, Brig-Gen N. 16, 26, 39, 42, 108, 110, 237–238, 240, 241, 251
Leech, Capt A.C. 38, 39, 41, 167, 179, 187, 209
Lee, Lt (RA) 108, 110
Leigh (town) 9, 36
Lemnos. *See* Mudros
Lindsay, The Hon. Mrs R.C. 19, 44
Littleborough 154
Lock, Lt A. 188
Lund, 2/Lt G.S. 95, 104, 113, 114, 117, 179, 188, 210

M

machine-guns 24, 71, 87, 91, 165, 171, 182, 184, 197
Maclure, Lt-Col A.F. 250
Magill, Capt J. 248
Malta 12–13, 156
Marie, 2nd Lieut., CEO 50, 51
Marriott, Lt-Col T. 248
Marshall, Brig-Gen Sir W.R. 82, 231–232, 238, 239–241
Mar Tepe donga 182
Maxwell, Lt-Gen Sir John 16
McCarthy-Morrogh, Lt-Col D.F. 74
McGeorge, 2/Lt T.L. 188, 210
McMahon, Sir Henry 16
Messervy, Lt R.F. 189, 210
Methuen, Lord 139, 140
Middlesex Regt, 8th Bn. 11
Milman, Major O.R.E. 248
mines 130, 132

Morrison, SM 179
Mott, Major 78
Mousley, Major J.H. 249
Mudros 138, 177, 212

N

Nevill, Capt T.N.C. 69, 83, 85, 241, 251
nurses 121, 138, 139

O

Ormsby, Brig-Gen V.A. 157
Ottoman army
  artillery 7, 21, 23, 27, 52, 54, 61, 64, 71, 75, 77, 79, 91, 92, 93, 99, 102, 105–106
  HCD's opinion of 94, 103, 105, 107, 119, 121

P

Parbold 55, 77, 153
parcels from home 37, 44, 50, 55, 61, 73, 77, 80, 82, 98, 102–103, 111, 115, 117, 125, 129, 133. *See also* food
Parker, 2/Lt A.S. 179, 188, 211
Parker, Lt-Col H.G. 251
Parker, Lt P.C. 35
Patricroft 9
Pearce, 2/Lt G.O. 189, 211
periscopes 28, 33, 39, 61, 67, 72, 108, 110, 112
Pilkington, Lt-Col C.R. 67, 68, 117, 118, 137, 176, 242, 251
Pink Farm 169
Porter, 2/Lt H.J. 173, 188, 211
Postlethwaite, Capt Dr J.M. 35, 118, 119, 134, 137, 243

Prendergast, Brig-Gen D.G. 250
prisoners of war 43, 78, 197

R

Redoubt Line 26, 91, 93, 163, 164, 168, 174, 228, 238, 241
Robinson, Capt T.C. 250
Rochdale, Lt-Col Lord 39, 42, 47, 52, 69, 138, 243–245, 250
Rogers, Capt H.M. 12, 28, 35, 45, 179, 187, 212
Ross, Capt 67, 68
Ruttenau, 2/Lt. 173
Rye, Lt-Col J.B. 250

S

Sanders, Capt J.M.B. 13, 15, 18, 22, 48, 51, 52, 55, 58, 60, 81, 88, 89, 92, 95, 99, 104, 118, 122, 134, 155, 178, 187, 212–213, 255
Sarpi 177
Second Battle of Krithia 21, 163
Seddon, Cpl 51
Sharples, Lt-Col W.E. 250
Shell Bivouac 29–31, 163, 168, 212
ships
  Danton 13
  German submarine 50
  HMS *Hibernia* 177
  HMS *Majestic* 36
  HMS *Minerva* 11, 12, 13
  HMS *Ocean* 11, 12
  HMS *Queen Elizabeth* 25
  HMS *Scorpion* 105–106, 118
  HMT *Corsica* 157
  HMT *Olympic* 156
  SMS *Breslau* 14
  SMS *Goeben* 14
  SS *Caledonia* 11, 155
  SS *Cuthbert* 178
  SS *Derfflinger* 19, 21, 156, 178
  troopships 11, 13–14
Simpson, Capt A.W.W. 36, 52, 187, 213–214
Skipworth, Lt P.J. 189, 214
Slaughter, Col R.J. 15, 248
Slaughter, Lt A. 52, 53, 188, 214
Smith, Albert, Labour Member for Clitheroe 53
snipers 23, 24, 27, 28, 32–33, 59, 91, 103, 107, 130
South African War 12, 16, 23, 36, 63, 144–150
Southampton 10, 11, 144, 154–155
Spencer, CSM W. 36, 215
Steinthal, Lt-Col W.M. 251
Stott, Lt T.M. 189, 215
Stuart, Pte A. 58, 216
Suvla 104, 106
Syers, Capt T.S. 99, 105, 186, 246

T

Taylor, Lt QM S. 35, 104, 117, 178, 188, 216
Taylor, Pte R. 132
Tenant, Lt-Col S.L. 249
Third Battle of Krithia 39–44, 52, 164–168, 180–181
torpedoes (land) 180
Torres Lines 97, 168, 174
trench mortars 57, 91, 92, 99, 105, 108, 128–129, 130, 132, 134, 186, 246
Trolley Ravine 175, 177
Tufnell, Col A.W. 57, 246–247, 248

INDEX

Turks. *See* Ottoman army; snipers

V

Valentine, Mr, vicar of Ramleh 20
Verdon, Lt F. 188
Vincent, Lt 180
Vineyard 40, 93–94, 228

W

Wade, Lt-Col D.H. 250
Walker, 2/Lt T.C. 21, 23, 38, 41, 179, 188, 217
Walker, Capt J.S.A. 21, 50, 52, 167, 179, 187, 217
Wall, Lt J. 187
Walmesley-Cotham. *See* Cotham, Capt J.
Welch, 127 Bde Ammo Officer 83
Wells, Major L.F. 249
Western Birdcage 174
Western Front 157–158
Wigan 1, 4, 6, 9, 28, 44, 47, 50, 64, 143, 144, 152, 154, 159, 251
Wigan Road 164, 166
Williamson, 127th Brigade Signal Officer 83
Winterbottom, Capt D.D. 90, 188, 218
Woods, Capt W.T. 31, 47, 48, 52, 95, 178, 187, 218

X

X Beach 96, 97, 168

Y

Y Ravine 108, 110, 115, 175, 176

'Grave. Gully Ravine.'
Lieut. C. Sartoris, 2nd Bn., The Royal Fusiliers.

www.ingramcontent.com/pod-product-compliance
Lightning Source LLC
Chambersburg PA
CBHW030334230426
43661CB00040B/1486/J